D0319730

BBC Sports Personality of the Year

Steve Rider with Martyn Smith

BBC Sports Personality of the Year

BOOKS

First published in 2003

ISBN 0 563 48747 X

Published by BBC Books, BBC Worldwide Ltd,
Woodlands, 80 Wood Lane, London W12 0TT

BBC Worldwide would like to thank the following for providing photographs and for permission to reproduce copyright material. While every effort has been made to trace and acknowledge all copyright holders, we would like to apologize should there have been any errors or omissions.

All images © **EMPICS** except:
© **BBC** pages 10, 14, 18, 22, 23 *below*, 31 *below left*, 34, 35, 40, 45, 51 *top,* 73 *below*, 76, 87, 88, 89 *below*, 92, 96, 98 *below*, 100, 104, 109 *below right*, 114, 115 *above*, 118, 119 *left*, 124, 128, 134, 136, 140 *left*, 142, 143, 147, 148, 160, 164, 165 *all*, 171 *left*, 172 *below*, 174, 178, 192, 198, 199 *below,* 204, 205, 208, 210, 211 *below left,* 221 *top*, 224, 228 *below*, 232, 238 *left*, 239 *top*, 240 *top left and below right*
© **Colorsport** pages 91, 109 *top*, 110 *below*, 126 *left*, 129 *below*, 130 *top*, 133, 151
© **www.sporting-heroes.net** pages 50, 80 *right*, 123, 185 *right*
© **Getty Images/Mike Hewitt** page 7

Excerpt from *Ovett: An Autobiography*, reproduced with the kind permission of Collins Willow

Commissioning editor: Ben Dunn
Picture research: David Cottingham

Produced for BBC Books by designsection, Frome
Editor: Lisa Hughes
Designer: Sue Lee
Printed and bound in Great Britain by Butler & Tanner, Frome
Colour separations by Radstock Repro, Midsomer Norton
Jacket printed by Lawrence Allen, Weston-Super-Mare

Contents

Foreword

By Paula Radcliffe, athlete and 2002 winner

'Standing in the centre of the BBC studio at the end of the 2002 *Sports Personality of the Year* programme, with the famous trophy in my hands and that emotional theme music playing, has to be one of the proudest moments of my sporting career so far.

'I am sure that the feelings have been exactly the same for all the previous winners, because they knew that this was the genuine endorsement of the British sporting public and, as such, one of the greatest accolades in sport.

'Like so many others I grew up inspired by the annual programme that would review all the sporting achievements of the year and seemed to bring the whole of British sport together.

'And knowing that the live studio audience was a cross-section of everything that was great about British sport, plus many international stars as well, just added to my special moment in 2002.

'This book follows the 50-year history of the programme and the iconic award, and offers a fascinating insight into how British sport has evolved, with many memories from some great performers.

'An athlete was the first winner, another athlete has been the most recent, and I would love to think myself worthy of the viewers' votes again in the future.'

Paula Radcliffe

In the beginning ...

A show is born ...

In 50 years it has become a pivotal night in the calendar, an annual excuse for fierce debate or outrage and a barometer for either Britain's sporting progress or its decline, but the birth of *Sports Personality of the Year,* back in the autumn of 1954, was low-key, even comical.

In the beginning there was *Sportsview*, the flagship of BBC TV's fledgling sports output. The programme was devised in 1954 by Paul Fox, later to become controller of BBC1, and the first show was broadcast on BBC1 on 8 April that year. It was in a memo from Paul Fox to the assistant head of outside broadcasts on 4 October 1954 that the idea of a *Sportsview* review of the year, including the results of a ballot for the sportsman and sportswoman of the year, was first advanced.

Paul Fox argued, quite correctly, that there had seldom been a year like this in sport. It had included not only the World Cup but also the heroics of Jim Peters in the Empire Games and, most glorious of all, Roger Bannister's sub-four-minute mile. However, within three weeks the idea had become somewhat diluted. The TV Sports Personality award, as it was now called, would be presented during an outside broadcast from the far more established *Sporting Record* awards, announced by the newspaper during a dinner at the Savoy Hotel.

Cecil Bear, the editor of what was a hugely popular sports weekly, welcomed the potential publicity, but in a letter to Peter Dimmock, the head of outside broadcasts, wanted to make his position clear: 'I reiterate that *Sporting Record* inaugurated the sportsman of the year idea eight years ago; that our ballot is nationally recognised, in the press and the BBC, as *the* ballot; that we spend a great deal of money and time in organising it; and that an independent award such as yours, made before a vast body of viewers, would cut across our ground.'

So, the newly created programme was starting with an immediate step backwards. *Sporting Record* had pulled rank and in a letter of 1 November, Peter Dimmock reassured Cecil Bear that, 'Our little trophy is merely designed to apply to the *Sportsview* programme and is limited to sporting personalities who have actually taken part in this programme.'

'There had seldom been a year like this in sport. It had included ... the World Cup, ... the Empire Games and, most glorious of all, Roger Bannister's sub-four-minute mile'

Paul Fox was adamant that, 'We gain nothing by joining the *Sporting Record* in the presentation of these awards.' In a memo to Dennis Monger, the head of outside broadcasts, he said, 'The one and, I can see, only advantage is that a crowd of sporting celebrities will be brought together and wined at the *Sporting Record*'s expense. But do we want so many people in the programme? I know that the half dozen stars we want at the most, Bannister, Chataway, Peacock, Richards etc. we can also get to the studio or have on film.'

In the early 1950s, it was the press and radio that were most influential when it came to sport, and *Sportsview* and its new award had much growing up to do, but the short article submitted by Peter Dimmock to Elwyn Jones, the editor of *Radio Times*, oozed confidence with its opening question, 'Who will be *Sportsview* Personality of 1954?'

It continued, 'When *Sportsview* became a regular weekly half-hour programme, it was decided to give viewers, who had so loyally supported this new programme with their suggestions and ideas, an opportunity to choose the outstanding *Sportsview* personality of the year. The only qualification was that the selected sportsman or sportswoman must have at some time during the year appeared in *Sportsview*.'

The piece then went on to explain the deadline for voting ('postcards only please') and how the winner would be presented with a model of a television camera mounted on a base as a trophy, which they would hold on to for one year.

So, for the first time the public were voting after a year that seemed totally dominated by the exploits of Bannister and Chataway. However, among other candidates suggested by the programme were footballing legend Tom Finney, heavyweight boxer Don Cockell, motor racing's Stirling Moss, golfer Dai Rees, the young jockey Lester Piggott and speedway rider Split Waterman.

Behind the scenes, more mundane preparations were continuing. The trophy, now a coveted symbol of the public's adulation, was commissioned from Mr John Procter of the Palace of Arts, Wembley. The requirement was for a model in the shape of a television camera, one sixth scale, for delivery just before Christmas, and the order solemnly stated, 'It will not be possible to run to more than £30 for this trophy.'

It was only on 11 November that the title of the programme was confirmed. In a memo to Paul Fox and Dennis Monger, the head of outside broadcasts pointed out that, 'The title of the retrospective *Sportsview* on 30 December must not include the word 'retrospect' ... This would mean a clash with the *TV News Retrospective* programme which is normally done at this time of year. The title which has been decided upon is *Sports Review of 1954*'. There was also a discussion about whether the award should be accompanied by prize money. The director of television entered the debate to suggest that the proposed £25 was 'very much on the high side'.

'The winner would be presented with a model of a television camera mounted on a base as a trophy'

The production and transmission schedule drawn up by Peter Dimmock was very precise: 'It is confirmed that at 8.24 I shall leave the *Sportsview* temporary studio to mount the presentation platform and make, very quickly indeed, the *Sportsview* trophy award ... I should think I could manage this in one and three quarter minutes at the outside.'

There was no need to agonise too much over what that temporary studio looked like. Fifty years on the *Sports Review of the Year* set would occupy teams of designers and builders, working flat out. In 1954 the property requirements called for a 'smart office desk, two office armchairs, no. 42, a black hand telephone, calendars, smart blotter, in and out trays and an ink stand and pens'.

At 7.45 p.m. on Thursday 30 December the announcer at BBC Lime Grove handed over to Peter Dimmock at the Savoy Hotel. From his red leather swivel armchair he looked at camera two and said, 'Good evening sports fans and welcome to our gala edition of *Sportsview*.' The announcement of the first BBC *Sports Personality of the Year* was less than 45 minutes away.

1954

Date 30 December 1954 • Location Savoy Hotel, London • Presenter Peter Dimmock
Editor Paul Fox • Producer Dennis Monger

1st Chris Chataway athlete
2nd Roger Bannister athlete
3rd Pat Smythe show-jumper

Overall winner

Chris Chataway had won three-mile gold in the 1954 Empire Games as well as 5000m silver at the European Championships. He went on to break the three-mile world record in 1955 and, in the same year, became ITV's first newscaster. In 1959 he went into Parliament as a Conservative MP, before retiring in 1974 to follow a business career.

There is no doubt that 1954 had been a historic sporting year, but there was still something disconcertingly familiar about the content of that first programme.

There was the faltering start the MCC was making to its winter Ashes tour in Australia and also the football World Cup, which had taken place that summer in Switzerland, with West Germany beating Hungary 3-2 in the final. In his 'upbeat' introduction to the World Cup report, Peter Dimmock said, 'Thanks to television's continental exchange, we were there for some of the matches and could see for ourselves the failure of both England and Scotland against other nations.'

Jaroslav Drobny's victory at Wimbledon, 16 years after his first appearance there, was hailed as the most emotional performance of the year. There were interviews with racing driver Stirling Moss and also Pat Smythe, whose most successful years on the European show-jumping circuit still lay ahead of her. Then the subject finally turned to athletics.

The production team initially assumed that Roger Bannister would beat the other

Above Roger Bannister and Pat Smythe came second and third respectively to Chris Chataway in the Sports Personality voting, but were consoled by winning the *Sporting Record* awards

main contender, Christopher Chataway. After all, Chataway was only the pacemaker when Bannister broke the four-minute mile at Iffley Road in Oxford, a run that secured him a legendary position in sporting history. However, it didn't secure him that first Sports Personality of the Year award, as the power of television – not for the last time – would strongly influence the viewers' choice.

Just a few weeks before those viewers were asked to make their decision, Chataway had produced an incredibly thrilling run to beat the seemingly invincible Russian, Vladimir Kuts, at the White City Stadium in London. Chataway took five seconds off the world 5000m record, was roared on by 45,000 home fans and, just as importantly, tracked every step of the way by BBC television cameras.

The drama of the evening had made a huge impact on the audience and when *Radio Times* asked its readers to send in their votes on postcards that run was still fresh in their memories. So at 8.26 p.m. Peter Dimmock announced that the first *Sportsview* Sports Personality of the Year was Christopher Chataway.

The presentation was simple, as had been promised, but then Lord Brabazon of Tara stepped forward to present the *Sporting Record* Sportsman of the Year award to Roger Bannister and the Sportswoman of the Year award to Pat Smythe. In its very first year, the BBC's 'small' award had provided much to discuss and debate.

By modern standards, it had been a rather routine, low key sort of programme, but as if mindful of its potential place in history, records of that night have been diligently kept. For example, 1954 is one of the few years for which a complete record of the voting survives. A total of 14,517 votes were cast and well over a third of them went to Chris Chataway. His lead over Bannister was significant, but the four-minute miler was barely 500 votes ahead of show-jumper Pat Smythe in third.

Although, in that first year, eligibility for the award was restricted to sportsmen or women who had appeared on *Sportsview* since its launch in April, the destination of the remaining votes offers an interesting profile of Britain's sporting enthusiasms in the early 1950s.

Geoff Duke, who once again dominated the 500cc motorcycling World Championship, was fifth, separating the footballing superstars Stanley Matthews and Billy Wright. It had been another World Championship year for cyclist Reg Harris and he polled 30 votes, ahead of the highest placed cricketer, Len Hutton, with 27. There were six votes for the twin world table tennis champions Rosalind and Diane Rowe, but no votes at all for rugby

Below Diane (left) and Rosalind Rowe were table tennis doubles world champions in 1951 as well as 1954
Right Jaroslav Drobny, Czech by birth, defected in 1949 and became a British citizen. He died in London in 2001, aged 79

Left Roger Bannister studied medicine at Oxford and used his medical knowledge to help him develop scientific training methods **Opposite** Geoff Duke on his Norton, one of many bikes he rode

Sir Roger Bannister remembers ...

'If it was a question of television coverage that decided the vote then I can understand that. The coverage of my race and Chris Chataway's win over Vladimir Kuts were very contrasting.

'It was only the foresight of Peter Dimmock that meant there was any coverage of the four-minute mile run at all. He had a single camera on a van in the middle of the track and those pictures have since become incredibly famous. I was especially keen to get back to the *Sportsview* studio the following night to help with the programme, which was one of the first in the series.

'Chataway's race against Kuts had everything and was seen by a big television audience. Kuts couldn't bear to be beaten and even claimed that he had become confused as to where the finish line was. I can see why the viewers got excited by all this – I did too. I never had any resentment about the award and became a huge admirer of the programme down the years.'

union and only two for golf, one apiece for Dai Rees and Henry Cotton.

Not only were the votes kept, but the audience research was also thorough and the results for Paul Fox, Peter Dimmock and their team were encouraging. It was estimated that the audience was 20 per cent of the adult population, equivalent to 62 per cent of the adult TV public, and the approval rating was 85, easily the highest figure *Sportsview* had achieved.

The main criticism was that the programme seemed 'rushed' in its attempt to be so comprehensive but, the audience research department's report said, 'Of particular interest to the viewers were the films of international football matches, the report of Pat Smythe's achievements in the world of show-jumping and the interview with her, and the presentation of the various trophies at the end of the programme.'

In a memo of 17 January 1955, Peter Dimmock congratulated everyone and said, 'I think we must come to an early decision about *Sportsview* 1955 ... The programme should also, in my view, be of one hour's duration. Could you please give this matter some very serious and urgent thought and then let me have your recommendations.' One of the most famous programmes in sports broadcasting was beginning to develop.

▸▸ **Lester Piggott** featured on the first programme as he was seen winning the Derby on 33-1 outsider Never Say Die, aged just 18. His direct association with the show was to continue until his final retirement, an astonishing 41 years later.

▸▸ In 1953, former Surrey and England batting legend **Jack Hobbs** had become the first cricketer to be given a knighthood. He had retired in 1934 with a record 197 centuries to his name.

Sporting roundup

Boxing Rocky Marciano was world heavyweight champion, having survived two difficult fights with Ezzard Charles.

Cricket Surrey had won their third consecutive County Championship and England had drawn their summer series against Pakistan.

Football Wolverhampton Wanderers won the League Championship and fellow Midlanders West Bromwich Albion beat Preston North End 3-2 in the FA Cup final. In Scotland, Jock Stein captained Celtic to the double.

Golf Peter Thomson won the Open at Royal Birkdale, having been runner-up in 1952 and 1953. It was the first of his five championships.

Horse racing Royal Tan won the Grand National.

Motor cycling Geoff Duke won the 500cc World Championship for the third time in four years.

Motor racing Juan Fangio won the Formula One title for the second time.

Rugby league Warrington won the Challenge Cup final.

Rugby union England, Wales and France shared the Five Nations Championship.

Tennis Maureen Connolly beat Louise Brough to win Wimbledon for the third consecutive year.

1955

Date 28 December 1955 • **Location** Savoy Hotel, London • **Presenter** Peter Dimmock
Editor Paul Fox • **Producers** Dennis Monger and Alan Rees

1st Gordon Pirie athlete
(no record of the second and third place winners survives)

On 28 December 1955, *Sportsview* returned to the Savoy's Lancaster Room to review the year and present the second Sports Personality of the Year award. The show had grown from 45 to 75 minutes and that gave Peter Dimmock, assisted by another regular sports presenter, Max Robertson, time to reflect on what had been a slightly disappointing 12 months for British sport.

Once again the format was a mixture of interviews and film clips as a number of sportsmen and women joined Peter Dimmock in the small studio that had been set up in the Lancaster's anteroom. The surviving script shows that they were all asked the same two questions: what is your outstanding memory of 1955 and what are your hopes for 1956? They were all allowed precisely 90 seconds to answer.

Donald Campbell was the first to be called from his dinner as he had set a new water speed record of 216 mph. He was followed by the two-wheel champion, Geoff Duke, and then England's cricket captain, Peter May, who was celebrating a year that had begun with England retaining the Ashes in Australia and then seen him lead the team to victory in a classic series against South Africa.

Dawn Palethorpe, or 'Miss Palethorpe' as she was addressed, was Britain's leading show-jumper; champion

Overall winner

Gordon Pirie had had a relatively lean season until he scored a resounding 10,000m victory over the great Emil Zatopek, but that prompted people to vote for him.

When he collected both the Sports Personality and *Sporting Record* awards, Pirie first expressed his surprise at winning and then made a short speech criticising sports journalists. This led to some vitriolic attacks on him in the press, most notably by Peter Wilson in the *Daily Mirror*, whose article was headlined, 'The poison in the heart of Gordon Pirie'. Wilson then went on to claim that the athlete was arrogant and conceited. However, Pirie was unrepentant and later said that he was glad that he had made his protest.

In 1956, Pirie went on to break three world records and win silver in the Olympic Games 5000m. In 1989 he was back at *Sports Review* to present the Team award, but sadly died of cancer two years later.

jockey Doug Smith briefly looked back at his successful season; and Peter Dimmock also talked to boxer Don Cockell about his brave encounter with Rocky Marciano. The viewers were able to see footage of that brutal contest for the very first time, as Cockell fought for the world heavyweight title in San Francisco, back in May.

Wolverhampton Wanderers hadn't been eligible for the first ever European Cup competition but Billy Wright was still able to talk about the club's stirring contests against Dynamo Moscow, which had been seen on the BBC in the autumn.

In other sports the British Lions had finished two apiece in the series in South Africa and Stirling Moss had become the first British driver to win the Grand Prix at Aintree, but he still finished second in the World Championship behind Juan Fangio.

Right Donald Campbell set his 1955 world record water speed on Ullswater in the Lake District, in *Bluebird K7*
Below Doug Smith, seen here after winning the 2000 Guineas at Newmarket on Our Babu, was champion jockey five times in all
Below right Peter May, one of England's finest ever batsmen, played for his country 66 times, captaining the team on 41 occasions

Left Chelsea played Sheffield Wednesday in their final home match of the season, winning 3-0 to clinch the First Division Championship. Here Wednesday keeper Dave McIntosh (right) tries to punch clear under pressure from Chelsea's Jock McNicol
Below left Peter Thomson, an Australian by birth, played a lot of his best golf in the UK and is a member of that select club who have won five Opens
Opposite Don Cockell (right) valiantly challenges the great Rocky Marciano for the world heavyweight title. Marciano emerged the victor to retain his title

It was motor sport that provided the tragic stories of the year with the death of Alberto Ascari at Monza and the awful toll of 83 fatalities at the Le Mans 24-hour race, caused when Pierre Levegh's Mercedes somersaulted into the crowd while travelling at 150mph.

Dai Rees reflected on yet another defeat for the British golfers in the Ryder Cup, but 1955 was also the year that the Open Championship was first seen live on British television. It was won by Peter Thomson at St Andrews.

Athletics had featured prominently on *Sportsview* throughout 1955 and steeplechaser John Disley, who, with Chris Brasher, was later to found the London marathon, spoke about his hopes for the Olympics.

For the second year in a row athletics attracted the viewers' votes and this time there was unanimity across the country: Gordon Pirie was crowned the second Sports Personality of the Year. He also collected the *Sporting Record* Sportsman of the Year award and Pat Smythe was once again voted Sportswoman of the Year.

▸▸ In 1955 **television facilities** were rather more basic than today and there were just two cameras in the centre of the Lancaster Room and two more in the small studio. The television mobile control room was set up in the cloakroom.

▸▸ The Scottish FA Cup final was televised live for the first time as **Clyde** beat Celtic 1-0 in a replay, having drawn the first game 1-1.

Sporting roundup

Football Chelsea were Division One champions for the first time. Newcastle United beat Manchester City 3-1 in the FA Cup final to lift the cup for the third time in five years.

Horse racing Quare Times won the Grand National and Phil Drake was first home in the Derby.

Rugby league Barrow beat Workington Town in the Challenge Cup final.

Rugby union Wales and France shared the Five Nations title.

Tennis Tony Trabert was Wimbledon men's champion and Louise Brough collected her fourth and final ladies title.

1956

Date 9 January 1957 • Location Savoy Hotel, London • Presenter Peter Dimmock
Editor Paul Fox • Producer Dennis Monger

1st Jim Laker cricketer

(no record of the second and third place winners survives)

Although one of the biggest stories of the year had been the Olympic Games from Melbourne, the BBC was unable to use any of the footage due to a dispute. This created a major headache for Paul Fox and his production team, but they got round the problem by interviewing some of the Olympians in the studio and by focussing on the domestic sporting stories of 1956.

Peter Dimmock began the show by linking into a film that featured no fewer than 16 contenders for the Sports Personality of the Year award, including athlete Derek Ibbotson, footballer Stanley Matthews and the cricketers Peter May and Denis Compton.

In many ways the previous year's award winner, Gordon Pirie, had had an even greater season in 1956.

Overall winner

Jim Laker was in the latter part of his international career when he came to Old Trafford for the fourth Test against Australia and completely rewrote the record books. The series was one apiece and he had already collected 20 wickets, including 11 in the previous game in Leeds.

In Manchester he returned the extraordinary bowling figures of 9 for 37 in Australia's first innings and 10 for 53 in their second, to help England to a resounding victory. His dominance was so great that in one spell in the first innings he took 7 wickets for 8 runs off 22 balls. Laker's Surrey team-mate, Tony Lock, took the other wicket in the match.

The BBC made strenuous efforts to get Jim Laker back from England's tour of South Africa, but the MCC declined the request to fly him home for three days and he was seen receiving the trophy from Peter May on film. After a long career as a BBC commentator, Jim Laker died in April 1986.

The finest performance of his career had come at Bergen in June when he raced stride for stride with Vladimir Kuts to break the world 5000m record by a massive 3.8 seconds. When it came to the Olympics, though, Pirie's preparations were hit by injury and Kuts beat him into the silver medal position.

It was a memorable games for Britain. Chris Brasher, who had been such a pacemaking support to Roger Bannister two years earlier, claimed an outstanding gold in the steeplechase. Terry Spinks, an 18-year-old Londoner, and Scotland's Dick McTaggart won boxing titles and 17-year-old Judy Grinham became the first British swimmer to win Olympic gold for 32 years. All were strong contenders for Sports Personality.

In boxing, several bouts were featured on the show, including the British-based West Indian light heavyweight, Yolande Pompey, seen losing in his attempt to win the world crown from the legendary Archie Moore. Moore was then shown losing to 21-year-old Floyd Patterson in his November battle for the vacant heavyweight crown, Rocky Marciano having retired as champion in April. Marciano had achieved the remarkable feat of remaining unbeaten throughout his entire 49-fight professional career.

Also with a chance of winning the main award were Manchester City's goalkeeper, Bert Trautmann, who broke his neck in his team's FA Cup final victory over Birmingham City, and Australia's Peter Thomson, who won the Open Championship for the third straight year. At this stage there was still no bar on international candidates.

The Busby Babes of Manchester United won the First Division Championship with 60 points, 11 more than Blackpool, their nearest rivals, and with an average team age of just 23. In the studio Peter Dimmock interviewed the England captain, Billy Wright, about Manchester United's outstanding young players.

Below Chris Brasher's lasting legacy is undoubtedly the London marathon, which he conceived after a trip to the States to run in the 1979 New York marathon. He died in 2003, aged 74
Bottom Judy Grinham was the first ever swimmer to hold European, Empire and Olympic titles simultaneously

From Wimbledon, Lew Hoad was shown vanquishing Ken Rosewall in the final. It was part of an amazing run of form for the 21-year-old Australian, who also won the French and Australian titles before Rosewall gained revenge and prevented him from taking the Grand Slam by beating him in the final of the US Open at Forest Hills. To add to an extraordinary year, Hoad also won three of the Grand Slam doubles titles. It was a good season for America's Shirley Fry, too. Famed for her doubles play, in 1956 she won the singles crowns at both Wimbledon and the US Championships.

Below Bert Trautmann was written off when he broke his neck in the FA Cup final, but the former prisoner of war fought his way back into the team. He made 545 appearances for Manchester City in all
Below right Dick McTaggart famously refused to turn professional and in 1964 became the first boxer to fight in three Olympics. He was later a national boxing coach for Scotland
Opposite Devon Loch (left), ridden by Dick Francis, taking Beacher's Brook for the second time. However, the horse unaccountably fell to lose the Grand National to ESB

At the end of the programme Peter Dimmock announced that the top names in the voting were Chris Brasher, Donald Campbell, Bert Trautmann, Peter May and Jim Laker. However, the final order was never confirmed, so all that is known for sure is that the top award went to a man who produced one of the most famous individual performances in sport – Surrey's off-spinner Jim Laker.

▶▶ This is the only time that **the programme** wasn't held in the year that it celebrated. This was because the *Daily Express* had purchased the Sportsman and Sportswoman of the Year awards from the *Sporting Record* and was unable to organize the event until January.

▶▶ The 1956 **Olympic Games** were split between two countries for the first time. Because Australia's quarantine laws prevented horses from competing in Melbourne, the equestrian events were staged in Stockholm. The British team won gold in the three-day eventing and bronze in the team jumping.

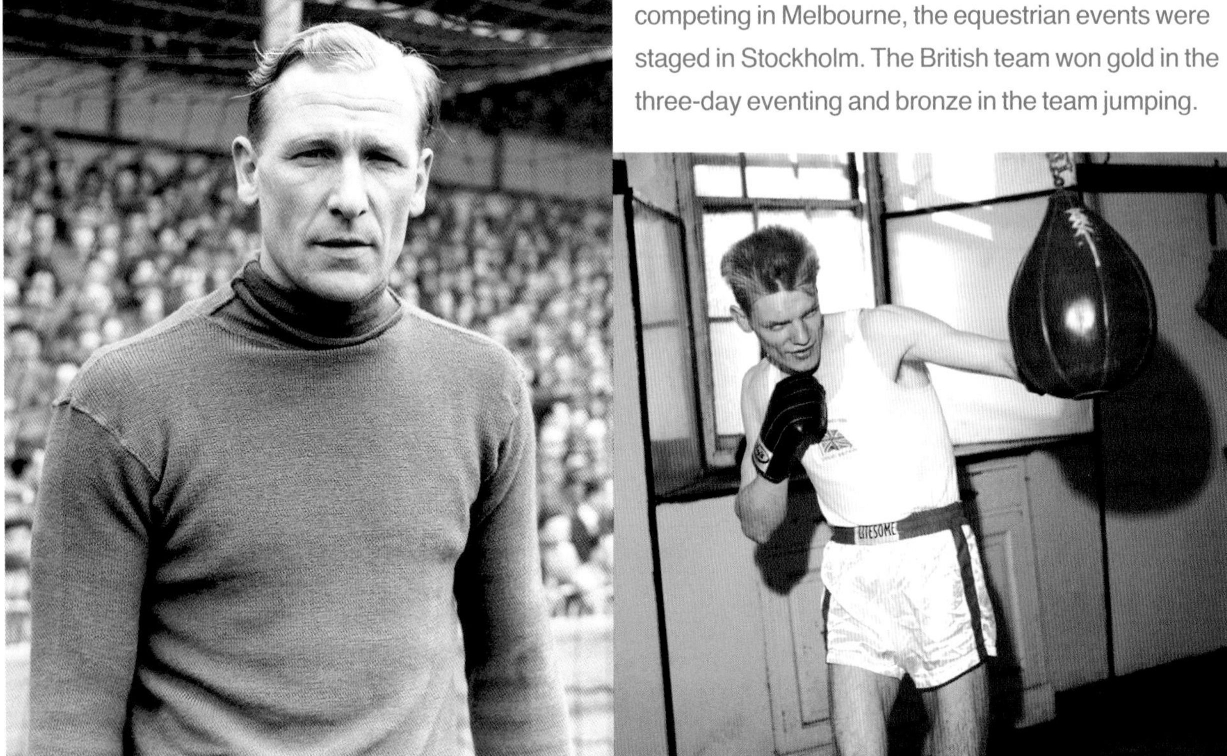

Sporting roundup

Cricket After 26 years and 45 matches, New Zealand finally won a Test match, when they beat the West Indies by 190 runs in Auckland.

Football In Scotland, Rangers won the Championship and Hearts the Cup, while in Europe, the first ever European Cup was won by Real Madrid, who beat Reims 4-3 in the final.

Horse racing The Grand National witnessed one of its most enduring mysteries: exactly why did the Queen Mother's horse, Devon Loch, fall to the ground while ahead of the field and with only 50 yards left to race? ESB won, but no-one remembers that.

Motor cycling John Surtees won the Senior TT at the Isle of Man and the first of his four 500cc world titles.

Motor racing In the Formula One World Championship, Stirling Moss was runner-up to Fangio for the second year in a row.

Rugby league St Helens won their first Challenge Cup trophy.

Rugby union Wales won the Five Nations crown.

1957

Date 12 December 1957 • Location Grosvenor House, London • Presenter Peter Dimmock
Editor Paul Fox • Producer Brian Cowgill

1st Dai Rees golfer

(no record of the second and third place winners survives)

Overall winner

The first Welshman to win the trophy, **Dai Rees** was runner-up three times in the Open and played in nine Ryder Cups between 1937 and 1961. He was also the non-playing captain in 1967. The 1957 victory was to be the only time that the USA lost the cup in a 52-year period of dominance.

The programme that had grown slowly in size and status now changed in location. 1957 saw the *Sportsview* Sports Personality of the Year award switched from the cramped confines of the Savoy to the grand acreage of the Great Room at the Grosvenor House in Park Lane.

Taking over as producer was Bryan Cowgill. In the next 30 years he would prove himself as one of the great television leviathans, but first of all, in partnership with editor Paul Fox, he had to prove himself with a year that had been more routine in comparison with the excitement of 1956.

Team sports provided many of the main stories and England's cricketers won a splendid Test series against the West Indies. Several of the players were also part of the team that won Surrey's sixth successive County Championship. Peter Dimmock interviewed the former Middlesex batsman Denis Compton about his long and sparkling career and his retirement. Compton's wider commercial activities had brought him fame beyond his sport and he was still clearly using the hair product that he so profitably promoted as he glistened under the lights of the small studio.

England's rugby union team also had a good season, having won their first Grand Slam since 1928. In football Manchester United dominated Division One, but were denied a historic treble when Aston Villa beat them 2-1 in the FA Cup final and they lost to Real Madrid in the semi-final of the European Cup.

Spurs' captain Danny Blanchflower was in the studio to pay tribute to the great Stanley Matthews, who had retired from international football at the age of 42, after winning 54 caps. Matthews was a candidate for the Sports Personality of the Year, as was Lester Piggott. He had had an outstanding 1957, winning the Derby and the 2000 Guineas on Crepello, as well as the Oaks on Carrozza.

Had there been an International award, the main contenders would undoubtedly have been Juan Fangio, who remained motor racing world champion, and Floyd Patterson, who had twice successfully defended his world heavyweight crown. It could also have gone to the South African golfer Bobby Locke, who was seen winning the Open at St Andrews, his fourth success.

At the start of the year, however, it was unlikely that many people would have tipped golf to produce the outstanding personality of 1957. It was a Ryder Cup year, but British and Irish golf fans had long abandoned any great optimism as the cup had been in American possession since 1935.

Top Denis Compton sweeps for a single in the last professional match of his career, as Middlesex play Worcestershire in the County Championship

Above Lester Piggott, on Crepello, is led in after winning the Derby. In all, he won the race a record nine times

Left Stanley Matthews, the gentleman player, was renowned for his politeness on the pitch and during his 36-year career was never sent off or even booked

Top Althea Gibson was so multi-talented, in 1959 she even released an album, entitled *Althea Gibson Sings*
Above John Charles, in his final season for Leeds before moving to Italy, powers a header towards the Arsenal goal
Opposite Juan Fangio drives his Maserati to victory in the German Grand Prix, to take his fifth World Championship in six years

When the Great Britain and Ireland team went into the last day at Lindrick in Yorkshire they required five and a half points from the eight final day singles and the odds looked stacked against them. It was then that the fighting qualities of the popular Welshman, Dai Rees, came to the fore and inspired them to one of the greatest final day performances in Ryder Cup history. Rees, who was also captain of the team, won both his matches and the Americans lost by three points, giving Britain and Ireland their first victory for 23 years.

Dai Rees' performance made such an impact on the British public that they voted for him in their thousands and in December he became the fourth person to win the Sports Personality of the Year trophy.

The programme ended with a dramatic flourish and a fanfare by four trumpeters from the Royal Military School of Music before the toastmaster, Mr John Mills, announced the arrival of the Ryder Cup team onto the stage. Peter Dimmock presented the BBC's award to Dai Rees, who then shook hands with his team before returning to the small studio to be interviewed at the end of the show. Athlete Derek Ibbotson and swimmer Diana Wilkinson won the *Daily Express* awards.

Dai Rees is the oldest person to receive the Sports Personality of the Year award. Born in Barry in March 1913, he was 44 when he collected it. He died in 1983.

Althea Gibson made history in 1957 when she defeated Darlene Hard at Wimbledon to become the first black winner of the competition. Having been raised in Harlem, Gibson had learned to box and play basketball, as well as tennis, and achieved further success as a golf professional. In 1957 she also won the Wimbledon doubles title with Hard and later that year took the US singles title as well.

Sporting roundup

Football John Charles played his last game for Leeds before signing for Juventus for a record British transfer fee of £70,000.

Horse racing Fred Winter rode Sundew to success in the Grand National.

Ice skating June Markham and Courtney Jones won the ice dance World Championships.

Tennis In the Wimbledon men's final Lew Hoad beat Ashley Cooper to retain the title.

1958

Date 10 December 1958 • Location Grosvenor House, London • Presenter Peter Dimmock
Editor Paul Fox • Producer Dennis Monger

1st **Ian Black** swimmer
2nd **Bobby Charlton** footballer
3rd **Nat Lofthouse** footballer

Overall winner

Ian Black had won three gold medals in the European Championships, as well as a gold and two silvers at the Empire Games. He went on to set various British and European records and the world record in the 440yds individual medley. He retired from competitive swimming in 1962 and later became a teacher.

Ian Black remembers ...

'I had won the Sports Writers' award and Sportsman of the Year but this was far and away the most important thing that I had ever won.

'Building up to the night I had serious doubts about whether I would win, but a few weeks before the programme Kenneth Wolstenholme appeared on *Sportsview* showing how to fill in the voting form. When Ken filled in the name of English footballer Nat Lofthouse this seemed to get all the Scottish voters behind me and they voted in their thousands!

'But even on the night I had my doubts. It was a black tie dinner and during the course of the meal certain individuals were taken off to the BBC studio to be interviewed by Peter Dimmock, but I was never asked. They called up Stirling Moss and Bobby Charlton but not me, so I assumed the winner must be one of them.

'When my name was called out I was astonished, especially as I received the *Daily Express* award that night as well. I was given the big trophy, which of course had pride of place in my home for a year. When that was taken away I wrote to the BBC asking if I could buy a small replica and they were kind enough to send me one for free.

'It is no longer in my home because in 2002, on St Andrew's night, the Scottish Sports Hall of Fame was set up in Edinburgh. I was one of the original inductees, so I donated my tartan dressing gown and Sports Personality of the Year trophy and they now sit proudly there.'

Grosvenor House was once again the venue for the broadcast and Peter Dimmock introduced proceedings from behind a desk in a side room with the now familiar opening lines of, 'Good evening and welcome to *Sportsview*'s gala night out.' One of the cameras then panned around the main banqueting room where the personalities were all seated in evening dress.

As well as a top table that featured Dai Rees, Roger Bannister, Judy Grinham, Derek Ibbotson and Pat Smythe, there were other tables themed by sport, including football, motor racing and swimming. Henry Cooper was at the boxing table with his brother George, and there was also a separate table for the ladies. However, Peter Dimmock explained that they deserved this because, 'It's been a wonderful year for Britain's sports girls.'

Indeed it had been and they had won a number of prestigious trophies, including tennis's Wightman Cup for the first time in 28 years. Golf's Curtis Cup was secured in August and at the Empire Games in Cardiff the British women's 4x100m athletics team and the medley relay swimmers had beaten the Australian favourites, setting new world records on both occasions.

Judy Grinham had played a key role in that swimming success but was now hoping to make a new career in films. In her chat with Peter Dimmock she revealed what had motivated her to come third in the European freestyle championship when she hadn't even anticipated a place. An overzealous official had tried to prevent her from competing as she wasn't wearing briefs under her costume and this had annoyed Grinham so much that it fired her up and helped her win the unexpected bronze.

But it was the tragic story of the Munich air crash that cast gloom over the whole of 1958. Eight Manchester United players and three officials were among the 23 who perished after their aircraft crashed on takeoff in February. The team were returning from a successful European Cup quarter-final against Red Star Belgrade and had stopped to refuel in Germany before continuing their journey to Manchester.

Below Manchester United line up for the European Cup quarter-final against Red Star Belgrade that preceded the Munich air disaster. Pictured are (from left to right) Duncan Edwards, Eddie Colman, Mark Jones, Ken Morgans, Bobby Charlton, Dennis Viollet, Tommy Taylor, Billy Foulkes, Harry Gregg, Albert Scanlon and Roger Byrne

Seventy days after the disaster they played in their second successive FA Cup final, their greatest victory being the fact that they made it to the match at all. In an emotional game, Bolton beat them 2-0 with Nat Lofthouse scoring both goals. If there had been a Team award, Manchester United would have been strong candidates. They won back-to-back league titles in 1956 and 1957 and twice reached the semi-final of the European Cup before that desperate night in Munich halted the progress of the magnificent Busby Babes.

Elsewhere in 1958 there were significant new faces and new developments. Although Peter Thomson won the Open Championship for the fourth time, at Royal Lytham, Arnold Palmer was winning his first major, the Masters, at the start of a career that would fundamentally change the face of professional golf.

Above Mike Hawthorn had a rather traditional dress sense and was known to prefer driving in a bow-tie, but crash helmets had been obligatory in Formula One since 1953

Opposite Pele tests French goalkeeper Claude Abbes in the 1958 World Cup semi-final. The slight but incredibly skilful young Brazilian got a hat-trick in 20 minutes in this match, which ended 5-2

In Stockholm that summer the world was introduced to another budding superstar in the shape of a 17-year-old footballer named Pele. He helped Brazil to their first World Cup success when they beat Sweden 5-2 in the final, and his incomparable talent took his sport to a previously unimagined level.

For the first time all four home countries made it to the finals, but the England captain, Billy Wright, acknowledged that his team were outplayed and deserved to go out. His most memorable moment of the year hadn't been in Sweden, however, but came when Wolverhampton Wanderers won the First Division Championship to give him his first league medal.

In Formula One, Fangio had retired and named Stirling Moss as his likely successor, but Moss faced fierce rivalry from Mike Hawthorn, who became Britain's first ever world champion. However, at the age of 29, Hawthorn decided to change direction and on the programme he spoke for the first time about his decision to retire. With his blond hair and dashing good looks he would have been perfectly cast in the more glamorous motor racing days that were to come, but he was tragically killed in a road accident on the Guildford bypass just a few weeks later.

As the show drew to a close it became very formal and a toastmaster introduced Peter Dimmock, who ascended the main stage. Surrounded by flowers, pipers and trophies he began by announcing that over 150,000 votes had been cast before he declared that the Scot who had become 1958's Sports Personality of the Year was the all-conquering swimmer, Ian Black.

▸▸ At 17, **Ian Black** remains the youngest ever winner of Sports Personality of the Year.

▸▸ **Grandstand** had begun broadcasting on BBC1 on 11 October 1958. The programme's arrival greatly increased the amount of sport on television.

Sporting roundup

Athletics The 20-year-old Australian, Herb Elliott, broke the 1500m and mile world records as he emerged to dominate middle distance running.

Boxing In America, Hogan Kid Bassey beat Ricardo Moreno in the third round to take the world lightweight title.

Cricket Surrey won their seventh successive County Championship.

Horse racing The Derby was won by Charlie Smirke on Hard Ridden. Mr What finished first in the Grand National.

Motor cycling John Surtees regained the 500cc World Championship. It was his second title in three years.

Rugby union England were Five Nations champions.

Speedway Barry Briggs retained the world title.

Tennis Ashley Cooper beat fellow Australian Neale Fraser in the men's final at Wimbledon and Althea Gibson defeated Britain's Angela Mortimer to retain the women's title.

1959

Date 16 December 1959 • Location Television Theatre, London • Presenters Peter Dimmock with David Coleman and Brian Johnston • Editor Paul Fox • Producer Brian Cowgill

1st **John Surtees** motor cyclist
2nd **Bobby Charlton** footballer
3rd **Ian Black** swimmer

Overall winner

In 1960, **John Surtees** went on to retain both his 350cc and 500cc titles, before switching to Formula One. He became the only man to win World Championships on both two and four wheels when he took the title for Ferrari in 1964.

John Surtees remembers ...

'When it came to awards, 1959 was a grand slam year for me because I was lucky enough to win all the top ones that were going. Not only did I win the BBC award but also the Sportsman of the Year and the Sports Writers' award, and because I was riding an Italian machine I was also made Italian Sportsman of the Year!

'What I remember most about the atmosphere of that 1959 programme, which maybe contrasts with today, was that we were all there because we loved what we were doing. Money and earnings were not an issue and we all felt a great sense of privilege to be in the studio audience.

'It was a difficult time for me because it was the year I had been introduced to driving a Grand Prix Vanwall by Tony Vandervell at Goodwood and my head was full of thoughts of making the switch to four wheels full-time, although I tried to avoid discussing it on the show.

'The following year I was driving cars one week and bikes the next, and I knew after the race at Monza in September that I had ridden my last race on two wheels. Most of those inside the sport seemed to know, but I chose the 1960 programme to make the formal announcement to the wider public, with the Madame Tussaud's waxwork in the studio to emphasize my change of sport. I'm sure that's long since melted down, but it's nice to have the things you've done remembered.'

In 1959, a move to the Television Theatre in Shepherd's Bush, combined with breaking away from the *Daily Express* awards, enabled the BBC's *Sports Review* to finally grow up. By organising the actual event as well as the show, the production team was able to base the programme on a full stage, bringing in cars and props to add greater variety to the 75-minute show. However, the *Sportsview* desk remained an essential element.

It hadn't been a vintage year, but the programme made the most of the limited raw material it had to work with. In particular, there was the studio appearance of Sweden's Ingemar Johansson, who had provided the upset of the year in defeating Floyd Patterson in New York to claim the world heavyweight title.

David Coleman appeared on the show for the first time, pointing out members of the 'greatest sporting assembly ever gathered'. These included the new England football captain Johnny Haynes, Danny Blanchflower, the Northern Irish captain, and Noel Cantwell who led Eire.

There was also a touch of theatre at the start of the show when, from behind large photographs of themselves, out stepped three great stars who had retired that year. Godfrey Evans had been England's wicket-keeper for a record 91 tests; Billy Wright captained England's footballers in 90 of his 105 internationals; and swimmer Judy Grinham was retiring at the age of just 20.

Motor racing played a major part in the show and six minutes of race footage illustrated the World Championship battle between Stirling Moss and Jack Brabham. It included Moss's second place to Brabham in the British Grand Prix, breaking down after one and a half laps in Germany, winning in Portugal and leading in the final race of the season in Florida, when yet again his car seized up. In a dramatic finish Bruce McLaren won that race when Brabham ran out of petrol on the last lap. Undaunted, the

Right Ingemar Johansson's reign as world heavyweight champion was brief as Floyd Patterson regained the title from him a year later
Below David Coleman's own athletic career was cut short by injury, but he went on to become a popular and enduring commentator

Australian got out and pushed the car 450m to the line, to be crowned world champion. In a recreation of that moment, Jack Brabham pushed his car into the *Sports Review* studio, where he was interviewed. Roy Salvadori's Le Mans-winning Aston Martin was then wheeled in, too.

The ten-minute boxing film that then followed included, in the words of commentator Len Martin, 'the punch of the year – Ingo's Bingo'. Viewers saw all seven times that Ingemar Johansson knocked down reigning world champion Floyd Patterson in the third round of their heavyweight title bout. Henry Cooper was then introduced as Britain's boxer of the year, having won and retained the British and Empire heavyweight titles.

Yorkshire had finally prised Surrey's fingers off cricket's County Championship trophy after seven years of domination. Their successful but retiring captain, Ron Burnett, and their new skipper, Vic Wilson, were both interviewed by Brian Johnston as members of their team were shown doing slip-catching practice in the studio.

On the track, Gordon Pirie beat Derek Ibbotson in the final 50m of their classic two-mile race at White City, while in Moscow a new star emerged when the British team took on the Soviets at the Lenin Stadium. Len Martin's commentary on the film was a little different in style from that of today, though, when he announced: 'The personality of the meeting is a pretty 19-year-old, Mary Bignal, the shapely lass from Somerset.'

John Surtees was the leading candidate for the 1959 award however, having had another outstanding season. He had become the 500cc world champion for the third time in four years, as well as retaining the 350cc title.

Peter Dimmock then stepped forward to reveal the top three places. The toastmaster had gone but the annual fanfare was retained. Swimmer Ian Black was third, Manchester United's Bobby Charlton was second, but the winner was John Surtees, rewarded by viewers for his unrivalled consistency.

Above Godfrey Evans, one of England's greatest wicketkeepers
Right Jack Burkitt, Nottingham Forest captain, holds the FA Cup after leading his team to victory over Luton Town, 2-1
Opposite Jack Brabham in his Cooper Climax. He was world champion three times, but is the only driver to have won the title in a car he constructed himself – the BT19 in 1966

▶▶ **Motor cycling** is one of 14 different sports whose stars have won the Sports Personality award.

▶▶ The International Cross Country Championship, which was held in Portugal in March, was the main outdoor race event of the year. **Fred Norris**, a 37-year-old miner from Bolton, led the British team to victory, but had to forfeit a week's wages in order to represent his country.

Sporting roundup

Cricket The Test year began with England losing 4-0 in Australia, but picked up when they beat India 5-0 in the summer.

Cycling Brian Robinson was Britain's leading cyclist, having won a stage of the Tour de France for the second successive year.

Football Nottingham Forest beat Luton 2-1 to win the FA Cup, even though they had lost Roy Dwight with a broken leg and had to play with ten men. St Mirren beat Aberdeen 3-0 to win the Scottish Cup, and both Rangers and Wolves reached the last eight of the European Cup, having won their leagues that season.

Golf Gary Player's first Open victory, at Muirfield, was also the first of his nine Majors.

Horse racing Parthia was first home in the Derby and Oxo won the Grand National.

Rugby league Wigan retained the Challenge Cup.

Rugby union France were outright Five Nations champions for the first time.

Tennis Alex Olmedo turned professional after winning the Wimbledon men's final against an unseeded Rod Laver, while Brazil's Maria Bueno won the first of her three titles when she defeated Darlene Hard in straight sets.

Peter Dimmock, presenter
remembers …

'People knew me as a sports presenter but that was really only a tiny part of what I did. My job was partly to provide the BBC liaison with the royal family, but I was also head of outside broadcasts and chairman of a programme committee on the European Broadcasting Union.

'When it came to *Sportsview*, Paul Fox would send me the script around 4.30 p.m. and I would do my best to re-write it in my own words. I really didn't know what the hell I was doing most of the time. It was same when it came to the *Review of the Year*, and the programme was a tribute to Paul Fox and his enthusiasm for sports journalism as well as sports broadcasting. He combined the two to make *Sportsview*, and once a year *Sports Review of the Year* pulled together the highlights.

'I soon became aware of the growing power of the programme and within a couple of years we had agents campaigning on behalf of their clients, and even trying to manipulate the voting, because they appreciated the importance of the prize in advancing a sports person's reputation and marketability.

'Others were also trying to cash in on the commercial possibilities of the show and I still cringe when I recall the *Daily Express* executive who stood up at the end of about the second or third *Review* programme and mentioned the name of the paper at least a dozen times in a minute and a half. The BBC was even more sensitive about commercial pressures in those days, compared to now, and I got a big telling off from a fellow called Williams in administration.

'In the early days we were dependent on the *Sporting Record* and the *Daily Express* providing all the food, drink and hospitality, but when the show moved to the Television Theatre, the BBC catering department took over. We would have a party on the stage after the show and pretty soon it was the party that all Britain's sports people and sports administrators wanted to come to, because there was simply nothing else like it in the calendar.'

Sir Paul Fox, programme editor, remembers ...

'It was outrageous, really, that Chris Chataway won that first award and not Roger Bannister, but it was all down to the power of the television pictures.

'The coverage of Bannister's four-minute mile was screened a day late and was shot by a single camera. By contrast, Chataway's victory over Kuts was an outside broadcast with dramatic pictures and 45,000 roaring him on in the White City stadium. The voters couldn't resist it.

'Peter Dimmock was the man who pushed the idea through and made the programme work. He was an amazing operator. Only 34 years old, assistant head of outside broadcasts and a great presenter and commentator, who had just made his name with his work on the Coronation. He'd been a commentator on racing and ice hockey and was just perfect on *Sportsview* and the *Review of the Year*.

'He was dapper and had special suits made that could handle microphone leads and all the hardware involved with the talkback, plus he had star quality. He was my boss four days of the week and I was his boss for one day.

'Len Martin was an Australian who had come here to see the Coronation and stayed for a long and distinguished career with the BBC. His was the ideal 'newsreel' voice and he was an essential part of the first *Review of the Year* and a familiar voice for many years to come on the BBC.

'I went into print on not being too happy about the *Sporting Record* tie-up. I felt we were bigger than that, but we got the venue and the guests and the party afterwards courtesy of them. Later it was changed to an association with the *Daily Express*, which was far more in keeping with the status of the programme.

'The first vote came in the days before the *Radio Times* printed coupons and I think they were a bit sniffy about the whole operation, so we called for postcards and my family and a few secretaries helped count them all up.'

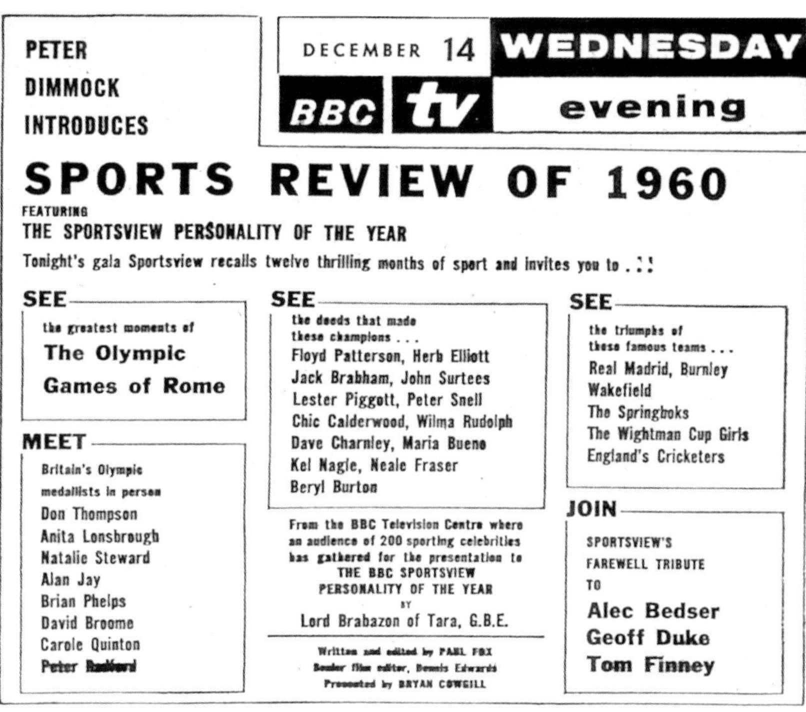

PETER DIMMOCK INTRODUCES

DECEMBER 14 WEDNESDAY

BBC tv evening

SPORTS REVIEW OF 1960

FEATURING

THE SPORTSVIEW PERSONALITY OF THE YEAR

Tonight's gala Sportsview recalls twelve thrilling months of sport and invites you to . . .

SEE

the greatest moments of
The Olympic Games of Rome

MEET

Britain's Olympic medallists in person
Don Thompson
Anita Lonsbrough
Natalie Steward
Alan Jay
Brian Phelps
David Broome
Carole Quinton
Peter Radford

SEE

the deeds that made these champions . . .
Floyd Patterson, Herb Elliott
Jack Brabham, John Surtees
Lester Piggott, Peter Snell
Chic Calderwood, Wilma Rudolph
Dave Charnley, Maria Bueno
Kel Nagle, Neale Fraser
Beryl Burton

From the BBC Television Centre where an audience of 200 sporting celebrities has gathered for the presentation to THE BBC SPORTSVIEW PERSONALITY OF THE YEAR BY Lord Brabazon of Tara, G.B.E.

Written and edited by PAUL FOX
Senior film editor, Dennis Edwards
Presented by BRYAN COWGILL

SEE

the triumphs of these famous teams . . .
Real Madrid, Burnley
Wakefield
The Springboks
The Wightman Cup Girls
England's Cricketers

JOIN

SPORTSVIEW'S FAREWELL TRIBUTE TO
Alec Bedser
Geoff Duke
Tom Finney

1960

Date 14 December 1960 • Location Television Centre, London • Presenters Peter Dimmock with David Coleman Editor Paul Fox • Producer Brian Cowgill

1st **David Broome** show-jumper
2nd **Don Thompson** walker
3rd **Anita Lonsbrough** swimmer

Overall winner

David Broome was a show-jumping legend who remained at the top of his sport for over 30 years. He was European Champion on Sunsalve in 1961 and then again in 1967. He defended his title in 1968 on Mr Softee, the same year that he won a second Olympic bronze. Broome was World Champion on Beethoven in 1970 and helped Britain to win the world team title in 1978. The following year he shared the BBC's Team of the Year award when the British show-jumpers won the European Championship.

David Broome remembers ...

'I look back now and wonder how I managed to get more votes than anyone else, but back in 1960 show-jumping was such a prominent television sport that it sometimes seemed as if it was on six nights a week, so people knew both the riders and the names of their horses.

'I was only a young lad but the viewers became familiar with me and my horse Sunsalve. Straight after he was given to me we took part in a big televised event at White City. We came second on the first night and on the following evening won the highly prestigious Kings Cup. From then it was just fantastic and we came third in the Olympics, where we were also clear in the team event.

'Sunsalve had the most fantastic temperament and could cope with anything, but I was still surprised to see him led on during the programme. My father had made all the arrangements and brought him to the studio without my knowledge, but I had no doubts that he could handle the strange surroundings and situation. My main worry was whether I could handle it, but I still look back on that night as one of the great accolades of my career.'

In 1960, *Sports Review of the Year* went another big step towards becoming the programme we are all familiar with. As the show went on air at 8 p.m., Peter Dimmock welcomed more than 200 personalities to the new Television Centre in West London and announced the introduction of two new trophies: the International award and the Team of the Year award.

Where football, rugby and athletics dominate today, in 1960 the public's viewing habits and sporting enthusiasms were very different. This was illustrated when the top three places were filled by show-jumping, race walking and swimming.

There were plenty of candidates in every category because it was Olympic year once again, with Rome staging a highly successful games. There had been regular coverage on the BBC for the first time and the fact that the show was now in its own purpose-built studio meant that many Olympic medallists were introduced on stage.

Britain had two gold medals to celebrate. Huddersfield's Anita Lonsbrough swam a perfectly judged race to win the 200m breaststroke in a world record time and Don Thompson, an insurance clerk from Middlesex, became an overnight hero with his courageous victory in the 50m walk.

David Coleman interviewed them both. Lonsbrough's remaining ambition, she said, was to win European gold in 1962. Thompson, meanwhile, explained that he had trained by putting an oil stove and electric wall heater in his bathroom, boiling a kettle and then exercising in there for 45 minutes at a time. He reckoned that he did this on 30 or 40 occasions in the four months before the Olympics in order to acclimatize himself to the Rome summer.

In international terms the star performers in Italy were the American athlete, Wilma Rudolph, with her three gold medals on the track, and the barefoot Ethiopian soldier, Abebe Bikila. He was unknown to the sporting world before the games, but won the marathon in an Olympic record time.

Above Wilma Rudolph suffered from polio as a child, but that didn't prevent her amazing athletic achievements

David Coleman introduced another section with two British world champions. He spoke first to cyclist Beryl Burton as she stood in her kit alongside her bike in the year that she won the world pursuit and road race titles. He seemed surprised that she could manage to compete at all, though, exclaiming, 'You've also got a job, you're a housewife and you've got a child.' Burton responded that she would happily turn professional if she was offered £20 a week and a pound a mile!

Meanwhile, a waxwork of John Surtees had been sitting on a motorbike beside them and Coleman now turned to it, saying, 'This is, of course, only a model, and already it is a model of the past. This is how you'll see him in the future – as a racing driver.' The camera then revealed Surtees in his racing car, as he announced his retirement from motorcycles. Just four years later he was motor racing world champion.

The winner of the seventh Sports Personality of the Year award was a rider of another kind and, thanks to the

Overseas winner

The first ever International Sports Personality of the Year was **Herb Elliott**, who was already a hugely popular figure in the UK. The 22-year-old Australian was one of the greatest ever middle distance runners, even though he was only on the world stage from 1958 to 1960.

In August 1958 he took an incredible 2.7 seconds off the mile world record. He also broke the 1500m world record in the same year and reduced it further in the Olympic final in Rome when, in his kangaroo hide track shoes, he destroyed an impressive field and finished almost 20m ahead of the Frenchman, Michel Jazy.

Elliott joined Peter Dimmock in the studio and explained that following his success in the Rome Olympics, he had retired from sport aged just 22 and gone to Cambridge University.

Team winner

The sensational 7-3 victory of Real Madrid over Eintracht Frankfurt in the European Cup final had been one of the highlights of the year, but they were not candidates for what was purely a domestic team award in the gift of the programme editor, Paul Fox. His decision gave the trophy to the **Cooper Motor Racing team** that had taken Jack Brabham to the World Championship for the second time. His team mate Bruce McLaren was runner-up.

Brabham had retained his title by winning five consecutive races, from June to September, and Peter Dimmock interviewed him in the studio as he sat in his race car, before presenting the first ever Team award to race director, John Cooper.

Opposite Beryl Burton dominated women's cycling – both pursuit and road racing – for quarter of a century. She died in 1996, aged 58, while cycling near her Harrogate home

viewers' love affair with show-jumping, it was David Broome. The 20-year-old showjumper had won an Olympic bronze medal on Sunsalve and regularly featured on *Grandstand*. Trumpeters played a fanfare to introduce the presentations as Peter Dimmock, with the final three on podiums in darkness behind him, read out the places. As Broome waited to be handed the trophy by Lord Brabazon of Tara, his Lordship launched into a five-minute speech of appreciation that included the line: 'To see a young man on a splendid horse jump about six foot is really very thrilling while you are sitting in your armchair.' A slightly bemused Broome then saw his own splendid horse brought into the studio and the pair of them trotted gently off the set as Peter Dimmock closed the show from behind the *Sportsview* desk.

▶▶ The now famous *Sports Review* **music** was first used in 1960. It's called 'Pioneer Trail', was composed by Charles Williams and was played by the Melody Light Orchestra. Williams was the resident composer for Gaumont-British Films during the 1930s and was responsible for many soundtracks, including *The 39 Steps* and *The Young Mr Pitt*.

▶▶ On the day that the show was broadcast the **West Indies** and **Australia** made cricket history in Brisbane when they took part in the first Test match to end in a tie.

Sporting roundup

Boxing Floyd Patterson made boxing history in June when he became the first man to regain the world heavyweight title. He knocked out Imgemar Johansson in the fifth round of their rematch.

Cricket England had a good year, winning 1-0 in the West Indies and beating South Africa 3-0 in the summer. The prolific partnership of Fred Trueman and Brian Statham accounted for 52 wickets in the five-Test series.

Football Burnley were Division One champions, while runners-up Wolverhampton Wanderers won the FA Cup by beating Blackburn Rovers 3-0.

Golf Australian Kel Nagle, the 100-1 outsider, won the centenary Open Championship at St Andrews. It was also a good year for Arnold Palmer, who came second in his first Open Championship and won both the US Open and the Masters.

Horse racing The Grand National was televised live on *Grandstand* for the first time and was won by Merryman II. Lester Piggott, still only 25, won his third Derby on St Paddy, on his way to clinching his first Jockeys' Championship.

Rugby league Wakefield Trinity beat Hull by a record 38-5 in the Challenge Cup final.

Rugby union England won the Triple Crown but shared the Five Nations championship with France.

Tennis Neale Fraser beat Rod Laver to win his first Wimbledon title and Maria Bueno beat Sandra Reynolds 8-6 6-0 to retain the women's crown.

1961

Date 13 December 1961 • Location Television Centre, London • Presenters Peter Dimmock with David Coleman, Harry Carpenter and Peter West • Editors Ronnie Noble and Leslie Kettley • Producer Brian Cowgill

1st **Stirling Moss** racing driver
2nd **Billy Walker** boxer
3rd **Angela Mortimer** tennis player

Overall winner

Stirling Moss (above left) won 16 of his 66 races from 1951–61 and was runner-up four times from 1955–58. He was third in 1959, 1960 and 1961, but was severely injured in a crash at Goodwood in 1962 and forced to retire. His sister, Pat Moss, was a leading rally driver, who also featured occasionally on the programme.

Stirling Moss was very happy to win, saying, 'I can't tell you how honoured I am to be here to receive this trophy tonight. I'm honoured on my own behalf and also because it is the first occasion that motor racing has managed to get at the top of the pile.'

The opportunities for televising sport were increasing all the time and 1961 was the most ambitious *Review of the Year* that the *Sportsview* team had yet attempted. Ronnie Noble and Leslie Kettley shared the editor's responsibilities and the soundtrack featured voices and reputations that would be the backbone of BBC Sport for years to come. Henry Longhurst, Peter O'Sullevan, Dan Maskell, Kenneth Wolstenholme, Eddie Waring, David Coleman and Brian Johnston were among those who voiced the films, and Harry Carpenter made his first studio appearance on the show.

There were no major international events in 1961 so the programme focussed on the wide range of sports that were now covered by the BBC. Three British sportsmen who had become world champions that year were introduced at the beginning of the show and, one by one, were revealed under a spotlight. They were the boxers Terry Downes (middleweight) and John Caldwell (bantamweight) and 21-year-old motor cyclist Mike Hailwood, who was the new 250cc champion.

In boxing, the domestic scene was dominated by November's amateur match between Britain and the USA. Amid a frenzied crowd at the Empire Pool, Wembley, Britain completed an extraordinary 10-0 whitewash, which included the then unknown 'blonde bomber', Billy Walker, flattening Cornelius Perry with a right and left combination in the first round of their heavyweight bout.

Having emerged as a major new personality, Walker trained with a punch bag as he was interviewed in the studio by Harry Carpenter. He had been given instant recognition by that televised fight but planned to stay amateur for a while longer. Always an incredibly popular fighter, Walker sadly never fulfilled his promise.

The quickest win of the year was by Dave Charnley, when he successfully defended his British, European and Empire lightweight titles by knocking out Welshman Darkie Hughes in just 40 seconds, including the count!

Richie Benaud's Australian cricketers had won the Ashes 2-1 in England that summer, but the high spot for many had been when Hampshire won the County Championship. They had played bright and adventurous cricket all year and the team were in the studio in their whites, along with their captain, Colin Ingleby-McKenzie.

Another candidate for Sports Personality of the Year was the motor cyclist Mike Hailwood. He had become the first rider to win all three main classes at the Isle of Man TT and was also the youngest ever 250cc world champion.

Hailwood was seen on film riding towards a camera, which then cut back to the studio to give the illusion that he had ridden straight onto the set. This worked pretty well, and the bike stayed upright, but Hailwood confessed to David Coleman that he had fallen off nine times that season. His ambition was to try and win the world 500cc title, an aspiration that he fulfilled the following year.

Jimmy Hill had led professional football toward the 1961 abolition of the maximum wage and the game had embraced a transfer system that took it into the modern, commercial age. Within a few months of its inception, Jimmy Greaves had left Chelsea for Milan and then moved on to Spurs, and Denis Law joined Manchester United to become Britain's first £100,000 player.

Tennis was still an amateur game and the young Australian Rod Laver collected the trophy but no money when he won the first of his four Wimbledon men's singles titles. However, the 1961 Championships will be remembered for the first all-British women's final since 1914, and both Angela Mortimer and Christine Truman were in the studio to watch the highlights on a small television set. The 20-year-old Truman had won the first set before picking up an injury that enabled Mortimer to take advantage and become the first British champion since Dorothy Round in 1937.

Angela Mortimer received enough support to place her in third spot, behind Billy Walker, but once again it was motor sport that had drawn most of the viewers' votes and the award went to one of the most enduring characters in British sport – Stirling Moss.

In fact, 1961 had been a difficult season for Formula One. The American driver Phil Hill won the motor racing World Championship in his Ferrari, but only after another horror crash had claimed the life of his team-mate, Wolfgang Von Tripps, and 11 spectators at Monza.

Left Mike Hailwood, who later switched to four wheels, received the George Medal for rescuing fellow driver Clay Regazzoni from his burning car when he crashed in the 1973 South African Grand Prix

Overseas winner

Valeriy Brumel won the International award at just 19, having twice broken the world highjump record that year. Peter Dimmock illustrated the achievement by standing under a highjump bar that was set at the new world record height of 7'4$^1/_2$".

A film was then shown of the Russian jumper receiving the trophy from David Coleman at the Institute of Sport in Moscow. Never one to understate, Len Martin's voice-over described the Russian as having, 'Gone further into space unaided than any other man!'

Brumel went on to win gold at the European Championships in 1962 and the Olympic title in Tokyo in 1964, to add to his silver medal from Rome 1960. In total he set six world records, but his career was destroyed in 1965 when he was a passenger on a motorbike that hit a concrete pillar and he needed more than 20 operations. Incredibly, he did manage to jump again, but never in international competition.

Team winner

Peter Dimmock introduced the Team award with the words, 'The year belongs to Spurs, the first club this century to complete the historic league and cup double.'

Indeed, there was only ever one real candidate for the second presentation of this trophy, and the **Tottenham Hotspur** team, including captain Danny Blanchflower (above), were in the studio, along with their manager, Bill Nicholson, having clinched the double by beating Leicester City 2-0 in the FA Cup final.

Below Angela Mortimer was partially deaf but said this helped her shut out distractions and concentrate when on court

Opposite Valeriy Brumel shared a birth date – 14 April 1942 – with the man who finally jumped higher than him, China's Ni Chih-Chin. This was a1970 jump of 2.29m, although the record wasn't ratified

Moss had performed very strongly throughout the year and he had won two races, including an epic performance at the Nurburgring when his skill took him to victory round the 170 curves on the 14-mile circuit. On straighter tracks, however, the superior power of the Ferraris proved unbeatable, but Moss's style and charisma made him one of the best known and loved sportsmen in Britain. The president of the International Federation of Football Associations (FIFA), Sir Stanley Rous, presented him with the award.

▸▸ Although athletics has dominated the domestic award with 16 wins, **Valeriy Brumel** was the first of only four people from track and field who have been presented with the Overseas trophy.

▸▸ In 1961 **Stanley Matthews** returned to Stoke City, where he had begun his career in 1930. He was described on the show as 'the reluctant middle-aged hero who persists as a living legend'.

Sporting roundup

Football In the home internationals, Jimmy Greaves scored one of his record six international hat-tricks as England beat Scotland 9-3 at Wembley.

Golf Arnold Palmer recorded his first Open victory when he finished one shot ahead of Dai Rees at Royal Birkdale.

Horse racing Aintree witnessed an epic finish as Nicolaus Silver beat the reigning champion, Merryman II, in the Grand National. It was the first time in 90 years that a grey had triumphed. There was a major upset at the Derby when the race was won by Psidium, a 66-1 outsider.

Rugby league St Helens beat Wigan 12-6 in the Challenge Cup final.

Rugby union France won the Five Nations, but the main story was the tour of the ruthless and intimidating Springboks. They ground down teams for 29 consecutive wins until they were eventually beaten by the Barbarians.

Harry Carpenter, presenter, remembers ...

'I had been with the BBC since 1949, but was still not full-time with them when I was first asked to be one of Peter Dimmock's co-presenters on the 1961 *Sports Review*.

'I remember that my first interview was with boxer Billy Walker, who had emerged as a new British heavyweight prospect. The shows were a very daunting experience as I was always worried that I might cock up in front of the audience of famous people. It was quite an odd programme to work on. For most of the year we would present from small, silent studios with just a handful of crew around us and then, for one night only, we had a live audience of several hundred of the country's top names staring at us.

'I was used to sitting behind a desk but with *Review* it was link, dash across the studio, look into a new camera and read another link. It was great fun to do, though. With Muhammad Ali that was very easy. All I had to do was set him going, sit back, wait for him to finish and then thank him!

'My strongest memory of Ali is from 1978, when I got an early morning phone call from Jack Oakman, who was the BBC Sport outside broadcasts admin chief. He said they wanted me to go and present Ali with the Overseas award in Mississippi, where he was making a film. When I protested that it was impossible as the show was in only three days time, I was told that a car was already on its way to pick me up. I was taken to Heathrow, got on Concorde, flew to New York, took a connection to New Orleans and a private plane flew me up the Mississippi river to Natchez. I interviewed Ali the next morning, gave him the award, grabbed the film and set off back to London. Having retraced my steps I got back just in time for the show.

'There are so many other great memories. I really used to enjoy interviewing Graham Hill and it was a great shame that he never won as he was both an outstanding sportsman and personality. Finding myself in the lift at Drury Lane with Red Rum was an unforgettable moment, and I loved doing the interviews with the boxers each year. I was so pleased each time that Henry Cooper won the trophy because he was, and still is, a very kind and generous man and a tremendous role model.

'How many programmes last 50 years? Very few I suspect. It's a show that's regarded very highly and the voting always fascinates people. I think that the name is a misnomer, though. The public believes they are voting for the outstanding sportsman or woman based on the feats they have achieved, not the outstanding personality – otherwise Chris Eubank would win every year.

'There are so many other great memories. I really used to enjoy interviewing Graham Hill and it was a great shame that he never won'

'After 25 years I did my last show in 1985, but then came out of retirement to present the 40th anniversary programme in 1994. That decade has gone very quickly. I love going back and meeting old friends and colleagues. It was great to work on a show that you knew a sizable part of the nation would be watching. It was a programme that mattered to people and I think it still does.'

BBC

1962

Date 19 December 1962 • **Location** Television Centre, London • **Presenters** Peter Dimmock with David Coleman and Peter West • **Editors** Ronnie Noble and Leslie Kettley • **Producer** Brian Cowgill

1st Anita Lonsbrough swimmer
2nd Dorothy Hyman athlete
3rd Linda Ludgrove swimmer

Overall winner

Anita Lonsbrough had a tremendous year, winning one European and three Empire golds, as well as setting two world records. She was only 21 when she collected the Sports Personality of the Year award and was also the first swimmer to receive an MBE when she was honoured in 1963. She retired from competition the following year. In 1965 Anita married the cyclist Hugh Porter and has remained closely connected to swimming through her work as a commentator and journalist.

Anita Lonsbrough remembers ...

'It was hardly surprising that swimming was prominent in voters' minds in this period because the BBC had a contract to screen one major swimming meeting a month, so we were never far from the viewers' attention.

'I had come third two years earlier and a lot of people felt I was the favourite to win this time, but on the night the BBC did their best to suggest to me that I hadn't. All the time they kept dropping hints that Dorothy Hyman had won and then before the show they called myself, Dorothy and Linda Ludgrove together and told us that it was between the three of us and to get a speech prepared. I didn't really bother because I was still convinced it was going to be Dorothy Hyman. But I was lucky enough to have won three golds and a silver at the Empire Games in the period just before voting started and I am sure this was what swung it my way.

'The trophy had pride of place on top of the television for a year but since then it has been replaced, not by a replica but by a horrible little wooden plaque with a medal on the front that is falling apart. But at least the memories are as strong as ever.'

The first eight winners of the Sports Personality of the Year trophy had all been men, but 1962 was the year that women's sport made its breakthrough in style, taking the first three places in the voting.

The men had their moments during the year, the most awesome being the manner in which Sonny Liston took the world heavyweight title from Floyd Patterson with a first round knockout. Patterson was floored after only two minutes six seconds, the third fastest time in world heavyweight history. One of the programme's regular guests, Britain's Terry Downes, lasted the distance but lost his world middleweight title to Paul Pender in Boston.

It was all grace and composure elsewhere, though. At Troon, Arnold Palmer won his second Open Championship by a six-shot margin. The elegant Rod Laver won Wimbledon for the second time and completed the first Grand Slam of the four major championships since 1938. Fellow Australian Margaret Court won three out of four, but was beaten in the first round of Wimbledon by a young Billie Jean Moffitt. Karen Susman beat Vera Sukova in the women's final.

The seventh football World Cup took place in Chile, but was marred by a violent and riotous game between the hosts and Italy that resulted in two players being sent off and several pitch invasions. Walter Winterbottom led his England team to the quarter-finals, where they were beaten by the outstanding Brazilians, who went on to retain the trophy by beating Czechoslovakia 3-1 in the final. Winterbottom later resigned after four World Cup campaigns and 139 matches in charge. He was replaced by a man who was to have a profound influence on British sport – Alf Ramsey.

Horses returned to the studio when Peter Dimmock interviewed Pat Smythe on Flannagan and David Broome on Mr Softee, following successful years for both, but neither rider was to feature highly in the voting at the end of the show. When it came to the viewers' choice for Sports Personality of the Year, the poll was dominated by British women on the track and in the pool.

Third-placed Linda Ludgrove had claimed double swimming gold at the Empire Games in Perth, winning both the 110yds and 220yds backstroke. Sprinter Dorothy

Below Sonny Liston, an ex-convict with a hard stare and alleged underworld connections, was a tough opponent
Right Arnold Palmer won 29 titles and $400,000 – an incredible sum given the small prize money on offer – during his peak of 1960–63

Team winner

Following an all-British battle for the title, in 1962 Britain once again had a world motor racing champion, with Graham Hill holding off the challenge from Jim Clark to clinch the crown in the final Grand Prix of the season in South Africa. During the programme a great piece of film was shown, which featured Graham Hill with a camera on his BRM car, doing a circuit of a track and commentating through all the gear changes and speeds. Hill's **BRM team** was honoured with the Team of the Year award and British motor racing was on the verge of a golden era.

Overseas winner

Donald Jackson was one of the best figure skaters never to win an Olympic title, although he did collect bronze in 1960. In 1962 he became the first Canadian to win the World Championship with an incredible display that saw him awarded a record seven perfect marks. He was also the first man to land the triple lutz in competition. He turned professional before the 1964 Olympics and won two further World Championships before returning to Canada to coach.

The award was presented to 22-year-old Jackson by Alan Weeks, at a live outside broadcast from Streatham ice rink.

Above Graham Hill pulls into the pits in his BRM after winning the Italian Grand Prix
Opposite Wakefield Trinity's Briggs is tackled by Huddersfield's Hayward in the Challenge Cup final. Wakefield won 12-6

Hyman came second, having had a prolific year. She won 100m gold, 200m silver and relay bronze at the European Championships in Belgrade, as well as completing the sprint double in Perth. The winner, however, was the sportswoman who had come third in the 1960 voting and Viscount Montgomery presented Anita Lonsbrough with the trophy.

▸▸ This is the only occasion in the programme's history when **sportswomen** have filled the top three places. Men have achieved this feat 21 times.

▸▸ The 1962 **Derby** was won by Neville Sellwood on Larkspur, but the race is largely remembered for a huge pile-up that brought a total of seven horses down, including the favourite, Hethersett. One horse had to be destroyed and six jockeys were taken to hospital.

Sporting roundup

Cricket England had beaten Pakistan 4-0 in the summer, while Yorkshire clinched their third County Championship in four seasons.

Football Spurs beat Burnley to retain the FA Cup and also made the semi-finals of the European Cup, where they lost 4-3 on aggregate to Benfica.

Horse racing Fred Winter won the Grand National on Kilmore.

Rugby league Eddie Waring described the action at Wembley as Wakefield Trinity beat Huddersfield in the Challenge Cup final.

Rugby union France retained the Five Nations title, but missed the Grand Slam when they lost 3-0 to Wales.

1963

Date 19 December 1963 • Location Television Centre, London • Presenters Peter Dimmock with Peter West, Harry Carpenter and Alun Williams • Editors Phil Pilley and Cliff Morgan • Producer Alec Weeks

1st Dorothy Hyman athlete
2nd Bobby McGregor swimmer
3rd Jim Clark racing driver

Overall winner

Dorothy Hyman had already collected 100m silver and 200m bronze at the Rome Olympics, and went on to add another bronze with Britain's 4x400m relay team at the 1964 Tokyo Olympic Games, before retiring from the sport aged just 23. She attempted to make a comeback but was barred because she had received proceeds from her autobiography. Later, however, she set up the highly successful Dorothy Hyman Track Club in Barnsley.

The 1963 *Review of the Year* was far grittier than any that had gone before. The staging and lighting made strong use of contrasting black and white images, suggesting that the programme had been influenced by the new movies and kitchen sink drama of the times. The films were more issue-led and the whole presentation felt as though it had skipped forward a generation.

Peter Dimmock opened the show by walking into a spotlight and then immediately introducing 'some of the champions and record breakers who won world or European supremacy in 1963'. The lights rose to reveal more than 50 people on the stage, all in their kit. They represented ice skating, angling, cycling, racquets, show-jumping, amateur golf, swimming and athletics. One other world champion had been unable to attend. Scottish sheep farmer Jim Clark had clinched the Formula One crown with three races to go, to become, at 27, the youngest driver to win the title.

It was also the year that the whole world learnt the names of Cassius Clay and Henry Cooper. Cooper briefly dumped 'the greatest' on the seat of his pants at Wembley in June, but the Louisville Lip soon recovered and stopped the badly cut Londoner in the fifth round, exactly as he had predicted.

Elsewhere in the heavyweight division, Sonny Liston beat Floyd Patterson again, this time in just 130 seconds, but the dangers of the sport were ever present and eight boxers died as a result of their injuries in 1963, including Davey Moore, the world featherweight champion.

In a vintage summer of cricket, 1963 saw Sussex win the first one-day final, beating Worcestershire in what was soon to become the Gillette Cup. But the West Indies were the stars of the summer and, with a side featuring Sobers, Kanhai, Griffith, Hall and Gibbs, they beat England 3-1. The series included the incredible second Test at Lord's, where Colin Cowdrey came in with a broken arm and two balls left. With six runs needed to win and one wicket left, David Allen blocked and the match was drawn.

A new departure for the show was an 'as live' interview in Cardiff, where Alun Williams was with the All Blacks squad. Demonstrating a more journalistic approach than was usual for the programme, their manager, Frank Kilby, expressed concerns that penalty kicks were becoming too dominant in the game.

Football was also treated very differently as Frank Windsor, better known as DS Watt in *Z Cars*, voiced a film that focussed on the fans and the problems that football was facing. Manchester United collected their first trophy since the Munich tragedy when they beat Leicester 3-1 in the FA Cup final, and Everton won the League Championship for the first time since 1939.

There was yet more success for Bill Nicholson's Tottenham Hotspur, who brought English football a little closer to its most glorious year. They became the first British club to win a major European trophy when they completed a 5-1 victory over Atletico Madrid in Rotterdam to win the European Cup Winners' Cup.

When the results of the voting were announced, Peter Dimmock revealed that Jim Clark was in third place, as swimming and athletics once again drew the viewers' votes. On this occasion, Scottish swimmer Bobby McGregor was second behind the previous year's

Below Jim Clark won 25 of his 72 Formula One races, two World Championships and the 1965 Indianapolis 500

Bottom Dorothy Hyman dips to win the women's 100m in a match against the USA at White City

Overseas winner

Jacques Anquetil was a cycling legend and in 1963 had won the Tour de France for the fourth time and the third year in a row. He went on to win it again in 1964.

The Frenchman had also taken Olympic bronze in the team road race of 1952 and in 1964 General de Gaulle awarded him France's highest decoration, the Chevalier of the Legion d'Honneur. He later became president of the French professional cyclists' union and retired to work as a gentleman farmer and in the media. He died of cancer in 1987, aged 53.

Team winner

The exhilarating style and talent of the **West Indies** squad resulted in them being named Team of the Year. England captain, Ted Dexter, presented the award to their captain, Frank Worrell, who had flown 5000 miles to appear on the show. He told Peter West about the huge motorcade and thousands of people who had welcomed them back to the Caribbean.

runner-up, Dorothy Hyman. McGregor, a popular 19-year-old architecture student, had become the first Britain to hold a sprint world record.

Athletics matches, rather than championships, had dominated 1963. The British team had taken on the US and competed in Hungary and Russia, and the star of the year had been Dorothy Hyman, who had won 16 consecutive sprint races. Introduced by Peter Dimmock as the 'Yorkshire lass' while trumpeters played a fanfare, Hyman seemed amazed to have won and thanked her friends, family, work-mates and club-mates. Former West Indian cricketing star, Sir Learie Constantine, was called upon to present the Sports Personality of the Year trophy.

Above Bill Nicholson, the Yorkshireman who took London club Tottenham to unprecedented European success
Opposite Rangers beat Celtic in the Scottish Cup final replay 3-0. Here Rangers' Davie Wilson scores after rounding the Celtic goalkeeper, Frank Haffey

▸▸ The only year in which cricket won the **team award** was 1963. Football has collected the trophy 12 times, while rugby union has won it outright on six occasions, with one shared place. The representatives of 15 different sports have been awarded it down the years, as well as the combined Olympic and Paralympic squads in 2000.

▸▸ Following the mass cancellation of football matches due to freezing weather, **the pools** companies created a panel of experts to forecast results. The first panel met on 26 January 1963 and consisted of Tom Finney, Ted Drake, Tommy Lawton, George Young and Arthur Ellis.

Sporting roundup

Football In Scotland, Rangers beat Celtic in the Cup Final to complete the double in front of more than 120,000 people at Hampden Park.

Golf New Zealander Bob Charles became the first left-hander to win the Open. He won the trophy at Royal Lytham.

Horse racing A doping investigation meant that the French horse Relko wasn't confirmed as the winner of the Derby until October.

Motor cycling Mike Hailwood retained his 500cc World Championship.

Rugby league Wakefield Trinity won their third Challenge Cup in four years.

Rugby union England won the Five Nations Championship.

Tennis Margaret Smith became the first Australian woman to win Wimbledon. Chuck McKinley won the men's title without dropping a set.

1964

Date 17 December 1964 • Location Television Centre, London • Presenters Frank Bough with David Coleman, Harry Carpenter and Peter West • Editor Cliff Morgan • Producer Alec Weeks

1st Mary Rand athlete
2nd Barry Briggs speedway rider
3rd Ann Packer athlete

Overall winner

Mary Rand's long jump on Wednesday 14 October in Tokyo had made up for the disappointment of coming ninth in Rome, in 1960, when she had been favourite. This time her leap of 6.76m brought her a new world record and Olympic gold. She also won silver in the pentathlon and bronze in the 4x100m relay to complete an extraordinarily successful games. Rand added another gold to her collection with the Commonwealth Games long jump title in 1966.

Forget the excitement to come in a couple of years – 1964 was perhaps the first year that a sporting event had united the nation. None of it was seen live, but each evening the strident 'Tokyo Melody' brought viewers more news from Japan of Britain's most successful Olympic Games to date. On 17 December, *Sports Review* celebrated those games and its own tenth anniversary with a different style of programme. Frank Bough succeeded Peter Dimmock as the main presenter in a show that was now sharper in both content and delivery.

As it began, Len Martin introduced Britain's five gold medallists, who were standing in giant rings at the back of the set. Mary Rand, Ann Packer and Ken Matthews were all duly lit and acclaimed, and Tony Nash and Robin Dixon slid in on their bobsleigh, having won Britain's first ever Winter Olympic gold at Innsbruck. But the good idea was slightly compromised when a waxwork dummy had to take the applause for Lynn Davies, because he was competing in Cuba.

Ann Packer had won the 800m in an astonishing finish that saw her storm past the leaders in the home straight to set a new world record of 2.01.1. She also broke the European record when winning silver in the 400m. Ken Matthews had easily won the 20k walk, but Lynn Davies exceeded all expectations when he beat the long jump favourite and world record holder, Ralph Boston.

David Coleman interviewed all the Olympians and was especially direct with Mary Rand, asking how much her post-gold offers had come to. She replied that they ranged from £15,000 to £20,000, but said she had turned them all down to stay an amateur as she felt that she could still improve. 'I must say, for a young mother that's a pretty brave decision to make,' was his response.

It had been a lively and successful year for our non-Olympians, too, and this was also reflected in the content and appearance of the programme. The emphasis was on relating British sports stars to their surroundings, so a mock boxing gym had been set up where Harry Carpenter interviewed Billy Walker and Henry Cooper, who were skipping; Howard Winstone, who was shadow boxing; and Terry Downes, who was on the punchbag. Harry described 1964 as the year 'Cassius Clay turned professional boxing into his own personal circus arena,' following his unexpected win over Sonny Liston to become world heavyweight champion.

When David Coleman introduced various members of the audience, he returned again to the subject of money and, in particular, how much Britain's leading golfer was earning. 'Neil Coles, one of our richest sportsmen – how much have you won this year Neil?' he asked bluntly. 'Officially, £7,400,' replied Coles. Times were different.

There was almost too much British motor sport success to celebrate. John Surtees had won the Formula One World Championship, Mike Hailwood collected his third 500cc world title and Barry Briggs was world speedway champion. In addition, Jeff Smith was world moto-cross champion, Phil Read and Hugh Anderson were motor cycling world champions as well, and for good measure Donald Campbell had set a new world land speed record. Many were in the studio, some with their machines.

England's ageing fast bowling legend, Fred Trueman, was in a gloomy mood when interviewed by Peter West. He was very disappointed to have been omitted from the squad that had been selected to tour South Africa and felt that English cricket was in a mess. England had lost that summer's Ashes series and Fred couldn't be consoled, even though it was the year of his record 300th Test wicket.

The audience were told that there was also a fair amount of gloom surrounding English football, with its crowd trouble, record sendings-off, accusations of bribery and falling attendances. England had been defeated 5-1 in Brazil and the prevailing view was that they were nowhere near producing a world class team for the 1966 World Cup.

Below Barry Briggs (right), speedway world champion, seen with the second and third placed riders and actress Janette Scott, who presented the prizes

Below right John Surtees, legendary world champion on two and four wheels, was the son of a motorbike salesman who never lost his love of tinkering about with engines

Overseas winner

In 1960, the unknown Ethiopian **Abebe Bikila** had won Olympic marathon gold and broken the world record while running barefoot. In 1964 he retained his crown, broke the world record again and was so fresh at the end of the race that he entertained the crowd with a fitness demonstration. Even more incredible was the fact that just six weeks before the race he had undergone a serious operation for appendicitis.

Bikila was one of the Ethiopian emperor's bodyguards and running clearly aided his career. He went to Rome a corporal and came back a sergeant; won again in Tokyo and was promoted to lieutenant. When he won the Overseas award it gave the opportunity for the most unlikely commentary line ever heard on *Sports Review*. It was delivered, with due deadpan reverence, by David Coleman: 'At the Imperial palace, Lieutenant Bikila goes to the throne room where the trophy is presented on behalf of BBC *Sportsview* by His Imperial Majesty, Haile Selassie the First, Emperor of Ethiopia.' This remains the only occasion when an emperor has presented one of the awards!

Injury caused Bikila to drop out of the 1968 Olympic marathon and the following year he suffered severe injuries, including a broken neck, in a car accident. Despite being paralysed from the waist down he continued to take part in sport from a wheelchair, but died four years later.

Team winner

As they had successfully defended football's Youth World Cup, the **England youth squad** were given the Team award. It was presented by Sir Stanley Rous, president of the International Federation of Football Associations (FIFA). The team, dressed in their kit, all appeared on stage inside a giant photo frame.

Opposite Lynn Davies, who hailed from Nantymoel in Wales, had jumped 8.07m in Tokyo to win his Olympic gold

But it was the Olympics that dominated the year and the programme, although the voting itself was curious. Lynn Davies failed to make the top three and Barry Briggs received more votes than both Fred Trueman and Ann Packer to give him second place. But no-one could beat the golden girl of British athletics, Mary Rand, the third woman in a row to win the Sports Personality of the Year trophy. Peter Dimmock returned to announce the placings, while the trumpeters played 'Tokyo Melody' in front of the Olympians with the gold medallists still standing in the rings! Lord Mountbatten made the presentation.

▸▸ The only wedding cake to be presented on the show went to athletes **Ann Packer and Robbie Brightwell**, who were getting married the following Saturday. They were stunned as a large, cake, complete with a replica Olympic flame on the top, was wheeled out.

▸▸ On 22 August 1964 **Match of the Day** made its debut on our television screens. The first programme was on BBC2, featured Liverpool beating Arsenal 3-2 at Anfield, and was presented by Kenneth Wolstenholme.

Sporting roundup

Football Bobby Moore lifted his first trophy at Wembley when West Ham beat Preston 3-2 in the FA Cup final. Liverpool won their first Championship since 1947 and Rangers clinched a second successive Scottish double.

Golf The Open was won by Tony Lema at St Andrews.

Horse racing Arkle beat Mill House in a wonderful finish to the Cheltenham Gold Cup.

Rugby league Widnes won the Challenge Cup for the first time since 1937.

Rugby union Wilson Winnery led the All Blacks to victory in all four Tests of their tour.

Tennis Mario Bueno beat Margaret Smith to clinch her third Wimbledon crown and Roy Emerson beat Fred Stolle in the men's final. He repeated the feat at both the Australian and US championships.

1965

Date 16 December 1965 • Location Television Theatre, London • Presenters Frank Bough with David Coleman, Harry Carpenter, Brian Johnston and Kenneth Wolstenholme • Editor Alan Hart • Producer Richard Tilling

1st Tommy Simpson cyclist
2nd Jim Clark racing driver
3rd Marion Coakes show-jumper

After the riches of 1964, 1965 was a more routine sporting year, but there was still plenty for the audience to applaud on the night of the show. As if to emphasize this, they were obliged to sit and clap for almost three minutes as Frank Bough opened by introducing a large group of British world champions, who all stood in front of giant images of themselves in action. Among the stars were Jim Clark and Tommy Simpson.

The programme included the almost obligatory appearance of a horse and rider, this time the World Championship winner, 18-year-old Marion Coakes, on Stroller. Frank Bough spoke to her about the disadvantages she experienced competing against much taller horses, before he nervously fed Stroller some sugar and led the animal off the stage.

A boxing ring had been erected so Harry Carpenter could introduce Britain's brightest boxing talent. Carl Gizzi, Johnny Pritchett, Maurice Cullen, John McClusky, Walter McGowan, Alan Rudkin and Pat Dwyer (the E-I-Addio Kid) all walked in to applause, but the year had been dominated once again by Cassius Clay. He had beaten Sonny Liston in their rematch but was furious about the criticism of the 'phantom punch' that had ended the fight.

Overall winner

Tommy Simpson had become Britain's first ever road race world champion and was hugely acclaimed all over Europe when he won the 167-mile event in Spain. Simpson had spoken to Frank earlier in the evening and said that he won because, unlike in the Tour de France, he was supported by a strong British team.

It was possibly the most surprising win in the history of the award as so little cycling was shown on British television, but the story of Simpson's achievement had caught the imagination of the sporting audience. He died just two years later during the Tour de France, aged 29. He had collapsed whilst climbing the steep Mount Ventoux and a combination of the heat and the effort required proved to be too much for his body to cope with. He was later found to have traces of stimulants in his body as well.

Britain continued to dominate the world of motor sport. Jim Clark had not only won his second World Championship, but had also gone to America with his Lotus team and become the first European to win the Indianapolis 500 for 45 years. Frank chatted to Clark, who sat in a Ron Harris Team Lotus.

They were joined by Graham Hill, who had been runner-up to Clark in the Formula One Championship. A few days before the show they had taken part in a special *Sports Review* race at Brands Hatch. Large camera tripods had been fixed to their vehicles and the footage of them speeding round the track was played.

David Coleman also spoke to Jackie Stewart, 'a new face here at our *Sports Review* gathering'. It was his first season in Formula One and he took advantage of the moment to tease Graham Hill about his age. This was the first glimpse of a double act that was to form an integral part of the show in future years.

Below Tommy Simpson, the first Englishman to wear the coveted Tour de France yellow jersey

Vin Denson, Tommy Simpson's riding partner, remembers ...

'We started racing in amateur time trials when we were in our late teens, but later on, in the professional ranks, the thing that set Tommy apart was his absolute determination.

'This was especially evident when he had a Union Jack on his epaulet or on his bike; he then became like a man possessed. I was with him in San Sebastian when he won the World Championship in 1965. He broke away with Rudi Altig of Germany, and there was no way that he should have had the finish or the stamina to win, but he simply didn't know any limits that day.

'We used to talk about how we were going to make cycling a far more high-profile sport in Britain and Tommy went a long way to achieving that. The manner of his death was a tragedy; the drug he took didn't kill him it was simply Tommy not knowing when to stop. I'd seen him reach that kind of barrier before and he seemed to enjoy pushing himself so far. After he had collapsed I rode past the scene a minute or so later without understanding how desperate it was, but apparently his last words to the spectators, before he lost consciousness, were "Put me back on my bike ..."

'I know how much winning the Sports Personality of the Year award meant to him, although I'm not sure he looked after the trophy. Shortly after winning it, he took it to Belgium but failed to declare it to customs. I was required to bring it back and had to conceal it beneath my daughter Natalie in her push chair ... she looked a bit uncomfortable but at least the trophy got back to where it belonged!'

Overseas winner 1

In 1965, the Overseas award was shared for the first time. **Ron Clarke** would never crown his career with a major title, but in 1965 the Australian distance runner was in the middle of an amazing span of performances that would see him set 17 world records over a six-year period.

He broke the 5000m world record three times and reduced it to 13.25.8 in a thrilling run in June. He also set new world bests for the 10,000m and 20,000m. David Coleman interviewed him 'as live' in Melbourne as he reviewed his extraordinary season.

Overseas winner 2

Gary Player was still in the early stages of what has been one of the longest and most prolific sporting careers, but his victory in the 1965 US Open had made him only the third player, after Ben Hogan and Gene Sarazan, to win all four of golf's Grand Slam Majors. He was the first non-American to win the event for 45 years. In total, Player won nine Majors, his last being the 1978 US Masters.

Team winner

The team of the year was a pretty straightforward choice for the new editor, Alan Hart. **West Ham** had completed a hugely popular victory against Munich 1860 in the European Cup Winners' Cup final at Wembley, although few people thought that the sight of Bobby Moore with the trophy was an omen for what was barely six months away. Kenneth Wolstenholme introduced the team and the cup in the studio. The chairman of Munich, Carl Brurnenmier, also presented Bobby Moore with a solid gold medal as a gift commemorating his team's sportsmanship.

Opposite Wales play Ireland on the way to winning the Triple Crown. Welshman Denzel Williams feeds the ball through to his scrum half, Clive Rowlands

There was one major prize that eluded Jim Clark in 1965, however, and that was the Sports Personality of the Year award, because the man who collected the trophy from Sir Stanley Rous that evening was Tommy Simpson. He had become the first British cyclist to make any kind of impression on the very competitive European road racing scene, and he had also become world champion. The tragic postscript to his career would come two years later.

▶▶ Alan Hart became the longest serving **editor** of *Sports Review*. He remained at the helm for 12 shows, before stepping up to become controller of sport at the BBC.

▶▶ Football League **substitutes** were allowed for the first time in 1965, but only for injured players. The first to be used, and a man forever immortalized in pub quizzes, was Keith Peacock of Charlton, who came on in a Second Division game against Bolton.

Sporting roundup

Cricket England had entertained two teams in one summer for the first time. They had beaten New Zealand 3-0 but lost 1-0 to the South Africans.

Football Sir Stanley Matthews had become the first player to be knighted. Liverpool beat Leeds 2-1 to win the FA Cup for the first time and Manchester United won the title. Kilmarnock were Scottish champions for the first time.

Golf Peter Thomson won his fifth Open. It was his last major victory and his second at Royal Birkdale.

Horse racing Arkle won the Cheltenham and Henessey Gold Cups to give the horse a record of 23 wins from 29 races.

Motor cycling Mike Hailwood won the 500cc motor cycling World Championship for the fourth straight year.

Tennis Margaret Smith regained her Wimbledon title against Maria Bueno and Roy Emerson retained his by beating Fred Stolle in the final.

Rugby league Wigan beat Hunslett 20-16 in the Challenge Cup final.

Rugby union Wales won the Triple Crown at the start of a decade of dominance.

1966

Date 15 December 1966 • Location Television Theatre, London • Presenters Frank Bough with David Coleman and Harry Carpenter • Editor Alan Hart • Producer Richard Tilling

1st **Bobby Moore** footballer
2nd **Barry Briggs** speedway rider
3rd **Geoff Hurst** footballer

Overall winner

Bobby Moore seemed born to collect trophies. In 1964 West Ham won the FA Cup; in 1965 he added the European Cup Winners' Cup and the *Sports Review* Team award; and in 1966 he lifted football's ultimate prize.

When Moore collected the Sports Personality of the Year trophy from minister of sport, Denis Howell, Peter Dimmock produced the World Cup from under the podium and shoved it under his right arm, so that he looked like a kid off *Crackerjack*! Moore went on to win 106 caps for England, 90 as captain, but died from cancer at the tragically young age of 51.

'1966 surely will forever be remembered as the year in which England's footballers won the World Cup and naturally that takes pride of place tonight. For the first time on television since July, you can enjoy again the moment which captivated the whole nation in the middle of the summer.' That was Frank Bough's opening script and it serves as a reminder of how easily we now take sporting repeats for granted.

So what else happened in 1966? The challenge for the *Sports Review* team was to produce a programme of breadth when the temptation must have been to let England's World Cup glory dominate the entire show. It was a difficult task but, on the other hand, it was a vintage sporting year. The voting public did their best to ensure that the wider sporting picture was represented and they

Right Arkle, ridden by Pat Taafe, clears the last fence on his way to winning the Gold Cup for the third consecutive year
Below Geoff Hurst controversially hits the bar and the referee decides the ball has crossed the line for England's third goal against Germany in the World Cup final

did it by once again supporting speedway rider, Barry Briggs. His army of fans was mobilized when Briggs won his fourth world title in Gothenburg. Amazingly, the Swindon-based New Zealander, who only came to Britain as an 18-year-old, found himself second in the voting, ahead of England's World Cup final hat-trick hero Geoff Hurst.

Briggs was in the studio with his machine, as were Jack Brabham, who, at 40, had won his third Formula One title, and the 29-year-old Yorkshire housewife Beryl Burton, who was cycling's new world pursuit champion.

There was no significant voting support for the Scottish boxer Walter McGowan, who had become flyweight champion of the world in June at Wembley. On the evening of the show he was flying to defend it in Bangkok, so Harry Carpenter interviewed him about his chances outside London Airport. Unfortunately they were not strong enough and he lost his title to Chartchai Chionoi just 15 days later.

Back in the studio Harry spoke to Henry Cooper, who had lost his world title fight against Cassius Clay in London in May. The British champion was knocked out in

Below Walter McGowan, surrounded by adoring fans, after beating Salvatore Burruni to take the world flyweight title

Team winner

The whole **England team**, except Nobby Stiles who had flu, appeared on stage with the World Cup as roars of 'England, England' were played into the studio. It was the show's longest burst of applause until Ali appeared in 1999.

David Coleman fronted the interviews and linked into the film report with the words, 'More and more people found themselves caring deeply about a game that they had never watched or understood before.' Eleven minutes of the final were shown to a nation who had not seen the footage since the afternoon of 30 July when England had beaten West Germany 4-2.

A shy Geoff Hurst still found it a fresh experience to talk about his hat-trick, while Jack Charlton revealed that he had been chosen for post-match dope tests on so many occasions that the testers had awarded him the Jimmy Riddle Challenge Cup.

Alf Ramsey was introduced to huge applause. He said he was very touched that Helmut Schoen, the manager of West Germany, was there to present the trophy and added that he was also very proud to be the players' team manager.

the sixth round, and then had also been beaten by Floyd Patterson. Clay was now known as Muhammad Ali and had 'a year of unbroken triumph' as he successfully defended his title five times. To demonstrate his new 'Ali shuffle' he shot a special film for the programme and was, as ever, confident that his move would be a success. 'This Ali shuffle is something that is sweeping the nation, throughout America old people, young people, ladies, men, all through the colleges; everyone is trying to do the Ali shuffle,' he proclaimed.

Lynn Davies had failed to get into the top three of the voting with his Olympic long jump gold in 1964 and he made it to only fourth place in 1965, despite his European

Below Eusebio scores Portugal's second goal in their World Cup group match against Brazil that ended 3-1. This meant the holders went out out of the competition at the first hurdle

Overseas winner 1

In 1966, the Overseas award was shared for the second time. **Eusebio** Ferreira da Silva was born in Mozambique, then known as Portuguese East Africa, and signed for Benfica in 1961. His team went on to dominate Portuguese football, winning the League title ten times between 1961 and 1973, as well as five domestic cups and two European Cups.

Eusebio had one of the strongest shots ever seen in football and, with nine goals, won the Golden Boot as the leading scorer of the 1966 World Cup. He scored from the penalty spot in the semi-final against England, but was stifled by Nobby Stiles and Portugal lost the match 2-1.

Overseas winner 2

In 1966 **Gary Sobers** led his West Indian team to a 2-1 victory over England in their five-Test series and established himself as the greatest all-rounder of all time. He scored 722 runs in the series at an average of 103.14. His innings included 161 at Old Trafford, 163 not out at Lord's and 174 at Headingly, as well as 20 wickets and 10 catches.

He was knighted in 1975. In 1982 he returned to *Sports Review* to give the trophy to Daley Thompson and in 1994 he presented the International award to Brian Lara.

Championship gold in Budapest. This made him the first athlete to hold European, Commonwealth and Olympic titles at the same time. Davies was in the studio and talked about how tough it was to be an amateur. For eight months he had been unemployed and living off benefits in order to train. He now had a job and had decided to keep competing, but it was very difficult to work and train properly, he said.

At the end of an exhilarating programme Frank Bough asked Peter Dimmock, who was now general manager of BBC TV outside broadcasts, to announce that Bobby Moore had been voted Sports Personality of the Year in, arguably, English sport's greatest ever year.

▸▸ **Bobby Moore** became the first person to win both the Sports Personality of the Year and Team awards. Steve Redgrave is the only other person to have collected both in the same year.

▸▸ **The Jockey Club** finally allowed women to hold a trainer's licence.

Above Frank Bough fronted *Sports Review of the Year* from 1962–82, presenting 19 editions of the show
Opposite Henry Cooper (left) raises his guard as Cassius Clay, now known as Muhammad Ali, aims a barrage of punches at Cooper's cut left eye. This precipitated the end of the heavyweight world title fight and Ali emerged the victor

Sporting roundup

Bowls David Bryant won the singles title at the first World Championships.

Football Liverpool won their second Championship in three years, while fellow Merseysiders Everton recovered from 2-0 down to beat Sheffield Wednesday 3-2 in the FA Cup final. In Scotland, Celtic's Double included their first title since 1954. They proceeded to hold onto it for the next nine years.

Golf Jack Nicklaus became the first golfer to win successive Masters at Augusta, going on to win the Open at Muirfield.

Horse racing Arkle was once again the horse of the year, having won his third Gold Cup. Anglo was first home in the Grand National and Scobie Breasley rode his second Derby winner in three years, this time on Charlottown.

Motor cycling Mike Hailwood won the 250cc and 350cc world titles.

Motor racing Graham Hill and Jim Clark filled the first two places in the Indy 500.

Rugby league St Helens were Challenge Cup winners.

Rugby union A dominant Wales won the Five Nations.

Swimming Linda Ludgrove set two world records and won three golds at the European Championships. Bobby McGregor also broke the world record when he won gold in the 100m freestyle.

Tennis Billie Jean King clinched her first Wimbledon title against Maria Bueno, and Manuel Santana became the first Spanish winner of the men's trophy, when he beat Dennis Ralston.

1967

Date 14 December 1967 • **Location** Television Theatre, London • **Presenters** Frank Bough with David Coleman, Harry Carpenter, Peter West and Cliff Morgan • **Editor** Alan Hart • **Producer** Fred Viner

1st **Henry Cooper** boxer
2nd **Beryl Burton** cyclist
3rd **Harvey Smith** show-jumper

Overall winner

This was **Henry Cooper's** year as he had successfully defended his British and Commonwealth heavyweight titles twice. In June he left Jack Bodell hanging over the ropes in round two and five months later Billy Walker was stopped in the sixth round to secure Cooper his third Lonsdale Belt.

When Harry Carpenter interviewed him in the studio, he said that after 14 years of boxing he still thought that the two fights against Clay were his best. He was now running a grocer's shop in North London and said, 'Even though I'm British champion, if I sell the ladies a dodgy apple they all want to come in and fight me.'

When Frank Bough opened the programme at the Television Theatre, he said, 'Our mission is to remember for you those sporting events that had you leaping about all over the place in the last 12 months, and then finally to present on your behalf, because you have done all the voting, the *Sportsview* trophy for the personality of 1967.' However, after the historic achievements of the previous year, any danger of a footballing anti-climax in 1967 was dispelled by Celtic, who created football history on behalf of Scotland with their victory over Inter Milan in the European Cup final in Lisbon. They were the first British club to win the competition.

The Celtic squad were gathered for a special outside broadcast in Glasgow with David Coleman and a host of other Scottish stars, including Bobby McGregor, Walter McGowan and the retiring athlete Menzies Campbell. It had been a good year for Scottish football as the national team had also beaten England 3-2 at Wembley in April, becoming the first side to defeat the champions since they had lifted the World Cup.

Horse racing had had a comparatively modest representation in the 12 years of the programme to date, but 1967 would provide some outstanding memories. Not least of these was the Grand National victory of the 100-1 outsider Foinavon, who emerged from the carnage of Aintree to record one of the most astonishing victories in National Hunt history. At the smallish 23rd fence, Popham Down, who had lost its rider at the first, swerved into another runner and brought down most of the field. Foinavon plodded on to win by 15 lengths. The horse was considered such a no-hoper that his owner hadn't even bothered to attend the race.

A contender for the International award might well have been golfer Roberto de Vicenzo who, to huge acclaim at Hoylake, won the Open Championship. It was a somewhat overdue first major championship, but not far behind the Argentinian was the promising young British player, Tony Jacklin.

New Zealander Denny Hulme was another contender, having won the motor racing World Championship by beating his boss, Jack Brabham, in a close finish to the season. Hulme steered his car into the studio and, with Brabham standing next to him, announced that he was leaving to join Bruce McLaren in an all-NZ team.

Two personalities who had close ties with the show had died that year and tributes were paid to both of them. Donald Campbell had been killed when *Bluebird* crashed on Lake Coniston during an attempt on the water speed record and cyclist Tommy Simpson, winner of the 1965 Sports Personality trophy, had died during the Tour de France.

The equestrian interlude in the studio was provided by Harvey Smith and Harvester. Smith spoke about his two champion horses and also the competitive nature of Yorkshiremen in the year that their cricketers had clinched their fourth County Championship title in six years. 'It isn't that we like winning, but just that we don't like being beaten,' he declared.

The presenter of the main award was Sir Francis Chichester, who had recently completed his single-handed round the world voyage on *Gipsy Moth IV*.

Consequently, he would have been oblivious to the boxing events that had attracted most viewers' votes.

Cassius Clay was now Muhammad Ali and for the first part of the year his presence continued to energize the heavyweight division. He won an

Below Foinavon, ridden by John Buckingham, takes the final fence to win the Grand National. What a day for celebration if you'd had the foresight to back it!

Bottom Denny Hulme adored motor racing in all its shapes and forms and in 1992 was taking part in the Bathurst 1000 Australian endurance race when he suffered a fatal heart attack, aged 56

Team winner

When **Celtic** defeated Inter Milan 2-1 to win the coveted European Cup it meant that the club had completed an extraordinary clean sweep of trophies, as they had already claimed the domestic treble.

Jock Stein's team were to remain Scottish champions for a further seven years in an unprecedented period of dominance that also saw them add the Scottish Cup in four of those seasons. Matt Busby presented Stein with the Team award (right).

Overseas winner

Australian jockey **George Moore** began riding in Australia in 1938 and rode his first Classic winner in England on Taboun in the 1959 2000 Guineas. He returned to England in 1967 and rode for Noel Murless, taking over from Lester Piggott as his number one jockey. Moore had a great season and rode 72 winners, including Fleet in the 1000 Guineas, Royal Palace in the Derby and the 2000 Guineas, and Busted in the King George and Queen Elizabeth Diamond Stakes.

Moore returned to Australia in 1969 and retired in 1971. He began training with great success in Hong Kong and his son, Gary, rode many of his winners. At 44 he was the oldest winner of the award, which was presented to him in Sydney by great Aussie cricketer, Bobby Simpson.

Opposite The All Blacks came and conquered. Against England at Twickenham they won 23-11. Here New Zealand's Ian MacRae is tackled and swiftly passes

ill-tempered contest with Ernie Terrell for the unified title and was then stripped of the belts for refusing the US draft.

In Britain, however, Ali had helped create the reputation of one of the most popular British sportsmen of the twentieth century. Britain's heavyweight champion had fought two brave contests with Ali and was still the dominant figure on the domestic scene. The viewers' choice was Henry Cooper.

▶▶ For the first time, Frank Bough was able to introduce three complete teams on the show. Jock Stein and **Celtic** were in Glasgow, while in London Colin Cowdrey and his **MCC** team appeared on stage, as did the **All Blacks**, who performed the haka in their blazers.

▶▶ On the day that the show was broadcast, the Lawn Tennis Association voted to change the rules of **Wimbledon** and 'go open'.

Sporting roundup

Cricket Overseas players were to be admitted into county cricket for the first time and in a very ropey recorded telephone call, Gary Sobers revealed on the show that he would sign for Nottinghamshire. England won both their summer series against India and Pakistan.

Football Spurs defeated Chelsea in the FA Cup final and Manchester United were league champions. It was to be their last title for 26 seasons.Third division QPR beat West Bromwich Albion in the League Cup final.

Motor cycling Mike Hailwood retained the 250cc and 350cc world titles.

Rugby league Featherstone Rovers won the Challenge Cup.

Rugby union The All Blacks beat England, Wales, Scotland and France, while France won the Five Nations.

Tennis At the last amateur Wimbledon, John Newcombe and Billie Jean King won the singles titles. Britain's Ann Jones was beaten by King in both the Wimbledon and US finals.

1968

Date 5 December 1968 • Location Television Theatre, London • Presenters Frank Bough with David Coleman and Harry Carpenter • Editor Alan Hart • Producer Fred Viner

1st **David Hemery** athlete
2nd **Graham Hill** racing driver
3rd **Marion Coakes** show-jumper

Overall winner

Following a fanfare from the trumpeters of the Royal Military School of Music, Peter Dimmock announced the top three and it was a genuinely surprised **David Hemery** who stepped up to collect the trophy. After winning the Olympic gold he didn't run the 400m hurdles again until 1972, when he won bronze, as well as silver in the 4x400m relay, at the Munich Olympics. After retiring, Hemery was a big success in the BBC *Superstars* series of the 1970s. In 1998 he was elected the first president of UK Athletics.

The 1968 Summer Olympics had taken place in Mexico City barely six weeks before the stars of sport assembled at the Television Theatre for what promised to be a wide-ranging *Review of the Year*.

On stage, they repeated the 1964 trick of having the five gold medallists standing in giant Olympic rings. Chris Finnegan (boxing), Bob Braithwaite (clay pigeon shooting), Rodney Pattisson and Iain McDonald-Smith (sailing, Flying Dutchman class) and Reuben Jones, Richard Meade and Derek Allhusen (three-day eventing) all took their places. Alongside them stood David Hemery, the 24-year-old athlete. Frank Bough described his gold medal and world record in the 400m hurdles as, 'one of the greatest Olympic performances of all time'. The action was reviewed and all the winners were interviewed, as was Marion Coakes, who had won Olympic show-jumping silver on Stroller.

Manchester United had provided the country with more glory when they followed the example of Celtic and became the second British club to win the European Cup. Their 4-1 extra-time victory over Benfica included one of the finest performances George Best had ever produced, but it would be another 34 years before Best would be individually honoured by the *Review of the Year* programme.

In rugby union, France had achieved their first Grand Slam, which just seemed to further emphasize England's lack of a Five Nations championship title for five years.

Leeds met Wakefield Trinity in the rugby league Challenge Cup and it was dubbed 'the watersplash final', due to Wembley's flooded conditions. It was probably called something stronger by Don Fox who, right on the final whistle, and having just been named man of the match, missed a kick directly in front of the posts that would have given Wakefield victory. Eddie Waring's 'poor lad' commentary line summed up the sympathy of a nation.

There was sympathy also for the dignified Argentinian Roberto de Vicenzo, who signed for a four instead of a three at the 71st hole at Augusta, costing him the chance of at least a Masters play-off. No such problems, though, for Gary Player who won his second Open Championship at Carnoustie.

Lester Piggott won the Derby on Sir Ivor. It was his fourth victory in the race and on a horse that he insisted was his best ever mount, but it was still not enough to see him placed in the top three of the end-of-year voting.

One notable absentee from the studio was a man who had been voted into second place three years before. Jim Clark had been killed in a Formula Two race at Hockenheim, aged just 32. He had won 25 of his 72 Grand Prix and was twice world champion. The 1968 motor racing season had tragically claimed the lives of four of the sport's top drivers.

Graham Hill had won his second World Championship and he joined Harry Carpenter in the studio next to his new car, complete with its huge aerofoils. They joked through the interview and talked about the car, its extra power and his age, 39. Hill said he wanted to carry on racing until he had had enough – and that proved to be many more years away. Strangely, though, they didn't discuss the death of Clark who had been Hill's friend and Lotus team-mate.

Despite the many distractions, the Olympics were

Below Bob Braithwaite, a vet from Lancashire, picked up his Olympic gold medal by missing the flying saucer targets just twice in 200 attempts

Bottom Graham Hill brought his car into the studio, but although state-of-the-art then, it doesn't look much like a modern machine now

Overseas winner

The Soviet Union's **Oleg Protopopov and Ludmila Belousova** were the first married couple to receive an award on the show. They won the Olympic pairs ice skating title in 1964 and 1968, as well as four successive world championships from 1965. They were both awarded the supreme accolade of Honoured Master of Soviet Sport, but in 1979 defected to Switzerland.

Team winner

Manchester United had fulfilled Matt Busby's dream when they won the European Cup and were the obvious choice for this award. Bobby Charlton talked about the emotions he had felt and he confessed that he had found the occasion better and more satisfying than winning the World Cup. 'To win the highest honour with your team-mates is unbeatable,' he said.

Busby sent a message to the show on film and Jack Charlton ignored any club or sibling rivalry to present the Team award to brother Bobby. Jack had also been a European winner in 1968 when Leeds beat Ferencváros in the European Fairs Cup final.

always going to be the highlight of 1968, not just in October in Mexico City, but also at the start of the year at the Winter Games in Grenoble.

For most, Grenoble will be remembered for the performance of Jean Claude Killy, who won all three alpine events. The *Sports Review* team were also enthralled, though, by the figure skating and gave the International award to the graceful Oleg Protopopov and Ludmilla Belousova, who successfully defended their Olympic pairs title. They were shown on film performing a special routine that had been recorded earlier at the Queens Club in London, before appearing in the studio to be interviewed by David Coleman.

In Mexico City there had been Bob Beamon's leap, Dick Fosbury's flop and the Black Power protests, but despite building up to the games with a string of records, there was still no major title for Ron Clarke to celebrate. The Australian was, however, on hand in the Television Theatre on the night of the show to present the Sports Personality of the Year trophy to Britain's star of those games, David Hemery.

▶▶ **Protopopov and Belousova** are the only married couple to receive the Overseas award.

Opposite Oleg Protopopov and Ludmila Belousova, known for their elegance and classical style, started the Soviet Union's, and then Russia's, almost complete dominance of the Olympic pairs figure skating event

▶▶ In 1968, cricket's D'Oliveira affair sent South Africa towards sporting isolation. Worcestershire batsman **Basil D'Oliveira**, a Cape Coloured by birth, was selected by the MCC to tour South Africa, but the host's apartheid policies meant his presence was unacceptable. As a result, the tour was cancelled. D'Olivera was interviewed by David Coleman and confirmed that he had been prepared to go to South Africa and toe the line, but that he had also been amazed by the support that he had received.

Sporting roundup

Athletics Jim Hines became the first man to run the 100m in under 10 seconds when he reduced the world record to 9.9 seconds in Sacramento, California, in June.

Boxing Henry Cooper regained his European heavyweight title when he beat Karl Mildenberger. Howard Winstone briefly held the world featherweight crown.

Cricket Gary Sobers hit six sixes in one over off Malcolm Nash for Nottinghamshire against Glamorgan. England drew the Ashes series, having beaten the West Indies in a winter tour that was interrupted by riots.

Football Jeff Astle became the first man to score in every round as West Bromwich Albion won the FA Cup by beating Everton in the final. Manchester City won the League Championship.

Horse racing Red Alligator won the Grand National.

Motor cycling Phil Read won the 125cc and 250cc world titles.

Tennis At the first ever open Wimbledon, Billie Jean King won for the third straight year, while Rod Laver beat Tony Roache for his first win since 1962.

1969

Date 11 December 1969 • Location Television Theatre, London • Presenters Frank Bough with David Coleman and Harry Carpenter • Editor Alan Hart • Producer Brian Venner

1st **Ann Jones** tennis player
2nd **Tony Jacklin** golfer
3rd **George Best** footballer

Overall winner

After the fanfare from the Royal Artillery State Trumpeters, **Ann Jones** looked shocked to hear her name announced. She had seemed destined never to win Wimbledon, having reached six semi-finals and been runner-up in 1967. In 1969 she also collected the Wimbledon mixed doubles and French doubles titles and was a member of 12 Wightman Cup teams, from 1957 to 1975.

Ann Jones remembers ...

'It is an award that I valued as much as anything else I won because it showed the direct approval of the public and it seemed to be a reward for all my hard work over the previous 12 or 13 years.

'On the night I was pretty convinced I hadn't won because Tony Jacklin had produced such a great achievement in winning the Open and was so popular. I think I mentioned in the speech that night that I had only seen a recording of myself beating Billie Jean King the previous Tuesday after the BBC sent me the film. I sat down with a glass of sherry and some cream cakes because I hate watching myself, and even with the recording I was by no means convinced that I was going to win the final point!

'I had the trophy at home for a little while and then the BBC gave me a plaque to keep, which has sat proudly on my television ever since, alongside the Wimbledon singles and mixed doubles trophies. The BBC plaque is looking a bit faded in comparison, but means as much to me as the other two.'

Television technology was moving fast and in 1969 the programme was able to review much of the sporting year in colour. There was also plenty of colour in the studio presentation when Frank Bough greeted Princess Alexandra as the programme's first royal guest of honour. She was seen at the start of the show, seated in a specially constructed royal box, surrounded by yellow flowers, ready to present the award. Little did anyone guess that in just two years time royalty would actually be receiving the trophy.

From a British point of view, the two stalwarts of the sporting summer, Wimbledon and golf's Open, had been comparatively unproductive during the post-war years. However, 1969 changed all that and when December came around Ann Jones and Tony Jacklin were in competition for the viewers' votes.

At the beginning of the show both were introduced to the audience as they, and several other British champions, stood beside their trophies. Jones and Jacklin were joined by the British Ryder Cup team, the gold medallists from the European Athletics Championships, members of

Left Tony Jacklin in fine form at the Open. His four under par total was enough to give him victory by two strokes over Australia's Bob Charles

Below Jackie Stewart in the cockpit of his Matra Ford. He has had a long and varied association with motor racing and, among other things, has campaigned tirelessly for safety in the sport

Overseas winner

In 1968 **Rod Laver** beat Tony Roche in straight sets to claim the first ever Wimbledon prize cheque of £2000. The following year, as part of a historic second Grand Slam, he retained his title against fellow Australian John Newcombe. Laver is the only male tennis player to have won the Grand Slam twice – as an amateur in 1962 and as a professional in 1969. David Coleman presented the Overseas trophy to him on film.

Team winner 1

In 1969, the Team award was shared for the first time. The European Athletics Championships in Athens had been a great success for the British team, who had won six gold medals. Lillian Board (above) had been outstanding, winning the 800m and running the anchor leg for the **women's 4x400m relay team** all on the same line.

The winning quartet of Pat Lowe, Rosemary Stirling, Janet Simpson and Lillian Board were all interviewed by David Coleman and, as the overall British women's team had been unbeaten all season, they were awarded the Team trophy. David Hemery presented it to their manager, Marea Hartman.

Team winner 2

Tony Jacklin featured again, as part of the **Ryder Cup team**, in company with Eric Brown, Peter Townsend and Brian Huggett. He reflected on the extraordinary competition and the putt that Jack Nicklaus generously conceded at Royal Birkdale's last hole, guaranteeing that the match finished tied. Eric Brown, the team captain, was then presented with the Team award, the second of the show, by Denis Howell, Minister for Sport.

Newcastle United's Fairs Cup-winning squad and the Formula One world champion, Jackie Stewart.

The first story to be recounted was Stewart's. In 1968 he had been runner-up as motor racing world champion to Graham Hill, but this time his five victories, in Spain, Holland, France, Britain and Italy, won him his first world title. The climax came at Monza, when he led a pack of four cars that seemed to cross the line together, as Murray Walker's voice hit its legendary peak.

A decent rivalry had built up between Stewart and Hill and the banter between them continued into the *Review of the Year* studio. Stewart had flown in from Johannesburg especially for the programme, while Hill was recovering from injury and entered the set in a motorized wheelchair. As Jackie Stewart sat in his race car, his great rival tried to interview him, but the conversation was rarely serious. The biggest laugh came when Hill asked, 'What particular advantage does this car have over the car that, for example, I was driving.' Stewart's deadpan reply was, 'Well, it's faster Graham.' The pair would be an indispensable double act on the show for several years.

It had been a good sporting year for the Welsh as Glamorgan won their first ever cricket County Championship and the national side won rugby union's Triple Crown. With Gareth Edwards and Barry John in partnership, they set out on a lengthy period of dominance in the Five Nations Championship.

Rugby union was introduced by Frank Bough with a reminder that the South Africans had faced anti-apartheid protests throughout their visit and that their 1970 cricket tour was now under threat. With a dramatic flourish and a smattering of applause, Bough read a newly issued statement from the MCC, stating that the South Africa tour would go ahead. It didn't.

The best goals of football's home international season were shown, including Bobby Charlton's classic long-range shot against Wales. It had also been another outstanding year of goal-scoring for George Best and after a montage of his 1968 highlights he joined the show live from a Manchester studio. He spoke of his

Right Lillian Board was the 'perfect girl next door' and in 1969 was showing enormous promise on the track, but her career was to be tragically cut short by illness

Below Rod Laver on his way to winning the Wimbledon title and actually earning something from the tournament for the first time

Manager of the Year

Football in 1969 had been dominated by Leeds United. Managed by **Don Revie**, they had won their first League Championship with a record number of 67 points, having lost just two games. A montage of some of their best goals was shown before Revie, looking like an old-fashioned trade union leader, was presented with a special Manager of the Year award, a tiny replica camera trophy, by David Coleman.

disappointment about Northern Ireland's failure to qualify for the 1970 World Cup finals and his sadness at the semi-retirement of Sir Matt Busby.

Manchester City beat Leicester City 1-0 in the FA Cup final, while third division Swindon Town pulled off a huge shock in the League Cup final by beating Arsenal 3-1. Newcastle achieved European success when they won the final of the Inter-Cities Fairs Cup 5-3 on aggregate against Ujpest Dozsa. In Scotland, Celtic completed the treble for the second time in three seasons.

Golfer Tony Jacklin was back in the London studio, telling the story of his Open Championship victory at Royal Lytham, where he became the first British player to win the Open since Max Faulkner in 1951.

The British performance of the year, though, had come from Ann Jones, who gave Britain its first Wimbledon ladies singles champion since 1961 and became the first left-handed player to win the title. A capacity crowd roared Jones back into the match after she'd lost the first set to Billie Jean King. Each one of that Centre Court crowd, and many more besides, sent in their postcards and stuck-down envelopes,

Above Gareth Edwards was capped 53 times for Wales, 13 of them as captain, between 1967 and 1978
Opposite George Best (left) runs at the Everton defence in an FA Cup match, while Alan Ball looks on

guaranteeing that Ann Jones would receive the Sports Personality of the Year award from Her Royal Highness Princess Alexandra.

▶▶ This was the first, but not the only, time that the **Team of the Year award** was shared. The other occasion was in 1991.

▶▶ There was a revolutionary cricket development in 1969, when the **John Player League** was launched on Sundays. The BBC called it the 'Country League' and it was regularly shown on BBC2. Lancashire were the inaugural champions.

Sporting roundup

Boxing The heavyweight division was in turmoil with Ali banned and the title unclaimed. Henry Cooper had fallen out with the British Boxing Board of Control (BBBC) and relinquished his British crown after a decade.

Cricket England had drawn a riot-torn tour in Pakistan and then beaten both the West Indies and New Zealand in the summer.

Horse racing Highland Wedding won the Grand National, while on the flat Lester Piggott had a sensational year, winning more than 200 races in seven different countries. The Derby was won by 20-year-old Ernie Johnson on Blakeney.

Rugby league Castleford beat Salford to win the Challenge Cup for the first time in 34 years.

1970

Date 16 December 1970 • Location Television Theatre, London • Presenters Frank Bough with David Coleman and Harry Carpenter Editor Alan Hart • Producer Brian Venner

1st **Henry Cooper** boxer
2nd **Tony Jacklin** golfer
3rd **Bobby Moore** footballer

With the World Cup in Mexico and the Commonwealth Games in Edinburgh, the 1970 *Sports Review of the Year* had no shortage of material. A new set meant that all the interviews were carried out on steps on the stage, while in the audience the collars and sideburns were growing.

It was, however, a year tinged with a great deal of sadness, especially when Lillian Board, one of the brightest stars of British athletics, succumbed to cancer at the tragically early age of 22. Her death came on Boxing Day 1970, ten days after the programme was transmitted.

Overall winner

Henry Cooper had an incredibly long career as a British sporting hero and had been an integral part of the *Sports Review of the Year* show for more than a decade. Apart from one brief break, he had been the British and Commonwealth heavyweight champion since 1959, was a three-times European champion and had twice fought Muhammad Ali. He has remained one of the most popular sportsmen in Britain, captained a team on *A Question of Sport* and in 2000 became the first boxer to be knighted.

Henry Cooper remembers ...

'I was going to the programme almost from the beginning because in 1954 my brother George and I had actually signed as professionals on Peter Dimmock's *Sportsview* programme. We were a bit like Audley Harrison these days but without the money, and I suppose the first invitations were as a result of that.

'Everything that happened with me and Cassius Clay helped, of course, and it was great to see Ali, as he became, popping up on the satellite every now and then – I knew that I would need to be ready with a line or two. My big regret was that a previous commitment meant that I wasn't able to be there on the night that Ali got the Sports Personality of the Century award.

'To win it twice was a great compliment and I had the two trophies on show for a long time, but since we moved to a smaller place they've been boxed up and stored away. My grandchildren or great grandchildren will unwrap them one day and be impressed.'

The year had also seen the first posthumous winner of the Formula One World Championship. Jochen Rindt was killed during practice for the Italian Grand Prix, but his form had given him an unbeatable lead in the title race. It was a more subdued Graham Hill who talked about Rindt and reflected on a season that had also taken the lives of Piers Courage and Bruce McLaren.

There were more upbeat events to celebrate, though, notably Tony Jacklin's victory in the US Open. This made him the first, and to date only, British player to win the title in the modern era. For a few glorious weeks, he held both the British and US Open titles, until Jack Nicklaus won the Open at St Andrews, courtesy of Doug Sanders's famous missed putt at the final hole of regulation play.

Brazil were irresistible in the World Cup in Mexico, beating Italy 4-1 in the final to win the competition for the third time in 12 years. England encountered Brazil on the way and pushed them close, thanks largely to Gordon Banks's classic save from Pele's seemingly goal-bound header. Banks and his England captain Bobby Moore spoke with David Coleman. Both felt that the standard of football had been higher than in 1966 and were very disappointed to have played well and still gone out.

Manchester City were candidates for team of the year after their victory over Gornik Zabrze in the European Cup Winners' Cup final, and their captain Tony Book and manager Joe Mercer were interviewed in the studio. The 1969 winners, Leeds, were out of the running , having let three possible trophies slip through their grasp in a calamitous 33 days.

In cricket, the South Africa tour had been cancelled and replaced with a series that saw England take on the Rest of the World. Yorkshire sacked Brian Close after he had led them to four County Championships, while another Yorkshireman, England captain Ray Illingworth, was interviewed live from Perth on a black and white feed. He was confident, he said, that England would win the Ashes.

David Broome, Britain's first show-jumping world champion and the 1960 Sports Personality of the Year, was joined on stage by Mary Gordon-Watson and her

Below Jochen Rindt had decided to quit racing at the end of the 1970 season, which made his death seem even more poignant
Bottom Pele scores the opening goal – Brazil's 100th in World Cup games – against Italy in the final. The match finished 4-1 to Brazil

1970

Overseas winner

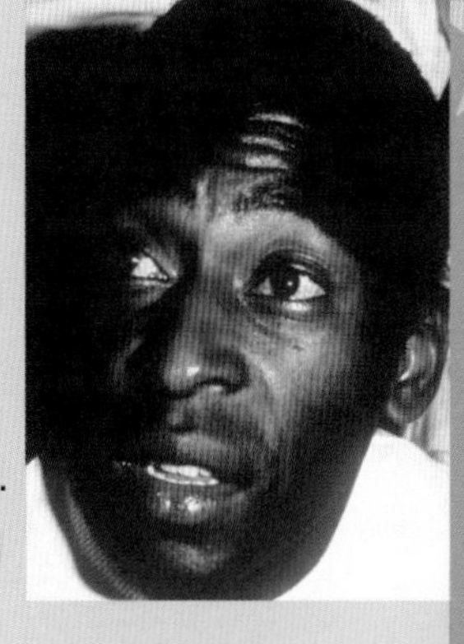

Pele had dominated the 1970 World Cup in Mexico and collected his second winner's medal. In 1958 he had scored a hat-trick in the semi-final and two in the final. In 1962 and 1966 injuries had restricted his appearances, but in 1970 he was masterful, scoring Brazil's opening goal in the final against West Germany (although for many the 'real' final was actually the quarter-final against England).

Pele went on to make the last of his 111 appearances for Brazil in 1971 and, after a spell in America, he finally retired with a record of 1281 goals from 1363 first-class games. The Overseas award was presented to him by the British high commissioner in Rio.

Team winner

The 1970 flat racing season had been dominated by **Vincent O'Brien, Lester Piggott and Nijinsky**. Piggott won his eighth Jockeys' Championship and as a team they won the 2000 Guineas, the St Leger, the Derby and the King George. He and trainer O'Brien were both in the studio to receive the Team award trophy from Lord Wigg, but despite the long tradition of equine guests there was no Nijinsky. The great horse had been retired to stud in America.

Opposite Lester Piggott passes the post to win the Derby. He described Nijinsky as possessing more natural ability than any horse he had ever ridden

horse, Cornishman. They had become three-day event world champions but the horse was very nervous and, to Frank Bough's horror, started making fresh 'deposits' on the set as he conducted the interview.

The Commonwealth Games received comparatively modest coverage in the programme, despite the many stirring performances that had taken place in the Meadowbank Stadium in Edinburgh, and none of the medallists featured among the frontrunners in the Sports Personality of the Year voting.

When Peter Dimmock announced the places, World Cup captain Bobby Moore was third and Tony Jacklin was runner-up for the second time. The winner, however, was to create a bit of history for the programme.

Henry Cooper was nearing the end of his career but remained the dominant figure in domestic boxing as he regained his British, Commonwealth and European heavyweight titles at the age of 36. The viewing public decided that as Our 'Enry was still the most popular star in British sport he would become the first person to be voted Sports Personality of the Year for a second time.

▸▸ Henry Cooper walked on stage to be given the trophy by **Colonel Sir Michael Ansell**, who promptly launched into a speech about his love of sport. As the minutes ticked by the stage manager was unable to wind him up as Sir Michael was blind. It wasn't until he had used up a magnificent eight minutes and 45 seconds of live BBC1 airtime that Peter Dimmock stepped in to hand over the trophy. This easily holds the record as the longest speech in the history of the show.

▸▸ **Tennis's tie-break** system was introduced in 1970, having been invented by James van Alen. It was first used in February at a tournament in Philadelphia.

Sporting roundup

Boxing Joe Frazier beat Jimmy Ellis in February to become world heavyweight champion.

Cricket Kent won the County Championship for the first time in 57 years.

Football Chelsea won the FA Cup, Everton the League Championship and Arsenal the Fairs Cup, their first major trophy in 17 years.

Rugby league Castleford retained the Challenge Cup against Wigan and Eddie Waring got very excited at the one try of the game: 'E's in, e's in, e's in, e's in, E'S IN!'

Rugby union The Five Nations title was shared by Wales and France.

Tennis It was an Australian double at Wimbledon as John Newcombe won his second singles title and Margaret Court her third.

Frank Bough, presenter
remembers ...

'In June 1964 I moved down from Newcastle to London and soon began to present *Sportsview*. A few months later I was at the Tokyo Olympics and then I found myself fronting *Sports Review of the Year*. It was an extraordinary time for me.

'I used to write my own script for the show and the editor would then chew it around, but in those days I wasn't allowed to say anything that wasn't related directly to the next link or interview. We had to play it very straight; say the words and move on.

'I do remember the routine on the actual day of the programme very well. In those early days it was at the Television Theatre on Shepherd's Bush Green and we used to rehearse in the morning before all going for lunch at a little Italian restaurant on the Goldhawk Road.

'In some ways it was a lot easier then as we had the rights to virtually every sport. If it wasn't on the BBC it almost wasn't worth showing and it was a great source of pride that we had all the action. It was a very exciting and different time to be working in television, especially as the show moved into the age of colour.

'*Sports Review of the Year* was seen very much as a celebration, so we tended not to cover deaths or tragedies as those were dealt with by the news programmes. The exception, of course, was the terrible series of events at the Munich Olympics in 1972.

'My favourite memories are based around two of the biggest personalities that we ever had on the programme and I'm sure that one of them, Red Rum, would have won the main award if horses had been eligible.

'I had presented *Grand National Grandstand* in 1977 from Aintree when Red Rum completed his famous third win. We had decided to bring him into the *Sports Review* studio but weren't sure how he would react. We had dealt with several show-jumping horses on the set down the years, but this was the first racehorse we had featured.

'When his trainer, Ginger McCain, led Red Rum in I remember thinking how totally composed he was despite all the cameras and the noise from the audience, who were giving him a huge ovation. He didn't seem fazed at all; just stood there and took it all in as the applause died down. I explained that Tommy Stack, his jockey, couldn't be there and that he was joining us from a live link in a Leeds studio. Immediately he spoke the horse's head whipped round, he stared straight at the screen and his ears pricked up. He absolutely knew who was talking and it became one of the best remembered moments in the show's history.

'I'm sure … Red Rum would have won the main award if horses had been eligible'

'I always thought it was a great shame that Graham Hill didn't win the trophy. I knew Graham very well off screen as well, and drivers like he and Jackie Stewart were so available to their audience. I remember how they would just pitch up in bars at Monaco after the race. Their chats together were always very good, all cut and thrust. They started when Hill came in a wheelchair having broken both legs and they always provided a lot of laughs for the audience.

'The other person who would surely have won was the athlete Lillian Board, who was absolutely charming. Lillian had a fantastic personality, but she was ill and died in 1970, when she was only 22. She had already won two European golds and an Olympic silver and it was a tragic loss as she was a terrific person.

'The programmes always overran as they were so unpredictable and there was always a note in the *Radio Times* warning that the other shows might be late.

'I remember two in particular. In 1970 I was in the wings helping to stage manage the closing when Mike Ansell was making the presentation. He really got into his speech, but because he was blind we had no means of winding him up. After about ten minutes we had to send Peter Dimmock on to literally hand over the trophy to Henry Cooper. The other occasion was when Prince Charles went on a bit when he was just supposed to present the award. No one ever advises you how to wind up the next king of England!

'I was privileged to meet so many wonderful sportsmen and women at the shows and at the parties afterwards. They were great years and have left me with many memories. I think that the show thrives because of the two continuums: the trophy and the music. There was always a debate about moving to modern times and changing the theme tune, and I expect there still is. It's synonymous with the show, though. You can't touch it.'

1971

Date 16 December 1971 • **Location** Television Theatre, London • **Presenters** Frank Bough with David Coleman, Harry Carpenter and Cliff Morgan • **Editor** Alan Hart • **Producer** Brian Venner

1st Princess Anne three-day eventer
2nd George Best footballer
3rd Barry John rugby union player

Overall winner

Princess Anne was an accomplished sportswoman who went on to represent Britain, in 1973, as a member of the British team in the European Three-day Event Championship in the Ukraine. In 1975 she won silver medals in Germany, both as an individual rider and as a team member, and the following year she competed in the Montreal Olympics.

For five years, Princess Anne was president of the British Olympic Association and in 1988 was elected to the International Olympic Committee.

Frank Bough introduced the show with the observation that this occasion was the only time that a lot of Britain's sportsmen and women got to meet each other. And even if they didn't get the chance to exchange many words during the actual transmissions, they have traditionally made up for it at the infamous after-show parties.

This was a time in British life when the stars were beginning to look more relaxed and the men's hair and sideburns were starting to extend downwards, just as the sportswomen's hemlines were going the other way. Frank's own look was getting a little racier and his sober grey suit was offset with a patterned red shirt and cream tie.

It was hardly surprising that Henry Cooper was invited back to be part of the show and present the main award. The big star of British boxing might have been popular the previous year, but there was overwhelming sympathy for him in 1971. Henry had been relieved of his three heavyweight titles in March by a controversial points decision in his contest against Joe Bugner, while Bugner's reign was brief and he lost all three belts in October when he was pounded by Jack Bodell.

In 1971 Muhammad Ali returned to centre stage, his suspension for refusing to do military service having been lifted. It proved to be a painful return as Ali suffered his first ever defeat in a bruising encounter with Joe Frazier at Madison Square Gardens that left him with a badly damaged jaw. Scottish lightweight, Jim Buchanan, was more successful at the same venue as he became the first British boxer to win and defend a world title in America for 50 years when, in September, he retained his crown against Ismael Laguna.

Elsewhere, Jackie Stewart won his second World Championship and played his part in another light-hearted studio interview with Graham Hill. There was huge laughter and warm applause throughout their six-minute chat.

It had been a very good cricketing year as Ray Illingworth led England to Ashes victory in Australia. Those images were in black and white, but the pictures were colour when the Australians had better luck at Wimbledon. Their new star was Evonne Goolagong, a 19-year-old who was described as 'the princess with a name like a peal of bells' by Harry Carpenter. She beat Margaret Court in the final, while John Newcombe defeated Stan Smith to retain his title, his third overall.

Football's main event had been Arsenal's double, a feat that in most years would have secured them the Team award. Their manager, Bertie Mee, and captain, Frank McLintock, were their main representatives in the studio, and there was a cup and league double for Celtic as well, so Jock Stein and Billy McNeill made the journey south to the Television Theatre. Surprisingly, no mention was made of the fact that 66 spectators were killed and 140 injured during a crush at an Old Firm match on 2 January 1971.

Manchester United had made a prolific start to the new season and David Coleman chatted with George Best, who was funny and relaxed and felt that the new refereeing clampdown had made it easier for forwards to score.

Horse racing had another vintage year with the emergence of Mill Reef, who won the Derby, Eclipse, King George and Arc. Jockey Stan Mellor was interviewed in the studio about the quest for his 1000th National Hunt winner. He had been stuck on 999 for

Below Evonne Goolagong was ten when she decided she was going to win Wimbledon – and win it she did, in 1971, and again in 1980
Bottom Graham Hill (left) and Jackie Stewart were a great double act and an established fixture in the *Sports Review* studio

Overseas winner

Entirely self taught, **Lee Trevino** had followed up his win at the US Open with victory in the 100th Open Championship at Royal Birkdale. Trevino resisted the famous challenge of the gentlemanly Mr Lu of Taiwan, but had proved himself an equally popular character with the British crowds.

In 1972 he successfully defended his title at Muirfield and went on to win the US PGA in 1974 and 1984. In 2001 he won a $1million prize with a hole in one at a par 3 challenge in Michigan. Harry Carpenter interviewed Trevino live from El Paso and his wife stepped forward to present him with the Overseas award.

Team winner

In rugby union, Wales had been invincible on their way to the Grand Slam, but the main story was that of the **British Lions** and their epic series win against the All Blacks in New Zealand. It was the first time they had beaten them and the entire squad was reunited in the studio. They gathered together in their touring blazers and treated the audience to a rousing version of 'Sloop John B', led by the Catweazle-like figure of John Taylor with his wild, frizzy hair and beard.

Cliff Morgan then interviewed several of the players, including captain John Dawes, Barry John and the manager, Dr Doug Smith. Despite the strong claims of the Ashes side, Arsenal and Celtic, the Lions were presented with the Team award by the New Zealand high commissioner.

three meetings and was clearly fed up with lugging the champagne around from course to course!

Equestrian events were still big box office and their profile was raised at Hickstead after Harvey Smith gave his, now infamous, V-sign after winning for the second year. The reaction against it was so strong that it took several weeks of meetings before he was finally awarded his £2000 prize.

Ann Moore won European show-jumping gold, while Princess Anne won both the team and individual golds on Doublet at the European Three-day Event Championship at Burghley. David Coleman interviewed her in the studio as Captain Mark Phillips looked on.

Opposite Charlie George (second on right), Arsenal's long-haired midfielder, shoots at the Liverpool goal. George got the decisive strike and, after extra time, the Cup final finished 2-1, making Arsenal became the second team to carry off the double

As the show drew to a close, Frank Bough announced that the main contenders in the voting were Princess Anne, David Bedford, George Best, Jim Buchanan, Barry John and Jackie Stewart. Then Peter Dimmock stepped forward to make the announcement and revealed the first ever royal winner. Henry Cooper presented the trophy to a slightly startled Princess Anne.

▶▶ This was the last time that **Peter Dimmock** announced the overall winner. He had done so for all 18 years of the show's existence, as well as presenting the first ten programmes.

▶▶ In January 1971 the first official one-day international cricket match was played between **Australia and England** in Melbourne. Each side had 40 overs and Australia won by five wickets.

Sporting roundup

Athletics David Jenkins won Britain's only gold at the European Championships and David Bedford set new European records for 5000m and 10,000m.

Football In a strong year for British teams, Leeds beat Juventus to win the European Fairs Cup and Chelsea lifted the European Cup Winners' Cup, having defeated Real Madrid in Athens.

Golf The Great Britain and Ireland Walker Cup team staged a fighting performance to record only their second ever victory over the United States.

Horse racing The Grand National was won by Specify, but the race was under threat as the owner, Mrs Topham, had turned 80 and the future of the course was uncertain.

Motor cycling Phil Read became 250cc world champion for the fourth time.

Rugby league Leigh beat Leeds in the Challenge Cup final.

1972

Date 13 December 1972 • **Location** Television Theatre, London • **Presenters** Frank Bough with Harry Carpenter • **Editor** Alan Hart • **Producer** Brian Venner

1st Mary Peters athlete
2nd Gordon Banks footballer
3rd Richard Meade three-day eventer

Whatever innocence sport seemed to have as it entered the 1970s was lost at the Munich Olympics in September 1972 with the murder of 11 Israeli hostages by Palestinian guerrillas. The games were suspended for 24 hours, but a long shadow was cast over the event that remains today. It wasn't just the Olympics that had been disrupted by terrorism and unrest. In rugby union, the Five Nations Championship had been abandoned as the situation in Ireland went into decline and both Wales and Scotland refused to play in Dublin. Sadly for the Irish, this came

Overall winner

Mary Peters retained her Commonwealth pentathlon title in Christchurch in 1974 and was made a Dame in 2000. In recent years she has managed many British athletics teams and she has spent much of her time in Northern Ireland, helping people from both sides of the community to use sport as a means of building friendships.

Mary Peters remembers ...

'I was told in advance that I was in the top three as the producers were very anxious to get me to attend. I didn't really expect to win though, as it was sometimes the case that the sportsmen and women of Northern Ireland were overlooked by the show. I can remember going to the BBC director general's party before the programme and then being led down to the studio.

'The strange thing about the Olympics was that we were so focussed and cocooned that we weren't aware of the other sports that were going on, so it was wonderful to be able to properly see and appreciate the footage of Olga Korbut for the first time.

'Everyone thinks that I had rehearsed my line to Princess Anne, but it was spontaneous and just came out. I was so thrilled when she gave me the trophy as it is so special.'

after they'd scored a notable victory over England at Twickenham. Amid all this, the gathering at the Television Theatre clutched at whatever optimism sport could still provide.

Some of it was to be found in the diminutive figure of the Soviet gymnast, Olga Korbut, the 17-year-old star of the Munich Olympics. History has shown that her life in gymnastics had not been quite as joyful as the exultant crowds in Munich assumed, but she nevertheless became the first woman to collect the International award.

The Olympics had not been especially memorable for Britain, but the outstanding success was Mary Peters. The Belfast secretary was in her third Olympic pentathlon, having always struggled to win a major title. However, she performed above all expectations in Munich and everything hung on the final event, the 200m, but she amassed a world record points total of 4801 to clinch first place by the narrowest of margins. There were also golds for Richard Meade and the British three-day event team, and for Rodney Pattisson and Christopher Davies in the Flying Dutchman class sailing.

Introducing the football section of the programme, Frank Bough described a game bedevilled by hooligans and falling gates, but there had also been some exciting play and Brian Clough and Peter Taylor were eager to talk about Derby County's League Championship win. They had finished just one point ahead of Leeds, who had beaten Arsenal 1-0 in the FA Cup final.

In Scotland, Celtic won their seventh consecutive Championship and completed their fourth double in six years, while Rangers won the European Cup Winners' Cup under a major cloud after fans rioted, leaving one dead and hundreds injured. Spurs became the first British club to win two different European trophies when they beat Wolves to lift the UEFA Cup.

Although Joe Frazier had twice defended his world title, there was only one real boxing star in the heavyweight division, and Muhammad Ali had had a good year,

Top Mary Peters putting the shot in the pentathlon. She won Britain's only athletics gold of the 1972 games
Above Olga Korbut gave her name to two gymnastic moves – a backwards aerial somersault on the balance beam (the Korbut salto) and a backflip-to-catch on the uneven bars (the Korbut flip)

Overseas winner

Olga Korbut was one of the stars of the Munich Olympics, winning gold on the beam and the floor, as well as with the USSR team. Overall, the 17-year-old gymnast was only seventh, having fallen from the asymmetrical bars, but it was her elfin features and smile that endeared her to millions of viewers.

In the 1976 games she won gold with her team and silver on the beam. She retired in 1977, became a coach and moved to America in 1991. Korbut returned to the *Sports Review* studio in 1999 and took part in the *Review of the Century* programme.

Team winner

Roger Bannister was on hand to present the Team award to the gold medal-winning Olympic **three-day event team** of Richard Meade, Mark Phillips, Mary Gordon Watson and Bridget Parker. Richard Meade had also been a member of the British team that had taken silver in Mexico, and in Munich he'd produced the highlight of a great Olympic career by winning the individual gold on Laurieston.

Opposite Mark Spitz won his seven Olympic golds in the 100m and 200m freestyle, 100m and 200m butterfly, 4x100m and 4x200m freestyle relays and 4x100m medley relay

winning all five of his fights. Harry Carpenter interviewed Ali, who was in an NBC studio in New York and was on great form, in a segment that was peppered with memorable quotes: 'Frazier's so ugly his face should be donated to the bureau of wildlife ... I'm not conceited – I'm just convinced ... My only fault is that I don't realise how great I really am ... I'd like to say you're not as dumb as you look Harry.'

But the fight Britain wanted to see was Ali against Joe Bugner, who had fought brilliantly to regain his European heavyweight title, especially after Ken Buchanan lost his world lightweight title to 21-year-old Roberto Duran at Madison Square Garden.

Also linking up with the programme via outside broadcast were trainer Ian Balding and Mill Reef, who had won the previous year's Derby and 2000 Guineas to become the dominant horse in European racing. A broken foreleg on the gallops had ended his racing career, but he was a very welcome guest on that evening's show.

Lee Trevino, by his own admission, had virtually conceded the Open title to Tony Jacklin as they approached the 17th at Muirfield, but then holed from off the green for the fourth time in the Championship. Trevino went on to successfully defend the title. Jacklin's resistance, and career, were shattered and he was never in contention for another major championship.

In previous years, Jacklin had featured strongly in the voting, but when Brian Cowgill, the BBC's head of sport, made the announcements it was Richard Meade in third place, with Gordon Banks in the runners-up spot. Princess Anne was then called upon to present the Sports Personality of the Year trophy to her successor, and Mary Peters deservedly stepped forward to collect it, making the memorable observation, 'Hasn't she kept it nice!'

▶▶ **Olga Korbut** is one of only seven women to have been presented with the Overseas award and was the first to win the trophy outright.

▶▶ No one has challenged swimmer **Mark Spitz**'s incredible tally of seven gold medals at one Olympics.

Sporting roundup

Cricket England retained the Ashes after their summer series against Australia was drawn 2-2. The star performance was by Bob Massie at Lord's, where he took 16 English wickets.

Cycling Hugh Porter won his third world cycling title, the professional 5000m pursuit.

Horse racing Lester Piggott clinched his sixth Derby on Roberto. Well To Do won the Grand National.

Motor cycling Giacomo Agostini won a record seventh successive 500cc World Championship.

Motor racing The 25-year-old Brazilian Emerson Fittipaldi became the youngest ever Formula One champion in only his second full year of racing.

Rugby league Great Britain beat Australia to win the World Cup for the third time and St Helens defeated Leeds in the Challenge Cup final.

Snooker Alex Higgins won the World Championship at his first attempt.

Speedway Ivan Mauger was one of the top six contenders in 1972, having collected his fourth world title in five years.

Tennis Billie Jean King beat Evonne Goolagong to win her fourth Wimbledon and Stan Smith beat Illie Nastase in a classic men's final. A financial dispute meant that Ashe, Laver, Rosewell and Newcombe were banned from the tournament.

1973

Date 12 December 1973 • Location Television Theatre, London • Presenters Frank Bough with Harry Carpenter, Jimmy Hill and Barry Davies • Editor Alan Hart • Producer Brian Venner

1st **Jackie Stewart** racing driver
2nd **Roger Taylor** tennis player
3rd **Paddy McMahon** show-jumper

Overall winner

Jackie Stewart had won 27 of his 99 starts in Formula One and was world champion in 1969, 1971 and 1973. He has gone on to have a long career as an owner and administrator in the sport, as well as continuing to have strong links with Sports Review of the Year.

This was a year crowded with memorable images. There was Poland's resistance against England at Wembley, Sunderland manager Bob Stokoe's victory celebration after the FA Cup final, Red Rum's first Grand National win and the famous try that was the first action of one of the most entertaining rugby matches ever.

That, of course, was the Barbarians victory over New Zealand at Cardiff Arms Park, which had begun with Phil Bennett's sidestep on his own 25 and then a sequence that went Williams, Pullin, Dawes, David and Quinnell before Cliff Morgan's commentary reached a crescendo with, 'Gareth Edwards, what a score ...' In the year of the first ever five-way tie in the Five Nations Championship, it gave hope that some kind of parity with southern hemisphere rugby was getting closer. However, 30 years on it's still getting closer.

It was football, however, that got most studio space at *Sports Review of the Year*. Pride of place went to the Sunderland team, who had become the first side since 1931 to win the FA Cup while playing in the Second Division. Ian Porterfield, the man who got the goal that beat Leeds United, was there, along with goalkeeping hero Jim Montgomery and the rest of the lads.

What England would have given for that kind of inspiration, though, as their 1-1 draw with Poland meant that they would not qualify for the 1974 World Cup. They were left to regret Peter Shilton's goalkeeping error and Jan Tomaszewski's astonishing heroics at the opposite end. It made Gordon Banks's appearance on the show all the more ironic, as he was interviewed live by a youthful Barry Davies after his testimonial match at Stoke.

Scotland had fared much better and qualified for their first World Cup Finals since 1958 when Joe Jordan headed in against the Czechs. It had also been a good year for Liverpool who celebrated a League Championship and UEFA Cup Double.

Wearing a pink-check jacket, Harry Carpenter linked into tennis, where the big story had been Billie Jean King's defeat of Bobby Riggs in the much hyped 'battle of the sexes'. At Wimbledon, King completed the clean sweep of all three titles for the second time.

A financial dispute between the players' representatives and the sport's governing body meant that most of the leading men boycotted Wimbledon. Illie Nastase and Britain's Roger Taylor were exceptions, and Taylor reached the semi-final, but the trophy was won by Jan Kodes. Tayor was introduced as a man who 'fought with his conscience and came down on the side of British tennis.' He was interviewed by Harry and said that he had no regrets about playing, even though it cost him money and lost him some friends on the circuit.

Meanwhile, away from controversy, a new word – 'tenneboppers' – was coined to describe the screaming girls who mobbed the 17-year-old blond Swede, Bjorn Borg.

Racing was well represented with Lester Piggott, Willie Carson, Terry Biddlecombe and Richard Pitman in the studio. Red Rum had won his first Grand National by just three-quarters of a length from the unlucky Crisp, but it was still a few years before Ginger McCain's famous horse would have his own starring role on the programme.

Show-jumping had always been heavily featured on *Sports Review* and in 1973 Paddy McMahon had won at both the European Championships at Hickstead and the Royal

Below Gareth Edwards said that he had only scored his famous Barbarians try against the All Blacks because he was scared of not being able to keep up with the ball, so he just kept running behind it
Bottom Roger Taylor, who reached the Wimbledon semi-finals in 1973, was appointed Britain's non-playing Davis Cup captain in 2000

1973

Team winner

Sir Stanley Rous presented **Sunderland** with the Team award following their famous FA Cup victory over Leeds at Wembley.

Overseas winner

Muhammad Ali won the first of his three awards in a year that had started well for him, with a win over Joe Bugner, and finished with a successful points victory against Rudi Lubbers. In between he had lost a split decision to Ken Norton, having boxed ten of the 12 rounds with a badly broken jaw.

Six months later Ali avenged the defeat and joined the programme live from Philadelphia, where he was training for his Frazier fight. He told Harry Carpenter that he hadn't taken the previous fight seriously and that, 'This time what I'm going to say might amaze ya, but I'm gonna retire Joe Frazier.'

Ali added that having his jaw wired up for six weeks gave him time to think rather than talk. He also said how much he loved England and that he would dedicate his next win to his British fans. Ali was then presented with the award by the former world heavyweight champion, James J Braddock.

Even at this stage in his career Ali was the most recognisable sportsman on the planet and it was to the production team's credit that they were able to make him such a regular on the show.

International Horse Show. It was to earn him third place in the voting for Sports Personality of the Year and was the last time than anyone from his sport finished in the top three.

In boxing, the biggest fight of the year was staged in Jamaica, when George Foreman knocked out Joe Frazier to become world heavyweight champion. Frazier was floored twice in the first round and four times in the second, including the knockout blow that Harry Carpenter said was the only time he had ever seen anyone literally knocked off both feet.

Another great career was coming to an end in 1973. Jackie Stewart announced his retirement at the end of a year in which he won his third World Championship. Despite finishing on top of the podium at five Grand Prix, it had been a dispiriting season in which the death of his Tyrrell team-mate, Francois Cevert, in practice for the final race of the season, hastened Stewart's decision to retire. In their annual chat, Stewart dropped a lot of hints to Graham Hill that he should take the same decision.

When the voting for Sports Personality of the Year was announced, it was Stewart, then, who received the famous trophy from Mary Peters – and television viewers and motor sport fans alike were glad to see him safely into retirement.

▶▶ **Jackie Stewart** is one of only three Scots to be voted Sports Personality of the Year. Ian Black (1958) and Liz McColgan (1991) are the others.

▶▶ On 28 April 1973, the final day of the season, **Jack and Bobby Charlton** both retired as players. Jack left Leeds to manage Middlesbrough and Bobby left Manchester United to manage Preston.

Opposite Red Rum, with Brian Fletcher in the saddle, jumps the last fence before going on to win the Grand National for the first time

Sporting roundup

Cycling Hugh Porter won his fourth world professional pursuit title.

Cricket Ray Illingworth was sacked as captain after England were beaten in the summer by the West Indies.

Football Jock Stein steered Celtic to their eighth successive Scottish Championship and Rangers won the Scottish Cup for the first time in seven years.

Golf Tom Weiskopf won the Open at Troon.

Motor cycling Phil Read was the 500cc world champion for the first time.

Rugby league In what was the highest scoring Challenge Cup final to date, Featherstone Rovers beat Bradford Northern 33-14.

Swimming David Wilkie collected gold and a world record in the 200m breaststroke at the World Championships.

1974

Date 11 December 1974 • Location Television Theatre, London • Presenters Frank Bough with Harry Carpenter • Editor Alan Hart • Producer Brian Venner

1st **Brendan Foster** athlete
2nd **John Conteh** boxer
3rd **Willie John McBride** rugby union player

Sports Review of the Year celebrated its 20th anniversary in confident mood. Amid the huge collars and large knotted ties, Frank Bough recalled memories of that very first edition and then turned the programme's attention to one of the major events of 1974, the Commonwealth

Overall winner

In 1974, **Brendan Foster** was just beginning a long association with BBC TV and the viewing public. He said that he accepted the trophy on behalf of his sport, the north and the north-east of England. During the 1970s he was Britain's most successful distance runner and collected medals at all the major championships, as well as setting many national, European and world records at 5000m and 10,000m.

Brendan Foster remembers ...

'I was still a schoolteacher in those days and had dashed to London for the show. I was running late and hurriedly got changed in the toilets at the theatre, but managed to cut myself shaving. It was quite bad and the only thing I could find to stop the bleeding was a very large plaster that I slapped on the middle of my right cheek. I had no idea that I was going to win and was taken totally by surprise when they read my name out. If I had known in advance I might have got rid of the plaster and also made a more rousing speech.

'I've been to many of the programmes since then and remember being with Paul Gascoigne and Steve Cram at the 40th anniversary show. There were photos of all the past winners around the studio and as we waited for a drink Gazza suddenly got very excited when he spotted mine. "Come here, come here," he yelled across the room. "Will you look at the size of that ******* tie!"'

Games in New Zealand. The home nations had won 35 gold medals and highlights included Ian Thompson's marathon win, Alan Pascoe's victory from the outside lane in the 400m hurdles, and a classic finish to the 5000m with Brendan Foster almost beating Ben Jipcho on the line, although Foster was further back in an epic 1500m in which Filbert Bayi smashed the world record.

Foster had more success, though, in the European Championships when he destroyed Lasse Viren to win the 5000m title, and there was also the pioneering work he'd done in establishing his home town, Gateshead, as a significant athletics venue. That was helped when he broke the world 3000m record at the opening of Gateshead's new all-weather track.

As well as the Commonwealth Games, it was also World Cup year, with the competition hosted and won by West Germany. Scotland were the only British representatives and went out without losing a game, having been held to draws by both Brazil and Yugoslavia. The star of the tournament was Johann Cruyff, but Holland lost 2-1 in the final and it was Franz Beckenbauer who lifted the trophy.

In the domestic game, Don Revie finally took Leeds to their second title in six seasons, after they had been runners-up three times. It also signalled the end of an era for the club as Revie took over the England side from the sacked Alf Ramsey. Revie's successor, Brian Clough, lasted just 44 days at Elland Road. Liverpool also lost their manager when Bill Shankley retired. They came second in the Championship, but finished as FA Cup winners when they beat Newcastle 3-0.

Harry Carpenter introduced several boxers, including Liverpool's charismatic John Conteh, who had just become our first world light-heavyweight champion for 25 years. Conteh won the vacant WBC title in October by beating the iron-hard Argentinian Jorge Ahumada.

Liverpool also featured in horse racing's main story, as Red Rum had completed his second consecutive Grand National victory at the city's Aintree race course. In the same year, Lester Piggott rode his 3000th winner and 22-year-old Pat Eddery became the youngest champion jockey for 49 years.

Princess Anne and Captain Mark Philips were in the show's audience and both were seen competing. Indeed, the latter was seen winning Badminton and being presented with the trophy by his mother-in-law, who also owned his winning horse, Columbus.

In an interview, Princess Anne revealed how easily pictures can be used to tell a false story. At the beginning of the programme, in the Commonwealth Games roundup, footage was shown of a weightlifter falling

Below John Conteh has his hands bandaged by his trainer, George Francis, as he prepares for his world light-heavyweight fight against Jorge Ahumada

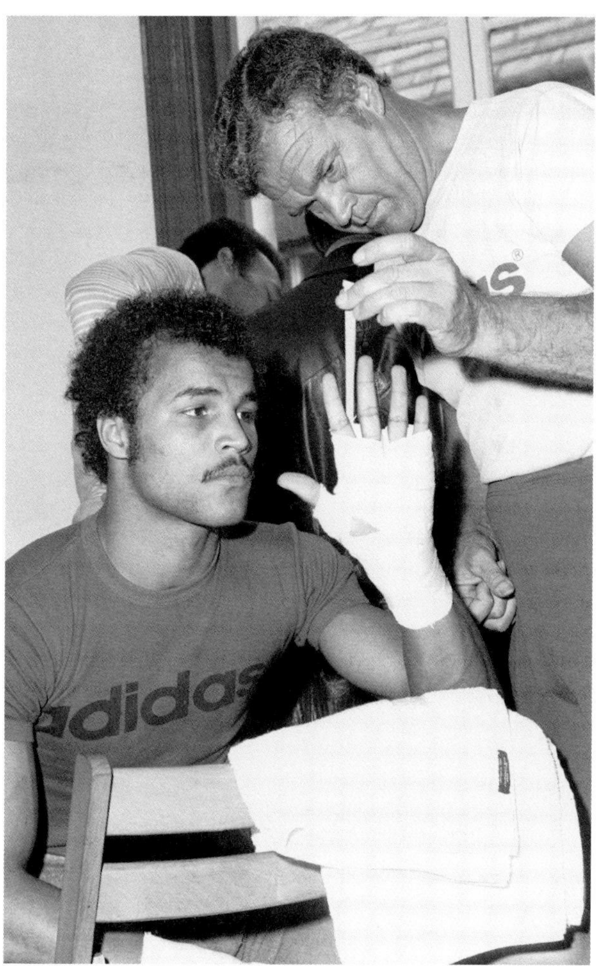

over and letting the bar and weights bounce freely down the steps of the stage. The suggestion in the commentary had been that the Royal couple had been in danger. However, Princess Anne pointed out that they hadn't even been there at that point and that they had missed all the medallists anyway, only seeing three late lifts!

When it came to the main award of the evening, Tony Preston, head of television outside broadcasts, announced the results and made a point of thanking 'the ladies who have to count all the votes'. The top three were Willie John McBride in third and John Conteh in second, but the winner was Brendan Foster, who received the award from Jackie Stewart.

▸▸ In the 20km walk, at the European Athletic Championships, **Roger Mills** became so dehydrated that he only just, agonisingly, wobbled over the line in fourth place. However, the bronze medallist was later disqualified, so Mills received his medal during *Sports Review*.

▸▸ England manager **Sir Alf Ramsey** had been sacked after losing just 17 out of 113 matches between 1963 and 1974. Having won the World Cup in 1966, he was knighted the following year.

Opposite Johann Cruyff (right), Holland's new star, gave Berti Vogts the runaround in the opening minutes of the World Cup final, but the defender eventually won the battle and Germany the match

Overseas winner

Muhammad Ali became the first person to win two Overseas awards after an extraordinary year in which both his fights became part of boxing folklore.

First he beat Joe Frazier, in their rematch, and then, in what is perhaps the most famous bout in history, he regained the world title by knocking out George Foreman in Kinshasa. The shock of the 'rumble in the jungle' was summed up by Harry's commentary line: 'Oh my God ... he's won the title back at 32!'

Ali was twice interviewed on a dodgy satellite link with Washington DC. The first attempt was abandoned due to unusable sound, but he returned later in the show, pretending to sleep and holding the Overseas award. He predicted that he would now beat Frazier and Foreman on the same night and talked about the rope tactics that were designed to wear Foreman out, before teasing Joe Bugner and warning him against being too pretty.

Team winner

Willie John McBride led the **British Lions** to South Africa in May and they returned unbeaten in 22 matches, having won the Tests 3-0 against the Springboks. It was an unparalleled success, as it was the first time in 78 years that a team had won a four-Test series in South Africa, and the squad were in the studio to celebrate.

The Lions sang an unrehearsed version of 'Flower of Scotland' and then Don Revie presented them with the Team award. Alun Thomas, their manager, received it with the longest handshake in *Sports Review* history. He clasped an increasingly uncomfortable looking Revie's hand for an impressive 42 seconds before asking for the trophy to be re-presented to Willie John McBride.

Sporting roundup

Cricket The English team, under Mike Denness, enjoyed a mixed year. They drew in the West Indies, beat India, saw the Pakistan series washed out and lost the first Ashes Test by 166 runs.

Cycling Eddie Merckx of Belgium won his record-equalling fifth Tour de France.

Football In Scotland, Celtic completed yet another double and won their ninth consecutive championship.

Golf Gary Player won his third Open title at Lytham, adding that to the second Masters jacket, which he had worn earlier in the year.

Motor racing Emerson Fittipaldi became Formula One World Champion for the second time.

Rugby league The year was dominated by Alex Murphy, who was both captain and coach as Warrington beat Featherstone Rovers in the Challenge Cup final and then completed the double by adding the Championship trophy as well.

Rugby union Ireland won their first Championship since 1951, thanks to the only away win of the competition, against England.

Tennis Wimbledon was badly affected by rain but was remembered for the 'young loves'. Jimmy Connors and Chris Evert were engaged and both won their singles crowns. Evert, 19, beat Olga Morozova, while the 21-year-old Connors beat 39-year-old Ken Rosewall in straight sets. Connors also won the US and French titles that year.

1975

Date 19 December 1975 • Location Television Theatre, London • Presenters Frank Bough with Harry Carpenter • Editor Alan Hart • Producer Brian Venner

1st David Steele cricketer
2nd Alan Pascoe athlete
3rd David Wilkie swimmer

Overall winner

In 1975, **David Steele** embodied everything that the creators of the award originally had in mind and he was presented with the trophy by Lord Killanan, the president of the IOC.

The sponsorship opportunities available to our sporting heroes in the 1970s were very different to those enjoyed by David Beckham and Denise Lewis today, and David Steele was rewarded with a lamb chop for every Test run that he scored that summer.

Steele only played one more series, against the West Indies in 1976, but after hitting a century in the first Test he struggled and wasn't part of the rebuilding process. He retired from first class cricket in 1984 but still regularly plays in charity matches.

David Steele remembers ...

'Winning the award proved that dreams could become reality, as I had been watching the show since I was a child and had thought it would be marvellous to be presented with the famous trophy. It was the second time that year that I'd had that feeling, as I had always dreamed of playing Test cricket for England and had finally achieved that ambition after more than a decade as a professional.

'I've always been in the printing business and found that the trophy helped me to get several new orders, because people wanted to come and have a look at it! I got to keep it for a year, but wasn't able to give the whole trophy back as my one-year-old son pulled a small bit off the back of the camera. I'd also won the *Daily Express* Sportsman of the Year cup in 1975, so I popped the piece in that for safe keeping. The next time I remembered where I had put it was when I saw the cup being handed over to James Hunt at the 1976 awards ceremony!'

In general, the Sports Personality of the Year award was about recognising the outstanding stars of its time, the career achievers and the big event performers. Occasionally, though, a complete outsider jumped into the frame, either by strength of character or by living the kind of unexpected dream that only sport can provide. That was certainly the case in 1975 with a grey haired, bespectacled 33-year-old Northants cricketer named David Steele.

England were struggling in the summer Ashes series and new young talent had been tried without success. It was time for a gamble, so the unassuming Steele got the call-up and became an instant national hero, with 365 runs in six innings at an average of 60.83, including a highest score of 92 in the third Test at Headingly. England still lost the series to Australia, but BBC viewers didn't forget his courageous performances.

A leading candidate for the Overseas award was Austrian Niki Lauda, who had won Ferrari their first World Championship since 1964, but in the studio, the main, desperately sad job for Jackie Stewart and James Hunt was to pay fond tribute to Graham Hill. He had been killed in a plane crash at the age of 46, just a month before. Twice world champion, Hill had been one of the star turns at *Sports Review* for many years and had only just retired.

The highlight of the domestic athletics season had been the Europa Cup semi-final at Crystal Palace, when Brendan Foster destroyed his rivals in the 5000m. Frank Bough spoke to Foster about the mass adulation that he was receiving from the British crowds, and he also interviewed hurdler Alan Pascoe, who had won 22 of his 23 races that year.

Only days before the programme, boxer John H Stracey had claimed the WBC world welterweight title with an outstanding victory over the Cuban, Jose Napoles, and he was linked up with Harry Carpenter via satellite from New York. It was the first time in 25 years that there had been two simultaneous British world champions and the other one, John Conteh, was in the studio.

Top Arthur Ashe was one of the founder members of the Association of Tennis Professionals, which forced tournament organisers to offer players bigger prize money
Above John H Stracey retired from boxing in 1978 and embarked on a new career as an actor and entertainer

Overseas winner

The International award could easily have gone to Muhammad Ali for the third straight year, but instead the accolade went to **Arthur Ashe**, who was making a similar kind of impact as Ali on the social fabric of sport. He wasn't the first black player to win at Wimbledon (that had been Althea Gibson in 1957), but he was the first black male, and his victory over the overwhelming favourite Jimmy Connors in the final was a triumph of tactics and dignity.

Ashe's consistency was such that he wasn't out of the US top three ranking for 11 years, but he suffered a heart attack in 1979 and retired the following year. From 1981 to 1985 he was non-playing captain of the US Davis Cup team and was a crusader for civil rights in America and South Africa.

Arthur Ashe contracted the HIV virus from a blood transfusion and became an incredibly eloquent campaigner for a cure, before dying of pneumonia brought on by AIDS in 1993.

Team winner

In 1975, David Wilkie (right) won two world swimming golds and Brian Brinkley won six ASA titles. Britain's **men's swimming team** had beaten all the state-sponsored Eastern European swimming squads and were now the second strongest team in the world, with only the USA above them. In recognition of this, the Team award was presented to the swimmers by mountaineer Chris Bonnington.

Wales continued to dominate rugby union, but were still unable to convince the production team that they were worthy of recognition by *Sports Review of the Year*, despite having beaten Ireland on the final day of the Five Nations to clinch their fifth outright title in ten seasons.

In football, the honours were spread around several of the less fashionable clubs. Derby County were Division One champions; West Ham beat Fulham to lift the FA Cup; and in Scotland, Rangers finally managed to end Celtic's decade-long domination of the Championship.

It was also the year of the first ever Cricket World Cup and a magnificent century by their captain, Clive Lloyd, inspired the West Indies to overcome a spirited Australian challenge and win the Lord's final.

Opposite Michael Angelow streaked at Lord's for a bet. Magistrates fined him £25 for his bare-faced cheek– the same sum he'd won in the bet

England's cricketers had begun the year being battered into defeat and disarray by the new Australian pace bowling combination of Jeff Thomson and Dennis Lillee, and the summer would provide precious little respite. That's why the game, and the *Sports Review* audience, were so happy to welcome David Steele as the very temporary saviour of English cricket and the worthy recipient of the 1975 Sports Personality of the Year award.

▸▸ Looking back on a season that included a classic home international in which he had spearheaded a 5-1 victory over Scotland at Wembley, England football captain, **Gerry Francis**, sported the largest shirt collar ever to appear on *Sports Review*.

▸▸ English Test cricket experienced its first ever **streaker** when Michael Angelow decided to strip off and hurdle both sets of stumps during the Ashes encounter at Lord's.

Sporting roundup

Boxing Muhammad Ali defeated Joe Frazier in the 'thriller in Manilla', the third and most bruising of their epic encounters. In July, Ali had beaten Joe Bugner on points in Kuala Lumpur.

Golf At Carnoustie, Tom Watson won his first Open championship, beating Jack Newton in a play-off.

Hockey The British women's squad won the Hockey World Cup.

Horse racing The Grand National was won by the Gold Cup winner, L'Escargot, ahead of Red Rum, a reversal of the previous year's finishing positions. Grundy won the Epsom and Irish Derbies, as well as the King George at Ascot. The latter was regarded as one of the greatest races of all time as Grundy held off the challenge from Bustino.

Motor cycling Italian rider Giacomo Agostini clinched his eighth and final 500cc world title.

Rugby league Widnes went into the Challenge Cup final as underdogs but pulled off a 14-7 win against Warrington to lift the trophy for only the second time since 1937.

Tennis At Wimbledon, Billie Jean King won her sixth title in an embarrassingly one-sided final against Evonne Crawley, while Virginia Wade and Ann Jones led the British team to victory in the Wightman Cup.

1976

Date 10 December 1976 • Location Television Theatre, London • Presenters Frank Bough with Harry Carpenter and Jimmy Hill • Editor Alan Hart • Producer Brian Venner

1st **John Curry** ice skater
2nd **James Hunt** racing driver
3rd **David Wilkie** swimmer

In 1976, Jimmy Hill joined Frank Bough and Harry Carpenter for the first time and the programme had seldom had so much outstanding sport to relive and recall. This was an Olympic year and there was British success to celebrate in both Montreal and Innsbruck.

In February, John Curry had become the first British figure skater to win Olympic gold by pushing back the artistic limits of the sport and winning his title with a performance of style and composure. In ninth place, Robin Cousins was also in outstanding form and British skating was poised to enter a golden era.

Innsbruck had also witnessed the sheer exhilarating aggression of Franz Klammer's victory in the men's downhill. His run was one of the most thrilling sequences of sports broadcasting and Klammer became an early contender for the International award.

In Montreal in the summer, it was the games of track doubles. Cuba's Alberto Juantorena won the 400m and 800m and the Finnish phenomenon, Lasse Viren, timed his finishes to perfection to become the first man to

Overall winner

John Curry's performance had been regarded as one that changed the whole concept of free skating and when he was interviewed by Frank Bough he described how he had set out to add an aesthetic dimension to the agility that the sport already demanded. Having also won the world title, he had now turned professional and was about to open a show in London's West End called *The Theatre of Skating*. John Curry tragically succumbed to an AIDS-related illness in 1994, aged just 44.

successfully defend the 5000m and 10,000m titles. In third place, Brendan Foster became the first British runner to win an Olympic medal at 10,000m. It was Britain's only athletics success of the games.

One of the best British performances came in the pool where Scotland's David Wilkie added the Olympic 200m breaststroke title to his World, European and Commonwealth successes. He became the first British man to win an Olympic swimming gold since 1908. He also won the silver medal in the 100m breaststroke, while the men's 4x200m freestyle relay team managed to clinch bronze.

We maintained our strong traditions in Olympic water sports with silvers for the men's eights, double skulls and Flying Dutchman class of boats, while Reg White and Jon Osborn added gold in the International Tornado class. White spoke with Frank Bough and reasoned that Britain always does well in these sports as water isn't taxed.

Jackie Stewart interviewed the new British Formula One champion, James Hunt, who had claimed his first and only world title, after a campaign which will be remembered for Niki Lauda's heroic return to action after a near-fatal crash at the Nürburgring.

Right Brendan Foster was asked, at the end of his athletics career, who was the greatest runner he had met. Lasse Viren was his reply
Below right James Hunt's main rival for the World Championship was favourite Niki Lauda, but fortunately for Hunt, Lauda's serious accident at the Nürburgring put him out of the running for a while
Below left Niki Lauda checks his Ferrari 312T2 before the start of the British Grand Prix, a race Hunt won fair and square, though he was later disqualified as his car had been rebuilt during the race

Stewart: 'You have had what one might call a sporting season in more ways than one.'

Hunt: 'Well, be more specific. Come on, you're on the telly.'

Stewart: 'All these ladies that we've seen you with this year – there have been great reports, [but] does it really help your racing?'

Hunt: 'I'll tell you what, it's been jolly heavy going ... the racing.'

Stewart: 'Just think how many Grand Prix I'd have won if I'd gone the same way!'

Hunt: 'Well, I told you and you wouldn't listen!'

It wouldn't be long before James would be joining Murray Walker on BBC Sport's Formula One commentary team. Another classy broadcaster was also emphasising her sporting credentials in the same year. Sue Barker won the French Open Tennis Championship, beating Renata Tomanova in the final, although it failed to merit a mention on the show. Twenty years on, Sue would be sitting in the studio as a key member of the *Sports Review* presentation team.

This was also the year in which British golf fans became aware of the name Severiano Ballesteros. The 19-year-old Spaniard had led golf's Open Championship at Royal Birkdale for three days, only to be overtaken by Johnny Miller in the final round, but his aggressive, inventive style and swashbuckling demeanour had already identified him as a superstar of the future.

Jimmy Hill linked into the football section by expressing his view that the sport had to encourage progressive attacking play to get the game back on its feet and spectators back into the grounds. Liverpool had done their best to achieve this on their way to their ninth League Championship and second UEFA Cup, and Second Division Southampton were the surprise winners of the FA Cup after Bobby Stokes scored the only goal against Manchester United in the final. In Scotland, Rangers completed the treble.

West Indies cricket captain, Clive Lloyd, was in the audience alongside David Steele. For his benefit year Lloyd described how he was going to be paid a pint of beer per run and a bottle of vodka per six. The previous year, Steele had been paid for runs in rather less exotic chops.

On the cricket field the England captain, Tony Grieg, saw his ill-advised comments backfire badly. He declared that, 'If the West Indies get on top they are magnificent cricketers. If they are down they grovel and I intend to make them grovel.' Viv Richards's 232 at Trent Bridge, 135 at Old Trafford and 291 at the Oval, alongside Michael Holding's 8 for 92 and 6 for 57 at the Oval, were just some of the reasons why it was the home side who suffered throughout a long, hot summer.

Opposite top Franz Klammer's death-defying gold run, in front of a home crowd, beat Swiss Bernhard Russi's by just a third of a second
Opposite bottom Mervyn Davies, who won 38 consecutive caps for Wales, always stood out, not just because of his skill and intelligence, but also because he wore a trademark white headband
Right Alberto Juantorena had a spectacularly long and very distinctive stride. As well as winning two gold medals, in Montreal he also set an 800m world record
Below David Wilkie was a naturally talented swimmer and the first to wear the cap and goggles combo that's now standard in the sport

Overseas winner

As with Olga Korbut in Munich, four years earlier, gymnast **Nadia Comaneci** was the star of the Montreal Olympic Games. Having won four gold medals at the 1975 European Championships, the petite 14-year-old Romanian went to Canada as favourite, but surpassed all expectations with strings of perfect tens being awarded to her throughout the competition. She won three golds, one silver and a bronze.

Four years later in Moscow, Comaneci had grown considerably but still managed to win a further two golds and two silvers before retiring in 1981. Yachtswoman Clare Francis presented her with the trophy in the London studio and, as it was her first ever non-competitive trip abroad, Frank Bough also gave her a bouquet of flowers.

Team winner

Every Olympic Games has its controversy and in Montreal it was the unlikely event of modern pentathlon that produced the headlines.

In fact, the **British modern pentathlon team** was at the centre of it all, because Adrian Parker and Jeremy Fox claimed that the épée of the Soviet contestant Boris Onischenko seemed to be recording illegal hits during the fencing stage of the competition.

The épée was examined and discovered to be wired with a circuit breaker, which allowed Onischenko to falsely register the hits. He was banished from the games, the Soviet team were disqualified and it all rather overshadowed Britain's eventual team gold in the event.

This was an unexpected success, but it was built on the great form of Fox, Parker and Robert Nightingale, and in the studio they received the Team award from Mervyn Davies.

Welsh rugby union had a mixed year. Wales won their seventh Grand Slam and their sixth title in eight years, but their captain, Mervyn Davies, was forced to retire in March after suffering a brain haemorrhage during a televised cup game between Swansea and Pontypool. Happily, Merv the Swerve had recovered from his near-fatal injury and was in the studio to thank the many well-wishers who had sent him cards and messages.

It had been a huge year of sport and Lord Mountbatten was in the studio to congratulate David Wilkie, who was placed in third, James Hunt, who came second, and John Curry, who was the first skater to be named Sports Personality of the Year.

▶▶ Since 1972, the **Team award** has gone to a group of medallists in seven of the eight Olympic years. The only exception was in 1980 when it went to England's Grand Slam-winning rugby union players.

▶▶ Just two days before they were due to begin, 20 African countries boycotted the **Olympic Games**. This was in protest at the participation of the New Zealand squad, following a decision by their rugby union team to tour South Africa in defiance of the sporting boycott that had been imposed.

Opposite Peter Collins won the individual speedway World Championship, aged 22, in front of 100,000 people at the Slaski Stadium in Katowice, Poland. In all, he won ten world titles

Sporting roundup

Boxing John H Stracey lost his world title to Carlos Palomino.

Football Czechoslovakia beat West Germany 5-4 on penalties in the European Championships final.

Horse racing Lester Piggott rode Empery to victory in the Derby. It was his seventh win. Rag Trade won the Grand National.

Motor cycling Barry Sheene had recovered from a horrific accident and was in the studio to talk about his 500cc World Championship.

Rugby league St Helens beat Widnes in the Challenge Cup final.

Speedway Peter Collins became Britain's first world champion for 14 years.

Tennis Chris Evert won her second Wimbledon title in three years when she defeated Evonne Crawley, and a 20-year-old Swede named Bjorn Borg beat Illie Nastase to clinch his first trophy in SW19.

1977

Date 14 December 1977 • Location New London Theatre, London • Presenters Frank Bough with Harry Carpenter and Jimmy Hill Editor Jonathan Martin • Producer Martin Hopkins

1st Virginia Wade tennis player
2nd Geoff Boycott cricketer
3rd Barry Sheene motor cyclist

Overall winner

Born in Hampshire but raised in South Africa, **Virginia Wade** had also won the 1968 US and Australian Open titles, as well as three Grand Slam doubles crowns, and in 1978 she helped Britain to win the Wightman Cup.

She looked stunned when her name was announced on the programme and said, 'This is the trophy that every sportsman or woman in the country wants to win.'

Her triumph against Betty Stove remains Britain's last singles success at Wimbledon.

There were no major set piece events scheduled for 1977, no World Cup or Olympics, but it still turned into a memorable year of sport with a succession of outstanding stories and the emergence of several future stars. It wasn't in recognition of this, but it was a stroke of good fortune that the programme chose 1977 to move into the more showbiz surroundings of the New London Theatre in Drury Lane. It was also the year that Martin Hopkins began a long run as programme producer.

Wimbledon was celebrating its centenary year and at one stage there were high hopes for an all-British ladies singles final. However, while Virginia Wade went through to the last two, Sue Barker lost in the semi to Betty Stove of Holland. Nevertheless, in the presence of the Queen in her Silver Jubilee year, Virginia delivered the Centre Court victory that the whole of British tennis had been waiting for. She lost the first set but fought back to win amid a raucous, party atmosphere on a court bedecked with Union Jacks.

In the men's final, Bjorn Borg won his second title in a classic five-setter against Jimmy Connors, and a young John McEnroe caught the eye of tennis fans when he arrived to play in the juniors but also made the main semi-final before losing to Connors.

Earlier in the year, there had been an equally emotional Grand National when Tommy Stack brought Red Rum home for a historic third victory at Aintree. The bookmakers had another painful day, because Red Rum was taking his place among racing legends with not only three wins but also two second places over a span of five years. There was a huge reception in Red Rum's home town of Southport and, of course, an equally memorable reception when Rummy made his appearance at the New London Theatre.

As Frank interviewed Stack, who, following a bad fall was in a wheelchair in a Leeds studio, trainer Ginger McCain brought Red Rum on to the stage and gave the show one of its legendary moments. As the horse looked at the screen and heard Stack's voice, it pricked up its ears. Frank commented that he was saying, 'I've met that fella before someplace.'

McCain explained how the horse, in his spare time, had turned on the Blackpool lights and opened hypermarkets, pubs and clubs. The intention was to have one more go at the National, but it didn't happen and Red Rum retired the following year. He continued to return to the course and when he died in 1995, aged 30, he was buried near the Aintree finishing post.

Tom Watson had been a strong candidate for the Overseas award when, at Turnberry, he had won his second Open championship at the last hole after a famous duel with Jack Nicklaus. The USA once again won the Ryder Cup, but this was the last time that Great Britain and Ireland would contest the trophy on their own. Next time it would be Europe taking on the USA. In the studio, we also were introduced to a very young-looking 20-year-old called Nick Faldo who was regarded as a great prospect. It took him over a decade but 12 years later he was back to collect the main trophy.

Australian media tycoon, Kerry Packer, had signed up many of the world's top cricket players and his 'circus' was doing its best to disrupt the sport, but hope for the future

Top Geoff Boycott, in his first match back since 1974, became the only English player to bat on all five days of a five-day Test match
Right Virginia Wade's tennis career spanned both amateur and professional eras and she played Wimbledon for 26 years, until 1987

Overseas winner

The great comeback story of the year was that of the Austrian driver, **Niki Lauda**. Badly burned, he'd battled back from his near-fatal accident the year before to win his second World Championship for Ferrari. He clinched the title in 1977, despite winning only three races, but his six second places enabled him to beat Jody Scheckter.

Lauda was a guest in the studio, along with his Brabham Alfa Romeo, and the Overseas award was presented to him by another man who had recovered from a high-speed accident, the British driver, David Purley.

Niki Lauda retired for two years from 1980 to set up Lauda Air, then returned to become world champion for the third time in 1984, this time in a McLaren. He won 25 races in total and finally left driving in 1985.

Team winner

The team of the year was **Liverpool**. They had beaten Borussia Mönchengladbach in the European Cup final. Liverpool had also won the League Championship for the second successive season and were only denied a treble when Manchester United beat them in the FA Cup final. The award was presented to the squad, which included Emlyn Hughes (above), by Jimmy Hill and Scotland's manager, Ally McLeod, who were at the team's Anfield Christmas party.

Opposite Kevin Keegan (right) is tackled by Berti Vogts of Borussia Mönchengladbach in the European Cup final. Liverpool's 3-1 victory came ten years to the day after Celtic had become the first British club to win the competition

came at Trent Bridge where an Australian collapse in the third Test was prompted by a young Ian Botham, who took five for 74 on his Test debut. England had won 3-1 in India before going to Melbourne to play in the Centenary Test. This included a great contest between Derek Randall and Dennis Lillee, and Randall's 174 is still regarded as one of the greatest innings ever played.

When the Australians toured in the summer, Mike Brearley took over as England skipper in his prototype head protector, and Geoff Boycott returned at Trent Bridge after three years of self-imposed exile. He promptly ran out the local hero, Derek Randall, and scored 107 and 80 not out. The script got even better in the next Test at Headingly, where Boycott's 191 enabled him to become the first player to score his hundredth first class century in a Test match. He was interviewed live by satellite from Lahore and said, 'It was the most magical part of my cricket career.'

At the end of an absorbing programme and an eventful year, Prince Michael of Kent presented the Sports Personality of the Year award to Virginia Wade.

▶▶ **Liverpool** are the only football team to have been presented with the Team award on three separate occasions.

▶▶ In 1977, the snooker World Championships moved to the Crucible Theatre in Sheffield and the first player to lift the trophy there was **John Spencer**. It was his third world title and he won it by beating Cliff Thorburn 25-21.

Sporting roundup

Boxing John Conteh was stripped of his world light-heavyweight title when he refused to defend it against Miguel Cuello.

Football England manager, Don Revie, quit and moved to the United Arab Emirates after failing to qualify for the World Cup. Scotland beat Wales in a play-off to qualify for the 1978 finals in Argentina.

Horse racing Lester Piggott had yet another great partnership, this time with the Minstrel, which gave him both the King George and his eighth Derby. He also won the Prix De L'Arc de Triomphe on Alleged.

Motor cycling Barry Sheene was 500cc world champion for the second successive year, winning six races on his Suzuki. George O'Dell and Cliff Holland won the sidecar title.

Rugby league Leeds beat Widnes in the Challenge Cup final.

Rugby union France won the Grand Slam, Wales clinched the Triple Crown and the Lions lost in New Zealand.

Speedway Peter Collins won the team and pairs world titles.

1978

Date 13 December 1978 • **Location** Television Centre, London • **Presenters** Frank Bough with Harry Carpenter • **Editor** Jonathan Martin • **Producer** Martin Hopkins

1st Steve Ovett athlete
2nd Daley Thompson athlete
3rd Ian Botham cricketer

Overall winner

Steve Ovett went on to fulfil his early promise and won 800m gold and 1500m bronze in the Moscow Olympic Games in 1980. He also broke the 1500m world record three times, the mile world record twice, and became the 1986 Commonwealth 5000m champion in Edinburgh.

Taking the programme to London's West End lasted exactly one show and in *Sport Review's* Silver Jubilee year it headed back to Television Centre, which was going to be its home for at least the next decade. The prestige of the programme was now unchallenged and Prince Charles was the guest of honour in a year that had thrown up a wide range of candidates for the Sports Personality of the Year award.

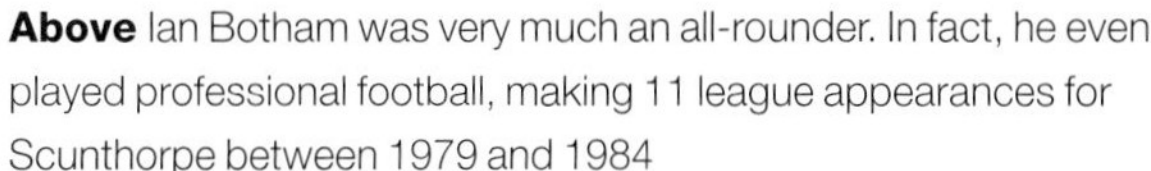

Above Ian Botham was very much an all-rounder. In fact, he even played professional football, making 11 league appearances for Scunthorpe between 1979 and 1984
Above right Bjorn Borg always favoured a wooden racquet, including when he returned to the seniors circuit in the early 1990s

None, however, had emerged from football's World Cup in Argentina. Once again England had failed to qualify and Scotland were unable to progress beyond the initial stage. They beat Holland, the eventual finalists, but failed against Peru and Iran. However, at least English football was gaining the flair and excitement of Osvaldo Ardiles and Ricky Villa as they were heading from the victorious Argentinian squad to Tottenham.

Domestic football had enjoyed an exciting season and Brian Clough led Nottingham Forest to their first ever title only a year after they had been promoted from the Second Division. As Ron Greenwood was confirmed as England's new manager, his eventual successor, Bobby Robson, was leading Ipswich to FA Cup final victory over Arsenal. Liverpool beat FC Brugge to become the first British team to retain the European Cup, and Rangers won yet another Scottish Treble.

The Commonwealth Games in Edmonton had produced 34 British gold medals and Frank Bough interviewed many of the winners in the studio, including athletes Daley Thompson, Allan Wells, David Moorcroft and Tessa Sanderson.

Ian Botham, at 22, was the star of England's summer series with Pakistan. At Lord's he had made 108 and taken eight for 34 ,before bagging 24 wickets in the three Tests against New Zealand. Frank spoke to Ian, via a satellite link with the England team's hotel in Australia. The Ashes Tests in progress were in opposition to Kerry Packer's World Series, but England would win the 'official' competition 5-1.

When he beat Jimmy Connors in straight sets to win the Wimbledon men's singles title for the third year running, many would have assumed that Bjorn Borg would have been a strong contender for the Overseas award. And there was also Martina Navratilova, who had

Overseas winner

Muhammad Ali was awarded the trophy for an unprecedented third time after another emotional year. In February, after a four-year reign, he lost his title to Leon Spinks, but later regained it in a rematch to become the first man to win the world heavyweight championship on three occasions. Harry Carpenter went to Mississippi to make the presentation in person.

Ali declared that there was no way he would fight again (he did), but that he was telling the American press that he might fight again so that they wouldn't take his title away. He waved, greeted Prince Charles and said he was proud to be the first man to win the Overseas award three times. Ali then complained about money and said to Harry, 'I love your show and I admire your style, but his pay's so cheap I won't see you for a while. Goodbye!'

Team winner

Paul Hutchins had coached the British **women's tennis team** to a memorable Wightman Cup victory over the USA, and also seen the **men's team** beat Australia in the semi-final of the Davis Cup. For that, he and both sets of players were presented with the Team trophy by Dan Maskell.

Opposite Leighton Rees collected £3000 – compared to the six-figure sums on offer today – when he beat John Lowe to win the first professional darts World Championship

beaten Chris Evert in three sets to take the first of her nine singles titles. Once again, however, Muhammad Ali was the dominant figure on the international stage and he collected the trophy.

Back in the studio, the Norfolk-based Lotus Formula One team performed a demonstration wheel change and their new world champion, Mario Andretti, joined them on a satellite link from Philadelphia. However, it was a also a very sad year for Lotus as the team's second driver, Ronnie Peterson, had died after a crash at Monza.

The Welsh rugby union team continued their relentless march towards sporting immortality by winning their eighth Grand Slam, but it still wasn't enough to get them the Team award. At the end of the season three of their legends – Phil Bennett, Gerald Davies and Gareth Edwards – all retired.

In fairness, the voting public came up with a surprise top three. Daley Thompson was third, Ian Botham second, and the winner was Steve Ovett, although he said himself, this season, in which he won the European 1500m title and beat Seb Coe to the 800m silver, should have ranked him merely as an outsider. After the announcement, the Prince of Wales then made an odd speech, in which he admitted that he hadn't seen any of the action before. He also said, 'I don't really know what I'm doing here, trying to give awards. This evening I missed three of my favourite ladies on the TV, the Three Degrees, in order to come here.'

▸▸ **Muhammad Ali** remains the only person to have been presented with the Overseas award on three occasions. Australian golfer Greg Norman has won it twice, in 1986 and 1993.

▸▸ Nottingham Forest's **Viv Anderson** became the first black player to represent England when he started against Czechoslovakia at Wembley on 29 November 1978.

Sporting roundup

Boxing John Conteh was the only British fighter to contend a world title but he lost a controversial bout with Mate Parlov on points.

Darts Leighton Rees of Wales won the first professional World Championship.

Golf At St Andrews, Jack Nicklaus won the Open Championship for the third time. Gary Player collected his third Master's jacket at the age of 42, 13 years after he had won the Overseas award.

Horse racing With no Red Rum in the field, Lucius won the Grand National in an incredibly tight, five-horse finish. Shirley Heights won the Derby and Lester Piggott, on Alleged, won the Arc for the second year in a row.

Rugby league Leeds defended the Challenge Cup against St Helens and Australia beat Great Britain 2-1 in the Test series.

Snooker All 17 days of the World Championships were televised for the first time and BBC viewers saw 45-year-old Ray Reardon win his sixth title.

Steve Ovett, winner, remembers ...

'My mother was getting calls from the BBC asking if I was going to be at the programme, which goes out live.

'She said that I would not be attending because I did not take part in this type of event. But then there were strong hints that I might win the award. That put me in a predicament. Declining to be part of the crowd did not worry me because that is going to upset no-one, but to win and not be there to receive the trophy would have been like accepting an invitation to a race and not turning up. Eventually we said I would go if I was the winner, which seemed to upset the BBC because traditionally no-one is told until the night, something I find hard to believe.

'"Yes, Steve has won it," came the whispered words. Panic set in at Harrington Villas since it meant I had to go out and buy a suit. At that time I did not own one because I was not in the sort of business where one was required. Father and Rachel also bought new clothes so it was a big family occasion. My mother did not go because she felt, rightly I believe, that it would have been hypocritical to be pally with people she was constantly rebuffing over the phone; my family has never stood for double standards.

'The BBC whisked us up to the Television Centre from Brighton in a Daimler and we were entertained in the executive suite before the programme. I found it a difficult occasion because I hate small talk and that was all there seemed to be; even the food seemed dangerous because it was things on sticks and I did not want to risk a stain on my suit being seen by millions. I still cannot bear those stand-up receptions where you have a glass in one hand, a plate in another and you need a third to consume anything. One man who made life easier that night was Cliff Morgan, head of sport at the time and a marvellous Welsh fly half in his day. My father took his autograph book and Cliff's name was the first to go into it. We then went into the studio.

'... to win and not to be there to receive the trophy would have been like accepting an invitation to a race and not turning up'

'I found the programme thoroughly entertaining. There were plenty of amusing and dramatic incidents from the year, and I enjoyed the way David Coleman, Frank Bough and Harry Carpenter operated. Their professionalism and the way they always seem to enjoy their work is something, which I admire. I was so absorbed that when Coleman homed in on me with some questions about what I might be doing next, I could only say something banal about wondering where I could get a drink. What with all those lights and a suit and a tie I was feeling a little hot.

'Normally the programme would run past midnight, but on this occasion there was an overtime ban by technicians and midnight was the witching hour. I was unaware of this as I mulled over what I might say in reply to Prince Charles, who was to present the trophy. When my name was announced I walked up to the dais, Prince Charles spoke about my performances and I had just begun to express my thanks and launch forth when one of the floor managers said, "Right, roll the titles, that's it." The programme was over and Ovett's speech to the nation was never heard.'

375

1979

Date 9 December 1979 • Location Television Centre, London • Presenters Frank Bough with Harry Carpenter, David Coleman and Jimmy Hill • Editor Jonathan Martin • Producer Martin Hopkins

1st Sebastian Coe athlete
2nd Ian Botham cricketer
3rd Kevin Keegan footballer

After Steve Ovett's success in 1978, it was his great rival, Sebastian Coe, who created the big impression in 1979, with a record-breaking spell in mid-summer. Coe was among the top celebrity guests at Television Centre, along with other great stars of this golden era of British athletics, Brendan Foster, Allan Wells and Daley Thompson.

Overall winner

Sebastian Coe won 1500m gold and 800m silver at both the Moscow and Los Angeles Olympic Games, and broke the world mile record twice more in 1981. In the 1986 European Championships he at last won an 800m title and added the 1500m silver as well. Coe was Conservative MP for Falmouth and Cambourne from 1992 to 1997 and was later elevated to the House of Lords.

It was a year dominated by powerful team performances, but strong individual personalities were also coming to the fore, and there was no one more engaging than Severiano Ballesteros. Aged just 22, the Spaniard became the twentieth century's youngest winner of the Open Championship. It was the manner of his victory, as he plotted an erratic, swashbuckling route around Royal Lytham and St Annes, that did most to help create the image that would be such a strong element of professional golf for the next 20 years.

However, even Ballesteros could not help the new European Ryder Cup team turn the tide against the USA. Even though Jack Nicklaus had failed to qualify for the team, the USA still won 17-11 at the Greenbrier in West Virginia.

England's cricketers had a great chance to win the World Cup at Lord's, but completely misjudged their challenge in the final and the West Indies, inspired by Viv Richards's undefeated 138 and Joel Garner's extraordinary spell of 5 for 4 in 11 balls, successfully retained the trophy.

Ian Botham joined the show live by satellite from Sydney, where it was 6.45 a.m. He had completed the fastest double (1,000 runs and 100 wickets) in Test cricket, reaching it in just 21 matches, and was now part of the England team who were taking part in day-night cricket for the first time. He said that he was enjoying it and had

had a good year, especially as Somerset had won the Gillette Cup and the Sunday League, their first trophies in 104 years.

Essex had also broken their duck and lifted their first trophies in 103 years, when Keith Fletcher led them to the County Championship and the B&H Cup. In was the start of an outstanding decade of success.

These were also great days for Brian Clough's Nottingham Forest side, who followed up their previous year's League Championship success by reaching the European Cup final, where the only goal of the game was scored by Trevor Francis, the first ever million pound player. Francis was in the audience and talked to Jimmy Hill about that victory over Malmo, as was SV Hamburg's Kevin Keegan, the European Player of the Year. He felt that the new England manager, Ron Greenwood, had given the players more freedom to express themselves, which in turn had led to the team's entertaining and winning performances. They had qualified for the finals of a major tournament, the European Championships, for the first time since 1970.

A classic FA Cup final saw Arsenal beat Manchester United 3-2, while Liverpool won the Championship and became the first British Club to sign a shirt sponsorship deal, with Hitachi. In Scotland, Celtic secured the Premier League title and Rangers lifted the Scottish Cup.

Britain also had many individual sporting champions and one of them, Welshman Terry Griffiths, had become world snooker champion at his first attempt. The 66-1 outsider had beaten Dennis Taylor and he joined Frank in the studio to demonstrate a whole range of trick shots in an item that lasted more than six minutes.

Also in the studio, but being less energetic, was James Hunt. Now retired, he had taken over the role of motor sport interviewer at the start of a colourful broadcasting career and chatted with Jackie Stewart about a Formula One season that had seen Ferrari claim yet another title, this time through Jody Scheckter. It would be the Michael Schumacher era before Ferrari could celebrate again.

Many of Britain's successful young athletes were in the studio and Allan Wells explained how he was considering using starting blocks for the first time, having become the fastest Britain ever over 100m. Daley Thompson had taken a year off decathlon to work on the individual

Below Trevor Francis of Nottingham Forest, repaying Brian Clough's faith in his value, heads the winning European Cup final goal past Malmo goalkeeper Jan Moller
Bottom Severiano Ballesteros quickly became known as a daring escape artist and a master at recovering from rough, trees or sand

Overseas winner

The summer had once again seen the brilliance of 23-year-old **Bjorn Borg** as he beat the fast-serving American Roscoe Tanner in five sets to win the Wimbledon Championship for the fourth consecutive year. The man who had ignited some of the younger passions of the Centre Court crowd received a slightly overdue International award from Illie Nastase.

Borg created Wimbledon history with a fifth successive title in 1980 by defeating John McEnroe in five unforgettable sets. When the result was reversed in the following year he retired and tried a number of business ventures, including his own range of underwear, before eventually renewing old rivalries by joining the masters circuit in the late 1990s.

Team winner

In equestrianism, the 1979 European Championships were won by the British **show-jumping team** of Caroline Bradley, Malcolm Pyrah, Derek Ricketts and David Broome. Consequently, continuing a long tradition of scaring presenters by bringing horses into the studio, Malcolm Pyrah arrived with Law Court and Derek Ricketts's wife, Pauline, brought along Hydrophone Coldstream, while the other riders were seen on film in Bordeaux. They were presented with the Team award by Dorian Williams.

Opposite Terry Griffiths, a former bus conductor and postman from Llanelli, had set his mind on simply qualifying for the 1979 snooker World Championship, so to win it was extraordinary

events and that stalwart of British athletics, Brendan Foster, had made his television commentary debut the previous day.

It was David Coleman who introduced the story of Sebastian Coe's incredible year. He had set new world records for the 800m on 7 July in Oslo, the mile on 19 July in Oslo and the 1500m on 15 August in Zurich. This made Coe the only man ever to hold all three records at the same time and he said that the toughest of the races was the 1500m, as he didn't have pacemakers to help him round. He was back at Loughborough University and in training for the Olympics, but hadn't decided what to run in Moscow.

Appropriately, there was another famous miler, Sir Roger Bannister, back on the *Sports Review* set and it gave him great pleasure at the end of the programme to present the Sports Personality of the Year trophy to a man who had advanced the world mile record still further – Sebastian Coe.

▸▸ **Sebastian Coe** proved to be incredibly popular with viewers and he was in the top three on four occasions. As well as winning in 1979, he was second in 1980, third in 1981 and second again in 1984. Ian Botham and Daley Thompson are level with Coe, while only Steve Davis has had more top three placings with a total of five.

▸▸ The **Fastnet race** in the Admiral's Cup was hit by a major storm that killed 15 sailors off the south west coast of Britain. Among those who survived the winds was the former prime minister, Edward Heath, who was competing on his boat, *Morning Cloud*.

Sporting roundup

Boxing Britain had two new world champions: Maurice Hope with the WBC light-middleweight title and Jim Watt who held the WBC lightweight belt.

Darts John Lowe beat Leighton Rees to win the World Championship.

Three-day eventing Badminton was won for the fourth time by Lucinda Prior-Palmer.

Horse racing First home in the Grand National was Rubstic. Willie Carson and Troy won both the 200th Derby and the King George.

Rugby league Widnes beat Wakefield Trinity in the Challenge Cup final.

Rugby union Wales won the Five Nations Championship for the fourth time in five years.

Tennis At Wimbledon, Martina Navratilova beat Chris Evert Lloyd to win for the second time and she also won the doubles with Billie Jean King. It was King's record 20th title.

1980

Date 10 December 1980 • **Location** Television Centre, London • **Presenters** Frank Bough with Harry Carpenter, David Coleman and Jimmy Hill • **Editor** Jonathan Martin • **Producer** Martin Hopkins

1st Robin Cousins ice skater
2nd Sebastian Coe athlete
3rd Daley Thompson athlete

In 1980, a year dominated by the Olympics, sport and politics met head on. The USA led a boycott of the summer games in Moscow, in protest at the Russian invasion of Afghanistan, and the British government tried unsuccessfully to stop our athletes from going. The team still took part in the games, but they did agree that no national anthem would be played and the Union Jack would not be raised when they won gold. Instead, they competed under the neutral colours of the Olympic flag.

Overall winner

Robin Cousins looked overwhelmed when John Arlott presented the trophy and said that it was a great thrill for him to win the award. He thanked his family, the Sports Aid Foundation, which had supported him financially, and his coaches.

Cousins later turned professional and continued to perform until 2000 when, at the age of 42, his knees began to give out.

Robin Cousins remembers ...

'I remember sitting in the audience thinking that it had been a great year, that it was lovely to be there in the studio and how nice it would be to watch Seb win his award. Figure skating was a minority sport and I had competed early in the year, so didn't think that I had a chance of winning, especially as the summer games had had such a high profile.

'When my name was read out I was totally shell-shocked and didn't really know what to say. After the show was over I stood shaking lots of hands, but still felt in awe of so many of the others in the room.

'I think that you always regard what you do as ordinary, as it becomes so run of the mill in your own mind, but to win the award was amazing. The trophy still sits proudly in my house – and is probably due for a cleaning!'

The absence of so many countries certainly helped Britain to enjoy one of its best summer Olympics ever, with gold in the pool for Duncan Goodhew and four athletics gold medals in the Lenin Stadium. Allan Wells became Britain's first 100m champion since Harold Abrahams in 1924 and, even without a boycott, Daley Thompson would have been tough to beat in the decathlon. As it was, he won it by a huge margin from his Soviet challengers. There was also the rivalry of Sebastian Coe and Steve Ovett – at its most intense in Moscow.

Against expectations, Ovett won the 800m when Coe ran one of the worst tactical races of his career. Coe was devastated but showed enormous character in getting it absolutely right to win the 1500m, while Ovett took bronze. British sport had been at the centre of the world stage and had provided enormous drama and excitement.

As well as winning medals, both athletes were in record-breaking form and on the same July evening in Oslo, Coe had broken the 1000m world record and Ovett had lowered the mile time yet further. The following month Ovett also reduced the 1500m record.

Many of the Olympic winners were interviewed in the studio, including Allan Wells and his wife Margot. She revealed that she'd been teased at work following her famous track-side cheering. Allan felt that he had proved that he was a worthy winner as he had beaten the best Americans later in the season.

Above Robin Cousins scored a perfect six in Lake Placid for his short artistic programme

Right Daley Thompson makes the 110m hurdles look easy. When he retired in 1992, he had never actually competed in a decathlon on English soil

Harry Carpenter's boxing section dealt with a year of mixed emotions. Alan Minter had beaten Vito Antuofermo to win the world middleweight title – the first British boxer to win a title in America since Ted Kid Lewis nearly 70 years earlier. Minter won the return at Wembley, before losing to Marvin Hagler, at the same venue, in front of a racist crowd who hurled beer cans into the ring. There was better news for our other two world champions, light-middleweight, Maurice Hope, who had twice defended his title, and lightweight, Jim Watt. When Harry interviewed Watt about his five successful defences in 18 months, he said that he didn't expect to box much longer. That proved prophetic as he retired after losing in the following June.

As well as the sad and ill-advised comeback fight of Muhammad Ali, Harry had to reflect on the tragic death of British bantamweight Johnny Owen, seven weeks after being knocked out in his world title challenge against Lupe Pintor.

Left Sebastian Coe (right), Steve Ovett (left) and Steve Cram – team-mates and rivals – in the 1500m final in Moscow. Coe ran a finely judged race and was the eventual victor, with Ovett third
Below Duncan Goodhew powers through the water to win Olympic gold in the 100m breaststroke
Opposite Alan Minter's (right) reign as world middleweight champion was relatively shortlived – Marvin Hagler (left) took the title from him the same year

Bjorn Borg was still in business at Wimbledon and won his fifth straight title, beating John McEnroe in one of the greatest finals the Centre Court had ever seen. It ran to 55 games and nearly four hours. In 'the most unashamedly feminine final for years,' as Harry Carpenter described it, Evonne Crawley beat Chris Evert to lift the plate for the second time and become the first mother to do so for nearly 60 years.

Terry McDermott and John McGovern were on hand to recall Liverpool's League Championship win and Nottingham Forest's successful defence of the European Cup. Meanwhile, Trevor Brooking chatted to Jimmy Hill about West Ham's success in the FA Cup and England's disappointment in the European Championships, when West Germany took the title yet again.

The sporting year had begun with the Winter Olympics in Lake Placid, where Britain's European figure skating champion, Robin Cousins, followed the magnificent example of John Curry four years earlier and won the men's title, amid some of the toughest competition the sport had ever assembled. Millions had supported Cousins throughout the late nights of the competition and an estimated four million had tuned in at 4am to see him clinch gold. This loyalty was reflected in the voting for Sports Personality of the Year.

When David Coleman interviewed him in the studio, Cousins was very emotional, because it was the first time he had watched the medal ceremony. Unlike his colleagues who took part in the summer games, he had been able to hear the national anthem and see the Union Jack raised in the winter equivalent.

Overseas winner

Harry Carpenter had the job of congratulating **Jack Nicklaus** on winning the Overseas award via a satellite link with Florida. Nicklaus had won the US Open and PGA Championships that year, but the trophy was presented as much in honour of a great career as for a season's work.

In all, Nicklaus won 20 Major titles, the final one being the US Masters in 1986. His three Open Championships came in 1966, 1970 and 1978, and he was also runner-up seven times. At 40, Nicklaus was one of the oldest winners of the Overseas award and he received it from another golfing legend, Sam Sneed.

Team winner

Bill Beaumont led **England's rugby union team** to the Grand Slam for the first time in 23 years and their first Championship since 1963.

In the studio, Mike Slemen and Bill Beaumont reflected upon their success, Beaumont feeling that it was due to a combination of an experienced team and a new coach and chairman of selectors. The assembled squad was then presented with the Team award by former international Dickie Jeeps, who had been a member of that 1957 Grand Slam-winning side.

It had been a splendid year for British sport, the BBC had reflected it all and chose one of its own to present the main award. In the year of his retirement as the voice of BBC cricket, John Arlott handed the Sports Personality of the Year trophy to Robin Cousins.

▸▸ **American sports stars** have dominated the Overseas award and been presented with the trophy on 18 occasions. Australia is next with seven winners. In all, 19 different countries have been represented.

▸▸ In 1980, the Billiards World Championship was held for the first time in nine years and won by 67-year-old **Fred Davis**. This made him the oldest ever world champion in any sport. His elder brother, Joe, had first claimed the title back in 1928 and had been world snooker champion in 1927-1947. Fred held the same title in 1948-49 and 1951-56.

Above Alan Jones won five (Argentinian, British, Canadian, French and US) of his 14 races to take the 1980 World Championship
Opposite Bill Beaumont (centre) leads the charge against Scotland at Murrayfield in February 1980. England's 30-18 victory won them the Grand Slam for the first time in 23 years

Sporting roundup

Cricket England lost the summer series 1-0 to the West Indies.

Darts Eric Bristow beat Bobby George to win the first of his five world titles.

Football Alex Ferguson steered Aberdeen to the Scottish Championship for the first time since 1955.

Golf Tom Watson won the Open for the third time and Severiano Ballesteros broke through another barrier to become the first European, and youngest player, to win the Masters at Augusta.

Horse racing The Grand National was won by Ben Nevis and Henbit gave Willie Carson his second successive Derby.

Motor racing In Formula One there was a new world champion from a comparatively new team, when Alan Jones won the title driving for the fledgling Williams team.

Rugby league Hull Kingston Rovers beat Hull in the Challenge Cup final.

Snooker Canadian Cliff Thorburn beat Alex Higgins to send the World Championship overseas for the first time.

1981

Date 9 December 1981 • Location Studio One, Television Centre, London • Presenters Frank Bough with Harry Carpenter, David Coleman and Jimmy Hill • Editor Harold Anderson • Producer Martin Hopkins

1st **Ian Botham** cricketer
2nd **Steve Davis** snooker player
3rd **Sebastian Coe** athlete

Overall winner

Ian Botham was the greatest match winner that English cricket has ever produced and he continued to play for Somerset, Worcestershire and Durham until he retired in 1993. He played in 102 Tests, scoring 5200 runs, taking 383 wickets and holding 120 catches.

Frank Bough opened the show with the lines, 'Since this is the Year of the Disabled we are delighted to welcome here tonight some of the sportsmen and women who stubbornly refuse to let their disability get in the way of them enjoying sporting competition.' Several sportsmen and women in wheelchairs were in a special area alongside Sir Douglas Bader, who was the guest of honour. On paper it may have been the Year of the Disabled but in practice it was the year of the Botham.

Ian Botham had started 1981 with his career apparently on the slide after leading England through a disappointing winter in the West Indies. Things had hardly improved by the time he arrived at Headingley in July, having resigned as captain after failing with the bat in the previous game at Lord's.

Former captain, Mike Brearley, returned to lead the side and helped to inspire, in his star all-rounder, a performance against Australia in the third Test that has become the stuff of legend. With three wickets left, England needed 92 runs to avoid an innings defeat. Survival seemed impossible, let alone victory, but then came Botham with his 149 not out, which followed the 6 for 95 he'd already taken in the first innings. His example energized and inspired England and with Bob Willis taking eight wickets for 43 runs, England came up with a victory that astonished cricket and confounded the bookmakers. Botham followed that with crucial wickets at Edgbaston, and a magnificent innings of 118 at Old Trafford, to guarantee an Ashes win for England and sporting immortality for himself.

Another name in the frame was Steve Davis, who beat Doug Mountjoy to win his first snooker World Championship. It was evidence of the sport's soaring popularity on television that the viewers gave him second place in the voting for Sports Personality of the Year. Harry Carpenter spoke to Davis about the changing image of younger players with their new hairstyles, flashy cars and tabloid tales. Davis felt that he hadn't changed and refuted accusations that the game was the sign of a mis-spent youth because, 'You never see snooker players going around and beating people up.'

Two previous winners, Seb Coe and Steve Ovett, were still in record-breaking form. Coe set new world records for the indoor and outdoor 800m, the 1000m and twice lowered the record time for the mile. In between, Ovett briefly held the mile record as well. When David Coleman spoke to Coe in the studio he talked about how breaking records was his greatest satisfaction, knowing that on that day you have run faster than anyone else has ever run. The 1000m was the hardest to break, but the 800m was his favourite, although, perhaps showing signs of his political future, he thought that his greatest satisfaction had come from being invited to address the International Olympic Committee conference.

Liverpool were contenders for team of the year, having maintained English football's domination of the European Cup with victory over Real Madrid in the final. Ipswich Town, who had won the FA Cup three years earlier, now added the UEFA Cup to their trophy cabinet. In the FA Cup final replay at Wembley, Spurs beat Manchester City 3-2 in a match that was famous for Ricky Villa's individual goal. In a time when overseas players were still a novelty in the British leagues, both Villa and Osvaldo Ardiles appeared together in the *Sports Review of the Year* studio.

Below Ian Botham was blessed with many nicknames, including Beefy, Guy the Gorilla and Iron Bottom, the latter due to the way in which Indian commentators pronounced his name

Special award

As Frank Bough said at the top of the show, 1981 was the Year of the Disabled and *Sports Review* reflected this with a special award. The inaugural London marathon had taken place in the spring and proved to be an event where both able-bodied and disabled athletes could compete on level terms.

Dick Beardsley and Inge Simonsen had crossed the line together, leading home the mass field of 7000 runners, including **Dennis Moore**, who had been blind since birth and was led round the course by a friend. In recognition of this achievement, and to mark the Year of the Disabled, Jimmy Saville presented with him a Special award.

Team winner

This was the year of Aintree's most romantic story as **Bob Champion** brought Aldaniti home for victory. Champion had recovered from cancer just a year earlier and Aldaniti had suffered from a series of injuries, but together they led the Grand National field right through the final circuit.

There was no doubt that, with the help of trainer Josh Gifford, they had forged an emotional bond as strong as any team, and little debate was required to name Bob Champion and Aldaniti winners of the Team award. It was a great sports story and also worked pretty well on screen, as was proved when John Hurt played Bob Champion in a feature film two years later.

Champion was interviewed by Frank Bough as Aldaniti was seen live on screen in his stable. Champion revealed that in 1977 he had predicted the horse would win the National and that he used the dream as a goal during his cancer treatment. He was presented with the Team award by Neil McFarlane, minister for sport.

There were definitely no thoughts of a team award for the European Ryder Cup team, though. Once again they were comprehensively beaten by the USA, after Dave Marr had brought across one of the strongest American sides ever assembled.

Ian Botham was the viewers' choice for 1981 Sports Personality of the Year and, although another great hero, Sir Douglas Bader, was on hand to present the award, Botham himself was with the England tour party in India. The trophy, a specially made replica, was presented to him by Mike Brearley and, by all accounts, a decent party ensued in both London and Bangalore.

Overseas winner

Chris Evert Lloyd beat Hana Mandlikova to win her third Wimbledon singles title. It proved to be her last victory, though, as she was beaten in three more finals to give her an overall record of three wins and seven runner-up positions.

The attempt to see her being presented with the award via a live satellite link to Florida went rather badly wrong and, after a number of technical problems, Chris Evert Lloyd became the first recipient to get her award by telephone.

Opposite Bob Champion on Aldaniti (right) clears the last fence and enters the home straight to win the Grand National

Ian Botham was the last cricketer to really make an impact on the voting preferences of viewers and, in addition to coming first in 1981, he was also second in 1985 after England won the Ashes. Since Geoff Boycott in 1977, the only other representative of our 'national summer sport' to make it into the top three is Graham Gooch. The England captain came third in 1990 following his innings of 333 and 123 at Lord's against India.

Sue Brown became the first woman to take part in the University Boat Race when she coxed Oxford to victory over Cambridge. She repeated the achievement the following year.

Sporting roundup

Boxing Jim Watt and Maurice Hope both lost their world titles and Cornelius Boza Edwards briefly held the WBC super-featherweight belt.

Football Aston Villa won the League Championship and Celtic took the Scottish title.

Golf The Open was held at Sandwich for the first time since 1949 and was won by the American Bill Rogers.

Horse racing Shergar won the Derby, ridden by 19-year-old Walter Swinburn, while Lester Piggott, at 46, won his tenth Jockeys' Championship.

Motor racing Formula One merited just 40 seconds on the show as Nelson Piquet became world champion.

Rugby league Widnes beat Hull Kingston Rovers in the Challenge Cup final. Eddie Waring retired from commentary and was warmly applauded in the studio.

Rugby union France won the Grand Slam for the third time in their history.

Tennis John McEnroe, already a Wimbledon hero after the part he had played in the previous year's final, won the title for himself by finally beating Bjorn Borg.

1982

Date 12 December 1982 • Location Studio One, Television Centre, London • Presenters Frank Bough with Harry Carpenter, David Coleman and Jimmy Hill • Editor Harold Anderson • Producer Martin Hopkins

1st **Daley Thompson** athlete
2nd **Alex Higgins** snooker player
3rd **Steve Cram** athlete

Overall winner

Daley Thompson caused a storm in the press who were critical of his outfit and his opening line: 'Well, the first thing that I'd like to say is that I feel like s**t.' This was not, perhaps, the way to earn tabloid plaudits. However, what has been forgotten is that he then recovered to make a generous and eloquent speech in which he paid tribute to the other athletes and the BBC, and acknowledged that sport as a whole is far more important than anyone in it.

This was the last edition of the programme to be presented by Frank Bough and the first to feature the voice of Desmond Lynam on the film reports. There was a strong theme to a lot of the sport that had taken place in the UK that year – rain. Such was the soaking that sport had endured that the programme began with a montage of just about every downpour caught on camera.

It was another frustrating World Cup for the home nations and the campaigns of England and Northern Ireland both stalled at the second stage of the competition in Spain. Paolo Rossi inspired Italy to their third success in a thrilling final against West Germany.

Despite some great action on the pitch, the domestic game struggled to cope with hooliganism and financial crisis amidst constant speculation of a breakaway super league. It had been, however, another successful season in Europe ,with Aston Villa becoming the fourth English club to win the European Cup. Liverpool's dominance continued as they won the League Championship and the Milk Cup; Spurs beat QPR to retain the FA Cup; Celtic were Scottish Champions; and Alex Ferguson added to his silverware at Aberdeen with the Scottish Cup.

The snooker world champion, Steve Davis, went out in the first round of the 1982 championship, losing 10-1 to Tony Knowles. This opened the way for the much-loved Irishman, Alex Higgins, to claim an emotional second title ten years after his first. Those emotions were still evident in the *Sports Review* studio when Alex was interviewed by Harry Carpenter about the family support that had helped him to succeed.

Also in the studio was motorcyclist Barry Sheene. In the summer he had survived a horrendous accident while testing at Silverstone, but the sight of Sheene riding his bike into the studio and talking about the photographs of his pinned-together limbs gave hope that Britain's favourite racer might yet compete again.

Others had not been so fortunate that year and in Formula One Gilles Villeneuve lost his life in a crash in final practice for the Belgian Grand Prix at Zolder. John Watson, driving for McLaren, gave a strong challenge to the eventual champion, Keke Rosberg.

There were more champions at the Commonwealth Games in Brisbane, most notably Allan Wells and Mike McFarlane, who shared a dead heat in the 100m. Daley Thompson's gold helped to complete his full set of Olympic, European and Commonwealth titles, plus a world record. Thompson had set that at the European Championships in Athens, where Steve Cram won the 1500m to add to his Commonwealth title. Cram had emerged from the shadow of Brendan Foster, who now sat alongside David Coleman in the BBC commentary box. David Moorcroft, another BBC voice of the future, also had a great year in 1982, knocking almost six seconds off the world 5000m record in Oslo, in addition to breaking the European 3000m record.

David Coleman interviewed several of the athletes, including Thompson, who explained that he had turned down the chance to carry the English flag at the Commonwealth Games because he didn't want to spend five hours on his feet just ahead of his competition.

The Australian rugby league team beat Great Britain 3-0 and went unbeaten in all 15 of their tour matches. At the Challenge Cup final, Hull and Widnes tied 14-14 and the moment of the match, if not the season, came when Stuart Wright intercepted a pass and ran the full length of the pitch on a straight run to score a try for Widnes. Hull won the replay to lift the trophy for the first time since 1914.

Below Steve Cram (left) and Sebastian Coe were both part of the men's 4x800m relay team that set a world record of 7.3.89 in 1982
Right Alex Higgins, known as the Hurricane because of the pace of his game, was the first player to take 15 reds with 15 blacks in the snooker World Championship, although he never managed the 147 clearance

Overseas winner

These were vintage days at Wimbledon and there had been another epic men's final, this time with **Jimmy Connors** beating the defending champion John McEnroe in five sets. It was his first win since 1974, although he had been a losing finalist three times in the intervening years, and he had gone on to win the US Open as well. Connors and his wife Patti were interviewed in Miami by John Barrett, and Connors's son Brett was given the honour of presenting the Overseas award.

Team winner

It had been an astonishing year for the Nottingham based skaters **Jayne Torvill and Christopher Dean**. The ice-dancers had attained 11 maximum scores at the European Championships and a further five maximums in winning the World Championships with their 'Mack and Mabel' routine.

In their white T-shirts, silver jackets and red neckerchiefs they were interviewed by Frank Bough before skating into the next studio to perform a new routine of 'Rock and Roll is Here to Stay' on a specially laid rink.

At the end of it they were presented with the Team award by the 1972 Personality of the Year, Mary Peters.

Opposite Chris Evert Lloyd, known as a consistent, baseline player, won 157 tournaments in her 18-year career. Only Martina Navratilova – whom Evert Lloyd played 80 times – has won more women's titles

Erica Roe took off on a different kind of run when, on a cold January afternoon, she streaked across Twickenham, where England were playing Australia. However, the main rugby union story of the year was confined to the back pages as Ollie Campbell inspired Ireland to the Five Nations title and the Triple Crown.

At Aintree, Aldaniti was one of ten fallers at the first fence and the Grand National was won by amateur jockey Dick Saunders on Grittar. At 48, Saunders was the oldest ever winner of the race, while Geraldine Rees became the first woman to complete the course.

Former West Indian cricket captain, Gary Sobers, was in the studio to make the presentation of the viewers' choice of Sports Personality of the Year. In a sports shirt, tank top, tracksuit bottoms and trainers, Daley Thompson stepped forward to collect it in his own distinctive style.

▶▶ **Frank Bough** had presented *Sports Review of the Year* for a record 18 programmes. He had calmly presided over horses in the studio, interviewed the biggest names in sport, introduced royalty, seen the incredible advances in television coverage and witnessed the change from amateur to professional in many major sports.

▶▶ During 1982's race to become the champion jump jockey, **Peter Scudamore** looked certain to secure the title when he had a bad fall and broke his leg. His great friend and rival **John Francome** drew level in the table and then retired for the season so that they tied on the same number of winners.

Sporting roundup

Boxing Larry Holmes, in what was judged to be his best ever fight, beat Gerry Cooney to retain the world heavyweight title.

Golf Tom Watson won the US Open and the Open at Troon. It was the fourth time he had collected the famous claret jug.

Snooker On 11 January, Steve Davis made the first ever televised maximum break of 147.

Tennis Martina Navratilova began her six-year residency on Centre Court when she beat Chris Evert Lloyd in the Wimbledon final. It was Navratilova's third singles title and she added her fourth doubles trophy as well.

1983

Date 11 December 1983 • **Location** Television Centre, London • **Presenters** Desmond Lynam with Harry Carpenter, David Coleman and Jimmy Hill • **Editor** Harold Anderson • **Producer** Martin Hopkins

1st **Steve Cram** athlete
2nd **Jayne Torvill and Christopher Dean** ice skaters
3rd **Daley Thompson** athlete

In 1983, Desmond Lynam inherited the main presenter's role and, for the next 16 years, put his own distinctive and debonair stamp on the programme. It was one of the quieter years of the decade for mainstream sport, but the absence of any one dominant event meant that there was a greater diversity of guests and features. There was also the first appearance of a man who was to become a regular interviewee on the show. A young heavyweight named Frank Bruno had won all ten of his fights that year and Des rather optimistically commented, 'Well, big Frank will have that world title in his sights in the not too distant future we hope.' In fact, it was to be another 12 years.

Overall winner

Steve Cram won the silver medal behind Seb Coe in the 1984 Olympic Games and then enjoyed a golden summer in 1985 when he set three world records in 19 days in the 1500m, mile and 2000m. In 1986 he completed the 800m and 1500m double at the Commonwealth Games and also won the European 1500m title in Stuttgart.

Steve Cram remembers ...

'I was very ill on the night of the show with food poisoning, but really wanted to win it, especially as I had come third the year before. I'd been told when I arrived that I was in the top three and might have to say something, which made it even worse, especially after Daley's speech the year before!

It was a great honour when I was given the trophy but after the photos and a quick beer I went straight back to the hotel to see a doctor. I always thought that if I won the award it would have pride of place in my home, but a few years ago my children found it in the cellar. However, it's now back out and on display.'

One of the year's highlights had been the first ever athletics World Championships. They were held in Helsinki and Britain's stars didn't disappoint, with Steve Cram producing the race of his life to win the 1500m and Daley Thompson confirming his dominance in the decathlon.

Cram had also won the 1500m at Crystal Palace in the European Cup final and in September he held off Steve Ovett at the same venue to win a classic televised race over the same distance. Ovett also had a strong year and reclaimed his 1500m world record, while the third of Britain's great middle distance runners, Seb Coe, broke the 800m and 1000m indoor world records.

A British tennis renaissance threatened briefly in 1983 with the emergence of Jo Durie, who reached the semi-finals of both the French and US Opens. The revival continued when John Lloyd won the mixed doubles with Wendy Turnbull and became the first British man to win at Wimbledon since Fred Perry in 1936.

The popularity of snooker was undiminished, helped in 1983 by Cliff Thorburn's maximum break in the televised World Championship. He was a guest in the studio, along with Alex Higgins and Steve Davis, who had regained the title at the Crucible. Des interviewed Davis, who talked enthusiastically about the sport's potential for international expansion. Unfortunately, it had only yet extended as far as Belgium.

Aberdeen performed better on the continent when they defeated Real Madrid in the Cup Winners' Cup final. Liverpool were League Champions for the sixth time in eight years and Manchester United beat a gallant Brighton in the FA Cup final, but England lost the one that mattered. A penalty by Allan Simonsen in September condemned England to only their third defeat at Wembley, and it meant that it was Denmark, not England, who qualified for the European Championships.

The national team also failed to qualify for the final of the Cricket World Cup, which was once again staged in England. Initially, another West Indian victory seemed inevitable, but the cup holders and favourites were bowled out for just 140 when chasing a modest target set by India. Kapil Dev, India's inspirational captain and all-rounder, lifted the trophy at Lord's.

Above Richard Noble and *Thrust II* continued the *Sports Review* tradition of bringing vehicles into the studio – on a grand scale

Horse racing was dominated by familiar personalities, although none featured in the end of year voting. The Grand National was won by Jenny Pitman's Corbiere, and in the Cheltenham Gold Cup Michael Dickinson achieved the astonishing feat of training the first five horses. Willie Carson, at 40, won the flat racing jockey's title and his great rival, Lester Piggott, at 47, won his ninth Derby on Teenoso, an incredible 29 years after his first victory on Never Say Die.

The appearance of Richard Noble and *Thrust II* in the studio further highlighted splendid achievement. Noble had reached 633.468 mph, reclaiming the land speed record, and Des was slightly startled to see a speedometer that went from 0-800 mph.

Team winner

Jayne Torvill and Christopher Dean had won World Championship gold when their 'Barnum' routine was given nine maximums for artistic impression. Des interviewed them and Chris explained the difficulties that they encountered in needing to change their act every year.

Their new one used Ravel's 'Bolero' and they had performed it at the British Championships. Chris didn't know why he had chosen this particular piece of music, but his and Jayne's interpretation of it would become one of the most iconic and viewed performances in British sporting history.

The pair were presented with the Team award for the second year in a row, the first time that this had happened in the show's long history, and it was given to them by Alan Weeks.

International Team winner

In 1983 the production team decided to create the International Team award. This was presented by Peter de Savary to **Alan Bond and the crew of *Australia II***. They had achieved an Australian ambition to wrest the Americas Cup away from the USA, who had held it for 132 years. Bond was in the studio and the rest of his crew joined the show on a live satellite link. It had taken him 13 years and four challenges to win the cup.

Overseas winner

The award stayed in America for a fourth successive year, following the emergence of the man who went on to become one of the greatest athletes of all time.

Carl Lewis won gold medals in the 100m and long jump before sharing an American world record in the sprint relay at the inaugural 1983 World Championships.

On the night of the show, Lewis was interviewed live by satellite from New York and became the only winner to receive the trophy from his mum and dad.

Opposite John Hewitt of Aberdeen, having come on as a sub, beats Real Madrid keeper, Augustin, to score the European Cup Winners' Cup final winner. The game finished 2-1 after extra time

However, at the end of the evening, Bobby Charlton, stepped forward to present the 1983 Sports Personality of the Year award to a fellow hero of the North East, Steve Cram.

▸▸ For the first time there were **silver plates** for the second and third placed personalities and it meant that all three people could now step forward and be acknowledged.

▸▸ **Bob Paisley** retired as Liverpool manager after nine years. He had won six League Championships, three European Cups, three League Cups and the UEFA Cup. Originally a bricklayer from County Durham, he joined Liverpool as a wing-half in 1939 and served the club as player, coach, manager and director, before he died in 1996.

Sporting roundup

Boxing Charlie Magri briefly held the WBC world flyweight title.

Golf Royal Birkdale staged the Open and Tom Watson won for the fifth time. Nick Faldo led the European money tour and the USA retained the Ryder Cup by one point.

Horse racing The winner of the 1981 Derby, Shergar, was kidnapped in February.

Motor racing Nelson Piquet held off Alain Prost to win his second Formula One title.

Rugby league In the Challenge Cup final, Featherstone Rovers beat Hull in one of the greatest ever upsets.

Rugby union France and Ireland shared the Championship and Scotland beat England at Twickenham to condemn them to the wooden spoon. In the autumn, England beat the All Blacks at Twickenham for the first time since 1936.

Tennis In addition to winning the US and Australian Opens, Martina Navratilova saw off a challenge from 18-year-old Andrea Jaeger in the Wimbledon ladies singles final. John McEnroe won his second men's championship, defeating the unseeded Chris Lewis.

Three-day eventing Lucinda Prior-Palmer won Badminton for the fifth time.

Desmond Lynam, presenter,

remembers ...

'I first started watching the show in the 1960s and when I went to television from radio I was invited once or twice to sit in the audience. I noticed that there always seemed to be a lot of tension in the studio.

'As well as the sportsmen and women there are lots of VIPs and administrators. That is a hard group to work with, as the viewer often sees them looking at the other people or up at the monitors. I knew that I wanted to relieve some of that tension and decided to try and do it a little more light-heartedly.

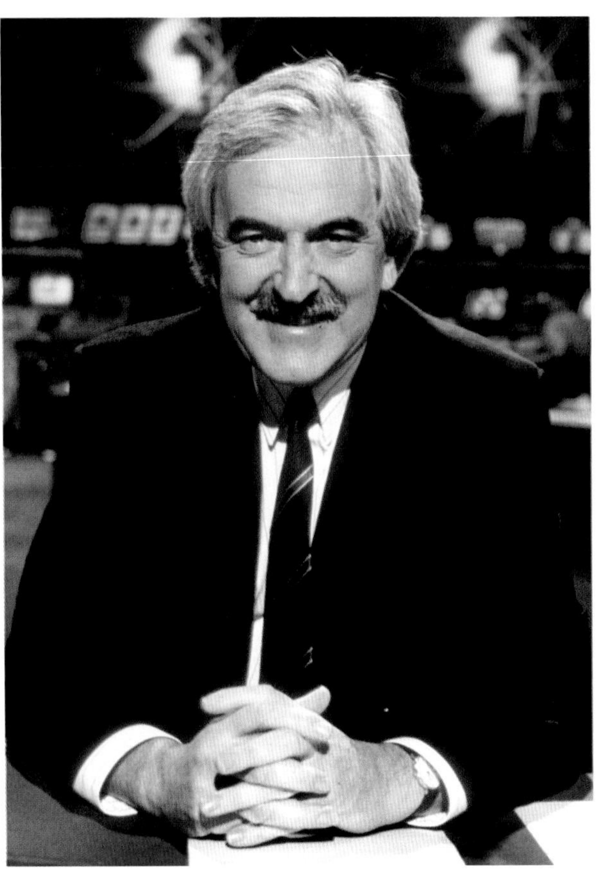

'It is an important award and a terrific live show to present, but I think it has sometimes lacked a bit of atmosphere. I've always thought that there should be members of the public in the audience. They would really lift it, give it a buzz.

'1983 was daunting. I was thrown straight in as the main anchor man in the year that Steve Cram won, and recall also having Richard Noble in the studio with his huge vehicle. They had just broken the land speed record and that at least gave us the opportunity for some banter.

'No interviews were rehearsed, not even the annual ones with Frank Bruno. We just had a technical run-through of our links and camera positions, so we were very dependent on people giving a reasonable interview. Jenny Pitman was always a joy as she is such a real personality. Sometimes people who had really sparkled when I spoke to them on *Grandstand* earlier in the year would just dry up on the night, when they were being stared at by so many famous faces. That was a problem that we always faced, so we just had to hope that we had picked the best people to chat to.

'That is one of the reasons why I loved interviewing the boxers. I always thought that they gave you both personality and size. They made such an impact on everyone who was there and that transmitted itself through the screen, and all the mock bragging made them entertaining. Riddick Bowe, Evander Holyfield, Chris Eubank and Frank Bruno were just some of my favourites. They never let you down.

'In 1996 we also had the Olympic sprint champions, Michael Johnson and Donovan Bailey, and you could feel the tension in the room between them. It was probably the only show where an editor could get guys like that to come on together.

'I did seem to be associated with the so-called stunts. I was the fall guy who had to make them work. There was a feeling that they should be there to be jokey and lighten the tension. Sometimes they worked, other times, such as the duck shoot (right), they didn't.

'One of the better ones almost broke my finger. After the farce of the Grand National that didn't count, the production team decided to get the actual starting gate down from Aintree. I was dressed in the regulation brown overcoat and black bowler hat and the effect was very good. But, as I pulled the starting lever down, my finger got caught and I bled my way through the rest of the show in considerable pain.

'I did seem to be associated with the so-called stunts. I was the fall guy who had to make them work'

'I always thought that Gary Lineker should have won the Sports Personality of the Year award. He won the Golden Boot in the 1986 World Cup and then helped England to the semi-finals in 1990, yet he didn't make it into the top three of the voting in either year. I thought that was a real shame, so it's ironic that he is now back helping to present the show.

'Having presented 18 *Sports Reviews* myself, I confess that I watched the 1999 show through gritted teeth, as I would have loved to have been there when Ali was the star of the night, but I had moved from the BBC earlier that year.

'I met Ali a lot in the 1970s, when I commentated on boxing on the radio, and had done loads with him over the years. In the mid-1980s he even rang up *Grandstand* once and asked if he could come on the show to prove he was fit and well.

'Looking back, the shows were great fun. The parties afterwards were always very entertaining and I met a lot of people I liked and admired and had wanted to meet. It's always good to see very famous people being in awe of other very famous people. Every programme was a little daunting, but very enjoyable once I got into them, although the best drink of the year was always the first lager at the end of *Sports Review*.'

1984

Date 16 December 1984 • **Location** Television Centre, London • **Presenters** Desmond Lynam with Harry Carpenter, David Coleman and Jimmy Hill • **Editor** Harold Anderson • **Producer** Martin Hopkins

1st Jayne Torvill and Christopher Dean ice skaters
2nd Sebastian Coe athlete
3rd Steve Davis snooker player

Desmond Lynam opened the show and introduced the Olympic medallists. He then illustrated the strength of our middle distance athletes by saying, 'You know it's 30 years since the first *Sports Review* celebrated the breaking of the four-minute mile back in 1954. Tonight we have three guests who can beat that barrier by over ten seconds.'

That was Coe, Ovett and Cram, and memories of the Los Angeles and Sarajevo Olympics could have filled the whole programme. For Jayne Torvill and Christopher Dean, Sarajevo, as expected, delivered their greatest triumph. 'Bolero' had pushed back the artistic boundaries of the sport and the judges awarded an astonishing nine

Overall winner

Torvill and Dean turned professional after the Olympics and spent a decade performing in their ice show around the world. They returned to the Olympics in 1994, after the rules were relaxed, and won bronze with their 'Let's Face the Music' routine.

Jayne Torvill remembers …

'Chris and I were first invited to the show when we became British champions and it used to seem like a really big thing to actually go to London and be in the same room as so many great sports stars.

'Then in 1982 we were asked to perform before being given the Team award. We adapted a routine that we used in exhibitions, called 'Rock 'n' Roll is Here to Stay', but it felt very strange. The studio was tiny, with no audience and no windows, and it was very odd knowing that so many people were watching it next door. At the end we had to skate on a plastic sheet into the main studio, so we were concentrating on not falling over and trying not to pant when we got the trophy from Mary Peters.

'It was wonderful when we won the Sports Personality of the Year award two years later. I remember we were surprised and honoured that Elton John was there to present it.'

maximum scores for artistic merit and a further three maximums for technical merit. Inevitably the gold was theirs, and they followed it with gold at the World Championships in Canada.

Even another boycott, this time by the Eastern bloc countries, failed to take the glitz off the Summer Olympics in Los Angeles. In the athletics stadium, Tessa Sanderson produced a timely Olympic record throw to beat Tina Lillak to the javelin gold, with Fatima Whitbread in third. Daley Thompson coasted to the gold again, becoming only the second decathlete to win the title twice. Sebastian Coe firmly established himself as one of the greatest middle distance runners of all time with his second straight victory in the 1500m. It was a new Olympic record and set the seal on his glorious career. Steve Cram took the silver medal.

Four former winners of the Sports Personality of the Year trophy – Coe, Cram, Ovett and Thompson – were brought together in the studio and an interview with David Coleman proved that it was team spirit as much as rivalry that had brought British athletics this golden era.

Steve Ovett had struggled with health problems all year, but was beginning to recover, although he was concerned that his dog still seemed fitter on their walks. Coleman noted that the three middle distance runners had now been in two Olympic finals together, but Cram gleefully doubted it could happen again as the other two were getting old.

But if one era of British sport was ending, another was just getting underway. There was British success on Lake Casitas in the coxed four rowing and, almost buried in the small print of the reports, was the name of Steve Redgrave, who had just claimed gold medal number one. Also in the studio was Britain's fifth Olympic champion, Malcolm Cooper, who had come first in the small bore rifle.

Special award

Lester Piggott was in the studio, having ridden to a record 28th classic success on Commanche Run in the St Leger. Des interviewed him as they viewed a clip of his first classic win, on Never Say Die, in the 1954 Derby. Sir Gordon Richards then presented him with a Special award to commemorate his achievements.

The summer had seen another stunning Wimbledon performance by John McEnroe, but there was no five-set marathon this time. Instead, Jimmy Connors managed to win only four games as McEnroe overwhelmed him in straight sets to take the trophy for the third time.

At Wimbledon it was the centenary of the Ladies Championship and for the first time a woman, Georgina Clark, umpired the final. The Centre Court crowd witnessed Martina Navratilova beating Chris Evert Lloyd again, and there was hope once more for British fans as

Below Ian Rush scores from the spot, after Liverpool's European Cup final against AS Roma ended in a 1-1 draw after extra time. The Italian side eventually lost 4-2 on penalties

Overseas winner

At St Andrews, **Seve Ballesteros** and Tom Watson fought it out in the final round of the Open Championship. A birdie at the final hole clinched one of the greatest victories of Seve's career. His exuberant celebration at the 18th added further to his vast army of fans and probably helped clinch the Overseas award, which was presented to him by Tony Jacklin.

Team winner

There had been great admiration for the **British hockey squad**, whose battle against the favourites, Australia, earned them Olympic bronze. It also made famous names out of goalkeeper Ian Taylor and goalscorer Sean Kerly, and earned them the 1984 Team award. They received it from Charles Palmer, chairman of the British Olympic Association.

Opposite Zola Budd was disqualified and then reinstated after colliding with Mary Decker in the Olympic 3000m final, but her athletics career never really recovered

John Lloyd and Wendy Turnbull held the mixed doubles title and Annabel Croft won the Junior Championship.

It was a mixed year for fans of other sports. Those north of the border were ecstatic as Scotland's rugby union team completed the Grand Slam and won their first outright championship since 1938. For English cricket followers the news was not so good, though. England had a terrible year – they lost their tours to Pakistan and New Zealand and were thrashed 5-0 by the West Indies.

Football's European Championships had been won in flamboyant style by the hosts, France, but there was the usual consolation for British clubs in Europe, with Liverpool reclaiming the European Cup on penalties against AS Roma.

After extra time, Spurs won the UEFA Cup against Anderlecht, but Watford provided the romance of the season by reaching the FA Cup final, although Everton beat them comfortably. The sporting credentials of Watford's chairman, Elton John, were now sky-high and he was called upon to present the Sports Personality of the Year award. And given the showbiz content of the year, it was very appropriate to see him give the award to the first joint recipients, Jayne Torvill and Christopher Dean.

▸▸ A regular on the show, **Seve Ballesteros** has won five awards. He was part of the Ryder Cup Team award winners in 1985, 1987 and 1995, and in 1997 was given a special trophy for sporting achievement by Colin Montgomerie.

▸▸ **Zola Budd** was an outstanding 17-year-old athlete from Bloemfontein who couldn't compete on the international stage because of the sporting boycott of South Africa. When it was discovered that one of her grandfathers had been British, her application for citizenship was rushed through and just three months later she found herself in the midst of controversy as a member of Britain's Olympic Team. The 3000m final saw her up against America's golden girl, Mary Decker. Unfortunately for Budd, there was to be no Hollywood ending to her story. She clashed with Decker, who was sent sprawling, was booed by the crowd and finished in seventh place.

Sporting roundup

Boxing Barry McGuigan retained his European title but Frank Bruno lost to James 'Bonecrusher' Smith and was thought to be almost finished as a fighter.

Horse racing Secreto won the Derby and Hello Dandy was first home in the Grand National.

Motor sport The year was dominated by two McLaren drivers: Alain Prost won seven races but lost by half a point to Niki Lauda. It was Lauda's third title.

Paralympics Britain's 224 competitors returned from Los Angeles with 238 medals.

Rugby league In the Challenge Cup final Widnes beat Wigan to register their fourth win in ten years.

Snooker Steve Davis beat Jimmy White 18-16 for his third title in four years.

Three-day eventing Lucinda Green won Badminton for the sixth time.

1985

Date 15 December 1985 • Location Television Centre, London • Presenters Desmond Lynam with Harry Carpenter and Jimmy Hill • Editor John Rowlinson • Producer Martin Hopkins

1st **Barry McGuigan** boxer
2nd **Ian Botham** cricketer
3rd **Steve Cram** athlete

Overall winner

Barry McGuigan (above right), affectionately known as the Clones Cyclone, defended his title twice, before losing it to American Steve Cruz in controversial circumstances in the Las Vegas heat of June 1986. Always a provocative spokesperson for the sport, he retired in 1989 and set up the Professional Boxers' Association.

If ever there was a year for *Sports Review of the Year* to become more solemn and reflective it was 1985, with the tragedies of Heysel and Bradford and the death of Scotland's manager, Jock Stein, casting gloom over sport in general and football in particular. However, on 15 December these events received an acknowledgment at the start of the football section and no more. The celebration of sport had to go on.

Britain had a new boxing world champion to be proud of. In June, at Loftus Road, in one of the greatest fights London had ever seen, Northern Ireland's Barry McGuigan had beaten Eusebio Pedroza on points to claim the WBA featherweight title. McGuigan was one of the main guests in the studio, showing his skills on the speedball for the benefit of the audience and reliving the tension and excitement of an amazing contest. Frank Bruno then joined them and told Des about his ambitions to win the world heavyweight title in 1986. He had become the European champion and his chances looked to have improved as three different men claimed to be world champion in that year.

Other less physical sports proved that they could generate similar tension – even snooker. Desmond Lynam explained that in 1966 there had been just 1 hour 28 minutes and 20 seconds of snooker coverage in the whole year. In 1985, encouraged by colour television, this figure had increased to 261 hours 15 minutes and one second. Much of that time had been spent on the best

Above left David Gower, known for his laidback batting style, hit three centuries in the course of the 1985 Ashes series
Above Dennis Taylor first wore his trademark big glasses in 1983. It can be no coincidence that he won his first major title a year later

World Championship final the sport had ever seen. As the clock went past midnight, an audience of over 18 million had seen Dennis Taylor complete his recovery from 8-0 down against Steve Davis to win the title on the final black of the final frame.

There was also joy for Scotland in the shape of Sandy Lyle, who, signalling the start of a great new era for the British game, had won the Open Championship at Royal St George's. Lyle had nearly turned victory into defeat with a fluffed chip from just off the 18th, and he was asked to reproduce this shot for the benefit of the studio audience on a plywood mock-up of the final green. The results were only slightly more reassuring.

Two horse racing legends, Joe Mercer and Lester Piggott, announced their retirements and there was a brief interview with the much younger John Francome. He had also retired, having become champion jump jockey for the seventh time.

England's cricketers were candidates for the Team of the Year, having had a great summer when, under the captaincy of David Gower, they regained the Ashes. After the political turmoil of the previous years, all their top players were available and all were on form.

Ian Botham was live in a Hollywood studio wearing an American football shirt and sporting a long, blond mullet. He had a go at the British press, said that he had

Overseas winner

The stranglehold that Jimmy Connors and John McEnroe had over Wimbledon was broken in 1985 by a 17-year-old unseeded German named **Boris Becker**. He had begun the year ranked 110th in the world, but at Wimbledon he beat Kevin Curren in the final to cause one of the greatest surprises of the sporting year.

Not only that but he had a strong personality and fluent English, as was evident when he received the Overseas award from Buzzer Hadingham in Munich.

Becker reached five more finals in the next six years, winning two of them. His last appearance as a finalist was in 1995, when he lost to Pete Sampras in four sets.

Team winner

Europe's golfers had wrestled the Ryder Cup from the USA for the first time since 1957. Sam Torrance rolled in a famous putt to make certain of the victory and the newly built Belfry became hallowed ground as far as European golf was concerned. The **Ryder Cup team** were in the studio to receive the Team award from three times Open champion, Henry Cotton.

Opposite Boris Becker, unseeded, dives to return the ball during his Wimbledon semi-final against Anders Jarryd, the fifth seed. Becker won this match and went on to beat Kevin Curren in the final

spoken to a couple of film producers about possible projects and talked about his first sponsored walk for leukaemia, from John O'Groats to Land's End. Looking ahead to the series against the West Indies, he felt that it would be very tight. It wasn't. England lost 5-0.

Jimmy Hill linked into the football section by recalling how Merseyside had dominated the year. Everton had won their first Championship in 15 years, with Liverpool runners-up, and the team then lifted the Cup Winners' Cup by beating Rapid Vienna 3-1. A unique treble was missed when they lost to Manchester United in the FA Cup final. Everton's dominance was confirmed when the awards were handed out. Peter Reid was the Professional Footballers' Association's Player of the Year, Neville Southall won the Football Writers' award and Howard Kendall was Manager of the Year.

None, however, were named among the six contenders for Sports Personality of the Year, as the list comprised Ian Botham, Steve Cram, David Gower, Sandy Lyle, Barry McGuigan and Dennis Taylor. There was a moment of slight confusion when 90-year-old Sir Stanley Rous announced the winner as 'Barry McCorchoran', but everyone knew that Northern Ireland's new world champion had been voted the viewers' favourite.

▸▸ **Sir Stanley Rous** had a long relationship with the programme and presented awards on five separate occasions across a 24-year span. One of the most influential and respected sports administrators of all time, he died in July 1986.

▸▸ Football was hit by two major tragedies in 1985. At Heysel Stadium in Brussels on 29 May, just before **Liverpool** were beaten 1-0 by Juventus in the European Cup final, 39 people died and over 400 more were injured in a riot. A fortnight before, **Bradford** were celebrating their Third Division Championship when fire broke out in a wooden stand. On that tragic afternoon, 56 people died.

Sporting roundup

Athletics Steve Cram broke the 1500m, mile and 2000m world records in the space of 19 days, and also won gold in the European Cup in Moscow.

Cycling Bernard Hinault won the Tour de France for a record-equalling fifth time.

Football In Scotland, Aberdeen retained the league title under Alex Ferguson, while Celtic won the Cup.

Horse racing The Grand National was won by the 66-1 outsider, Last Suspect, while the leading flat jockey and trainer combined to win the Derby when Steve Cauthen rode Henry Cecil's Slip Anchor to victory at Epsom.

Motor racing Alain Prost won the Formula One World Championship and, after 72 races, Nigel Mansell won his first Grand Prix, the European, at Brands Hatch.

Rugby league The 50th Challenge Cup final to be played at Wembley was judged to be the best to date as ten tries were scored when Wigan beat Hull 28-24 to lift the trophy for the seventh time

Rugby union Ireland took their third title in four years.

Tennis In the women's final at Wimbledon, Martina Navratilova met and defeated Chris Evert Lloyd for the fifth time, despite losing the first set.

1986

Date 14 December 1986 • Location Television Centre, London • Presenter Desmond Lynam with Steve Rider
Editor John Rowlinson • Producer Martin Hopkins

1st **Nigel Mansell** racing driver
2nd **Fatima Whitbread** athlete
3rd **Kenny Dalglish** footballer

In 1986 I was lucky enough to be invited to join Desmond Lynam as presenter of a programme that, for me, had been an annual television highlight for as long as I could remember. I had joined BBC Sport from ITV the previous year and, although in 1986 I had presented Wimbledon, the Open Championship and the Commonwealth Games in Edinburgh, nothing quite prepares you for the sense of responsibility you feel when fronting a programme that is so much part of people's lives.

Overall winner

Nigel Mansell said winning Sports Personality of the Year was a complete surprise, thanked the BBC, the fans and his Williams team, and made a special point of thanking his wife. He had some difficulty in holding the trophy, though, as his arm was in plaster following a crash while testing.

I was lucky in that once the show was under way, one of the key interviews I was required to do was with Nigel Mansell, whom I had got to know pretty well when he had been driving for Lotus. Now, though, he was a World Championship challenger with Williams.

Certainly the Williams team would never forget 1986. Boss Frank Williams, confined to a wheelchair after a car crash in France, visited the *Grandstand* studio at 4 a.m. on 26 October, hoping to see Mansell crowned world champion in the final race of the season in Adelaide. Instead, he saw Mansell's title hopes disappear in a shower of sparks as his left rear tyre exploded. It was a difficult moment to interview Frank Williams and it wasn't much easier to get Nigel to talk about the incident two months later.

Reflecting on Mansell's misfortune , Mel Smith and Griff Rhys Jones, whose 'head to heads' were popular at the time and who had been brought in to strengthen *Sports Review*'s light entertainment spin, commented, 'Poor old Nigel – a man's hopes dashed all because of a little bit of burst rubber.'

However, it was the 'hand of god' that had dashed England's hopes in the World Cup finals in Mexico. Diego Maradona's interventions, both legal and illegal, put England out of the competition in the quarter-final.

Argentina went on to regain the cup with a 3-2 victory over West Germany in the final. Northern Ireland and Scotland had been eliminated at the first stage.

Boxing had a new star as 20-year -old Mike Tyson became the youngest ever world heavyweight champion. Frank Bruno seemed on the wane, though, as he had lost to Tim Witherspoon, but better news had come at other weights with Lloyd Honeyghan beating Don Curry to become world welterweight champion in the boxing upset of the year. His sixth round victory in Atlantic City was seen as the best ever win by a British boxer abroad.

The light entertainment continued with a hockey penalty shoot-out between Sean Kerly and Ian Taylor from the British squad and Emlyn Hughes and Bob Wilson from *Football Focus*. It was a revenge opportunity for Bob as his show had been postponed earlier in the year to allow a hockey international to be shown, but the footballers' mockery of the heavy padding required soon vanished as they lost 5-2.

The Commonwealth Games in Edinburgh, meanwhile, introduced us to Liz Lynch, later to become Liz McColgan, and the rivalry of Tessa Sanderson and

Above right Fatima Whitbread's world record, set at the 1986 European Championships, was a staggering 77.44m
Right Diego Maradona (left) punches the ball past England goalkeeper, Peter Shilton, in the highly controversial 'hand of god' incident. Argentina won the World Cup quarter final match 2-1

Special award

Although not officially recognized as such, this was effectively another Team award, which the **British men's 4x400 relay squad**, who had won gold at the European Championships, received from David Hemery. All six members of the squad were interviewed by Des, including Brian Whittle, who had run his leg in just one shoe.

Overseas winner

Although he will probably be remembered as golf's 'nearly man', **Greg Norman** won his first Open Championship at Turnberry in 1986. He was also runner-up in the US Masters and US PGA. The Overseas award was presented to him in America by his Florida neighbour, Arnold Palmer.

Team winner

Liverpool had clinched the double by beating Everton 3-1 in the Merseyside FA Cup final. They were only the third club in the twentieth century to complete the feat, and their Championship victory had been their sixth in eight years. Jimmy Hill had the job of interviewing player-manager Kenny Dalglish and his squad at a Christmas party at Anfield. When presenting the Team award, Jimmy's task was made no easier by the Father Christmas outfit he was required to wear.

Opposite Kenny Dalglish (left) outpaces Everton's Paul Bracewell and Peter Reid in the FA Cup final. Despite Gary Lineker giving Everton an early lead, Liverpool won this half of their double 3-1

Fatima Whitbread was growing. That was resolved in Fatima's favour at the European Championships when she claimed javelin gold with a world record throw. There were also golds for Linford Christie, Seb Coe, Daley Thompson, Jack Buckner, Steve Cram and Roger Black.

Jump jockey Jonjo O'Neill was also a studio guest, having prompted unprecedented Irish celebrations when he brought Dawn Run home to victory in the Cheltenham Gold Cup. Tragically, the horse died three months later from a fall in France. Jonjo was now fighting a different battle, against illness, and as well as describing how Dawn Run had given him his best ever finish and greatest reception, he talked about his cancer treatment. Bob Champion, who had been down the same road, sat next to him, offering support and encouragement.

The English cricket team was again in crisis, having lost to the West Indies in the winter and India and New Zealand in the summer. Ian Botham had also been suspended after admitting that he had smoked marijuana. The comments from Smith and Jones were: 'Do you think Botham can win the BBC Sports Personality of the Year?' 'No, the best I can think is that he can be joint winner!'

Botham had, inevitably, returned in style and took a wicket with his first ball against New Zealand to equal Dennis Lillee's world record of 355 scalps. Then, ten balls later, he broke it. Just for good measure he followed that with one of the fastest ever Test match half-centuries, but later that season resigned from Somerset when they didn't renew the contracts of Viv Richards and Joel Garner.

Henry Cooper, the first Sports Personality of the Year double winner, was called up to present the 1986 version. He named Liverpool's Kenny Dalglish in third and Fatima Whitbread in second, but the viewers had been most thrilled by the season-long exploits of Nigel Mansell.

▸▸ **Ballyregan Bob** became the first, and to date, only dog to appear in the studio. The greyhound had just completed 32 consecutive wins.

▸▸ **Viv Richards** hit the fastest ever Test century off just 56 deliveries against England at his home ground in Antigua in April. It took 41 scoring strokes to bring up his 20th Test hundred.

Sporting roundup

Boxing Dennis Andries won and defended the light-heavyweight title but Barry McGuigan lost his crown to Steve Cruz in the heat of Las Vegas.

Football Celtic won the Scottish League and Aberdeen lifted the Scottish Cup for the fourth time in five years.

Golf Jack Nicklaus won the US Masters, 23 years after his first Green Jacket and at the age of 46. Britain's Curtis Cup Team beat America for the first time in 30 years.

Horse racing Richard Dunwoody rode his first Grand National winner on West Tip, while Walter Swinburn achieved his second Derby victory, this time on Sharastani.

Rugby league Castleford beat Hull Kingston Rovers in the Challenge Cup final and the legendary commentator Eddie Waring died, just five years after his retirement.

Rugby union Scotland and France shared the Five Nations title.

Snooker Joe Johnson surprised everyone by winning the World Championship as a 150-1 outsider.

Tennis Martina Navratilova won her seventh Wimbledon singles and added her fifth doubles title with Pam Shriver, her seventh in all. Boris Becker retained his title, defeating Ivan Lendl in the final.

1987

Date 13 December 1987 • Location Television Centre, London • Presenters Desmond Lynam with Steve Rider Editor John Rowlinson • Producer Martin Hopkins

1st **Fatima Whitbread** athlete
2nd **Steve Davis** snooker player
3rd **Ian Woosnam** golfer

Golf had undoubtedly been a headline event in 1987, so some kind of golf stunt seemed appropriate for the programme. Consequently, we decided to use one of those new-fangled computerized simulators and have a charity shoot-out between the year's leading personalities. In rehearsals, both Des and I were able to achieve nothing better than our usual 180-yard high slice. When Ian Woosnam did much the same during the live show, our doubts about the technology set in. However, Nick Faldo set the target, Nigel Mansell and Steve Cram tried to be competitive, and Frank Bruno had easily the fastest swing but failed to make contact at all. In total, £1,300 was raised for Jonjo O'Neill's cancer charity and the programme had fulfilled at least part of its growing light entertainment brief.

Overall winner

The first individual sportswoman to pick up the award in a decade, Fatima won Olympic silver the following year but injury cut short her career soon afterwards. Since retirement she has been involved in sports marketing and development.

Fatima Whitbread remembers ...

'It was a very proud moment when I held the trophy as it was considered to be the main award to win. It was a wonderful evening and I remember that six of us were told that we should prepare a few words as we were the main contenders.

'I had won Britain's only gold medal at the World Championships and I think that I probably got most of the athletics vote, which helped. There were so many great names in the running in 1987 that to win was a real achievement and stands out as one of the highlights of my career. The small replica trophy still sits in my home.'

It had earlier fulfilled a bit more when Nigel Mansell, last year's winner and a part-time special constable, brought the trophy to the studio in a police car, accompanied by the *Z Cars* theme. If anything, Mansell's reputation had grown in 1987 as he took six races, including the British Grand Prix at Silverstone after a fantastic duel with Nelson Piquet. However, he still failed to win the World Championship.

As well as Europe successfully retaining the Ryder Cup with a historic victory at Muirfield Village in Ohio, there had also been some outstanding individual performances in golf. These included Nick Faldo's 18 final round pars to win the Open Championship at Muirfield and Laura Davies becoming the first British player to win the US Women's Open. Although he didn't win a major, Ian Woosnam had the richest season the sport had seen, winning eight tournaments and over $1.8 million. All were in the studio to reflect on their achievements – and experience the humiliation of the golf simulator.

The racing world was shocked by Lester Piggott's three-year jail sentence for tax evasion; Peter Scudamore dominated the national hunt season; while on the flat, Steve Cauthen beat Pat Eddery to the Jockeys' Championshipon the last day of the season. Reference Point was the horse of the year, winning the Derby and the King George; Maori Venture won the Grand National; and Des conducted a welcome interview with Jonjo O'Neill, who had a full head of hair once again and was now, thankfully, recovering from cancer.

In tennis, Pat Cash made his famous climb through the centre court seats at Wimbledon to receive the congratulations of his family after beating Ivan Lendl in the men's final, and in the mixed doubles Jeremy Bates and Jo Durie became the first British champions for 51 years.

The inaugural rugby union World Cup had been held in Australia and New Zealand in June. Wales beat England in the quarter-final and eventually took third place in the competition, while Grant Fox kicked the All Blacks to

Top Pat Cash beat Ivan Lendl in straight sets to win the Wimbledon title. 'Pat cashes a Czech' was the theme of the next day's headlines
Above Ian Woosnam (right) and caddy Phil Morbey line up a putt

victory in the final against France, although the French could take some consolation from their Five Nations win earlier in the year.

Australia had beaten England by seven runs in the final of the fourth cricket World Cup, in Calcutta, in a year that had begun well for England's cricketers as Mike Gatting led them to the Ashes and Chris Broad was named International Cricketer of the Year. But then it all went wrong, as they lost in the summer to Pakistan, before a descent into farce and bad feeling in Faisalabad with the infamous finger-wagging session between Gatting and umpire Shakoor Rana.

In boxing, British world champions Lloyd Honeyghan and Denis Andries had come and gone. Mike Tyson was now the undisputed heavyweight champion of the world and Frank Bruno, in his studio interview with Des Lynam, nervously revealed that he was being lined up as an opponent for Tyson the following year. In 1987 he had beaten slightly lesser opposition in the form of the ageing Joe Bugner.

Judged by the standards of recent years, the athletics World Championships in Rome had been a disappointment, with Steve Cram and Daley Thompson both beaten and Britain's only gold medal coming from Fatima Whitbread in the javelin. She, however, was a hugely popular winner and at the end of the evening Colin Cowdrey handed her the famous Sports Personality trophy.

Overseas winner

Martina Navratilova won her eighth Wimbledon as part of her season-long duel with Steffi Graf, and it was her old rival Chris Evert who presented her with the Overseas award in America. Dressed in a dark blue leather, military-style outfit, Martina admitted that until recently she had never actually heard of it, but was grateful anyway!

Team winner

The European achievement of successfully defending the Ryder Cup at Muirfield even eclipsed what had happened at the Belfry two years earlier and captain Tony Jacklin was in the studio to take the applause, along with Eamonn Darcy, who had holed the putt that finally secured the victory. They had won on American soil for the first time in 60 years and it was pretty much a formality that the **European Ryder Cup team** would win the Team award. Peter Alliss made the presentation.

▶▶ Many vehicles have appeared in the *Sports Review of the Year* studios down the years, but in 1987 it was the turn of the sidecar world champions, **Steve Webster and Tony Hewitt**, and their weird-looking machine.

▶▶ Canadian sprinter **Ben Johnson** made a startling impact at the World Championships when he beat Carl Lewis to win the 100m title in a new world record time of 9.83 seconds. However, his place at the top was to be short-lived and the following year saw him stripped of the title.

Opposite Stephen Roche was only the fifth rider in cycling history to win the French and Italian tours in the same season

Sporting roundup

Cycling Stephen Roche, a 27-year-old Dubliner, became the first Irishman to win the Tour de France.

Football Graeme Souness led Rangers to their first title in nine years and St Mirren won the Scottish FA Cup. Everton were League Champions and Coventry beat Spurs 3-2 in the FA Cup final.

Motor racing Derek Bell recorded his fifth win in 13 years at Le Mans.

Rugby league Halifax won their first Challenge Cup since 1939, but Wigan won all the other rugby league trophies, thanks to 62 tries by Ellery Hanley.

Snooker Steve Davis lifted the World Championship trophy for the fourth time.

Those studio set pieces ...

The obligatory stunts

Through at least 30 years of *Sports Review of the Year* there was an obligation to interrupt the action and achievement with stunts that portrayed the stars in relaxed, fun-loving mode and delivered light entertainment along with the sporting review.

The philosophy was that neither the programme nor its participants should be seen to be taking themselves too seriously but, in reality, as the ideas became more and more cliche-ridden, these interludes were generating more cringes than meaningful insights. Des Lynam's relaxed, dry humour helped stars and audience survive the embarrassment, but when he departed in 1999 it was seen as the perfect excuse to ditch all the clumsy comedy and get back to the straightforward journalism.

In doing so, though, *Sports Personality of the Year* lost much of the eccentricity that set it apart from other programmes and producer Martin Hopkins, for one, felt that such interludes had been essential. 'They gave the programme a chance to change gear and the production team a chance to use their imagination – to me the studio stunts were the highlight of the show.' This from a man who had presided over a cavalcade of sporting fashion, choreographed Baddiel, Skinner, the Lightning Seeds and an enthusiastic line-up of footballing youth and orchestrated the notorious duck shoot.

'It all seemed doomed when the BBC's resident safety officer shot himself in the foot with one of the guns'

The 1988 fairground stunt was a bid to pit the skills of our gold medal shooters from Seoul against some far from trigger-happy volunteers in the audience. But even before this particular spectacle marked the nadir of studio entertainment, it all seemed doomed when, as floor manager Chris White recalls, 'The BBC's resident safety officer shot himself in the foot with one of the guns.'

Producer Alec Weeks had felt a similar sense of foreboding almost three decades earlier when, with the programme safely ensconced in the BBC Theatre, he 'threw the kitchen sink' at the 1964 post Tokyo Olympic show. He says, 'It was my idea to build the rather rickety ramp on which the bobsleigh gold medallists, Tony Nash and Robin Dixon, would make their entrance. The ramp ran over the audience's heads and the safety people made it clear to me that if one nut or bolt fell on to the audience, then the legal implications would be my responsibility.

'On top of this I had also persuaded boxer Terry Downes to do a sparring session in the middle of the studio, except that I had overlooked the fact that Terry Downes didn't spar, he just hit people, and the poor guy we put in with him took the most fearful punishment.

'In the same show we had produced a giant wedding cake for Ann Packer. It was the programme that had everything, and in the end it did all work. People seem to think that this was the great pioneering age of sports broadcasting. Well, it was, as long as you got the pioneering right; if you got it wrong, you were out.'

Over the years, Formula One played its part with its wheel changes and car builds, and golf was also a regular source of stunts. In 1985 a mockup of the 18th green at Royal St George's was built in the studio, complete with the swale behind the green that almost caught out Sandy Lyle on his way to winning the Open Championship. Sandy reproduced the shot perfectly on the night, but a couple of years later our Ryder Cup golfers were caught out by a malfunctioning computer golf simulator that gave all our top stars a violent slice.

And then, after the penalty shoot-outs, with Bob Wilson losing his dignity in the hockey goal and Peter Shilton ultra-competitive in the football version, and the celebrity attempt to reproduce Jeremy Guscott's British Lions drop goal, the ideas ran out.

Paul Davies, the programme's current producer, does not mourn their passing. 'Every year the ideas were more and more of a struggle and if the ideas don't come naturally then quickly its odds on they're not going to work. Ending the stunts meant there was one less area where the programme could go seriously wrong and it probably means that the studio audience – and possibly the audience at home – can relax a bit more. I'm not saying that we won't go back to a light-hearted studio set piece if the idea is strong enough, but for the time being we're concentrating on slightly slicker things.'

Top John Surtees (left) on his bike. But hang on, what a hoot! That's actually a waxwork standing next to David Coleman and Beryl Burton
Middle Tony Nash, Robin Dixon and bobsleigh slide in safely
Above Anne Packer, Robbie Brightwell and that cake
Opposite Frank Bruno gets teed off with the golf simulator

1988

Date 4 December 1988 • **Location** Television Centre, London • **Presenters** Desmond Lynam with Steve Rider
Editor John Rowlinson • **Producer** Martin Hopkins

1st **Steve Davis** snooker player
2nd **Adrian Moorhouse** swimmer
3rd **Sandy Lyle** golfer

It was another Olympic year and the games had taken place in Calgary and Seoul. Following the age-old tradition of the show, Britain's gold medallists were welcomed onto the stage at the beginning of the evening.

The studio stunt potential offered by Eddie Edwards' exploits in the Olympic ski jump competition were – mercifully – resisted. Instead, Britain's shooters, Malcolm Cooper and Alastair Allan, who had won gold and silver in the small bore rifle, were persuaded to give their sport some extra exposure by taking part in

Overall winner

Steve Davis was in the middle of a match and thought he was just being lined up to give an interview for the show, so he was very surprised to be presented with the trophy and incredibly disappointed that he wasn't in the studio. He retained his world title the following year.

Steve Davis remembers ...

'It would have been nice to have been there in the studio, but getting awards can sometimes be embarrassing, because you are surrounded by so many great winners. It's always very much dependent on the sports that people watch and also their timing in the leadup to the voting.

'I'm very proud that I won it, though, especially as it showed just how popular snooker is with the viewing public. I'm amazed that I came in the top three on five occasions and that is a great accolade for our sport. However, we must also remember all the other talented sportsmen and women who don't get the recognition because their sports don't get the same television coverage.'

a studio-based charity duck- shooting competition. It all helped divert attention from some of the more gloomy issues to emerge from Seoul.

This, of course, was the year that sprinter Ben Johnson was exposed as the sport's biggest drug cheat, following his explosive performance in the 100m. Linford Christie, who was eventually awarded silver, was among Des Lynam's interviewees. Christie felt that becoming the first European to break the 10-second barrier for the 100m was easily the best part of his year.

Among the other contenders for Sports Personality of the Year was Adrian Moorhouse, who had emulated Duncan Goodhew eight years earlier by winning gold for Britain in the 100m breaststroke. And there was the small matter of a second gold medal for Steve Redgrave, alongside Andy Holmes in the coxless pairs. However, Redgrave hadn't done enough to figure in the voting yet. Our other Olympic champions were Mike McIntyre and Bryn Vaille, who maintained Britain's strong tradition in Olympic sailing when they won the star class. The Paralympics had been a great success in Seoul and I interviewed the remarkable Tony Jarvis, who gave a bowls demonstration using only his feet, live in the studio.

This was also the year of the Laurie Sanchez goal and the Dave Beasant penalty save that saw Wimbledon beat Liverpool in the FA Cup final. Liverpool had the consolation of a ninth league title in 13 years, but there were no European trophies for British football to celebrate as English clubs were still banned following Heysel, and Holland had won that year's European Championships.

It was a bad year, too, to be appointed an England captain. The cricket team went through four as they lost heavily yet again to the West Indies, while their rugby union counterparts

Below Sandy Lyle's golfing career probably peaked in 1988, when he won three tournaments on the US Tour, including the Masters
Bottom Ayrton Senna, the Brazilian who won three Formula One World Championships, started off racing go-karts at the age of four
Opposite Eddie Edwards achieved lasting distinction when the International Olympic Committee passed what's known as the 'Eddie the Eagle' rule. This states that to qualify for the games, would-be participants must finish in the top half of an international competition

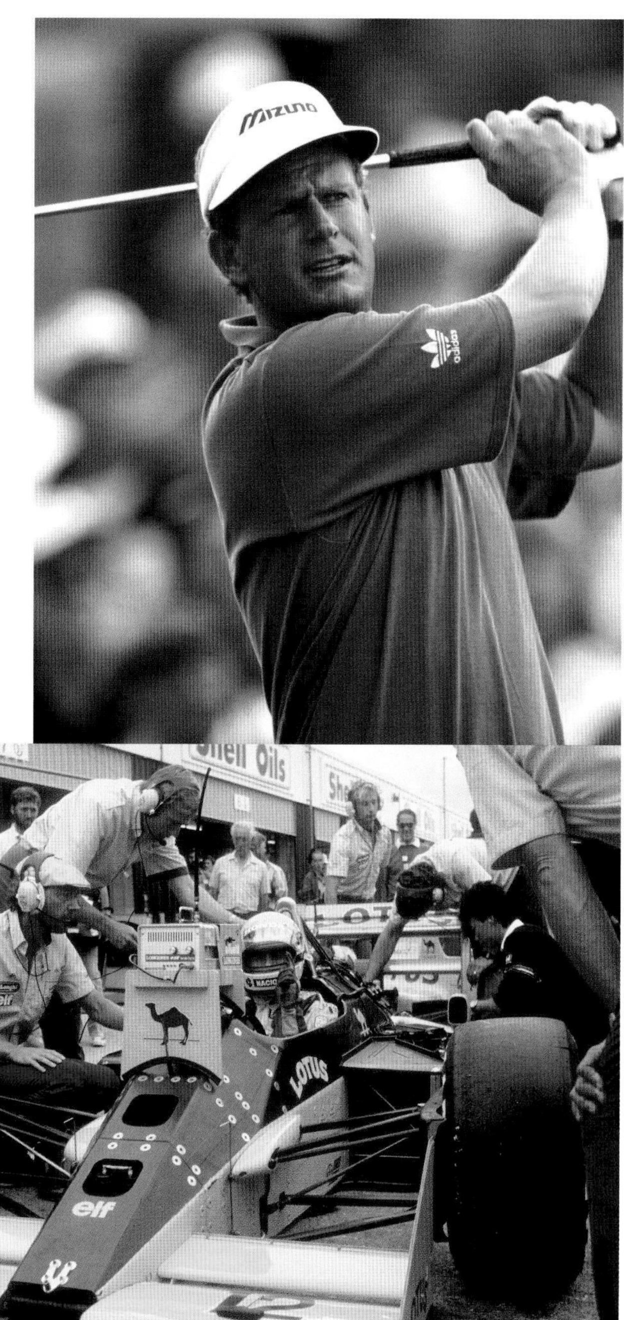

Overseas winner

As tennis returned to the Olympics after a 64-year break, there was a gold medal for 19-year-old **Steffi Graf**. That rounded off an amazing Grand Slam year for Graf, as she joined Margaret Court and Martina Navratilova as winners of all four major titles in one season. To add further glory, Fred Perry gave her the Overseas award.

Team winner

With their performance at the Olympics, the **British hockey team** had caught the public's imagination once again. The core of the squad that had taken bronze in Los Angeles was still together, led by Richard Dodds, and with stars like Sean Kerly (above right) and Imran Sherwani they beat Germany to win Britain's first ever hockey gold.

Barry Davies's commentary line, 'Where were the Germans? And frankly who cares?' once again generated applause from the studio audience, as did Seb Coe's presentation of the Team award.

Opposite Sean Kerly (left) completes his hat-trick and scores the winning goal in the semi-final against Australia at the Seoul Olympics

were led by five different men. The final one was Will Carling and he inspired them to victory over Australia at Twickenham.

British boxing had some success stories, though, with Lloyd Honeyghan beating Jorge Vacca to regain his welterweight title and Duke McKenzie becoming the IBF flyweight champion. Des called out Frank Bruno for their annual chat, but Frank had been frustrated by a difficult year that consisted only of training. He was also disappointed that not even his panto plans had worked out but, as ever, he hoped to fight Tyson soon.

We then gave into temptation and spoke to Eddie Edwards, live from Canada, where he had just come 73rd out of 73 in a ski-jump competition. His parents were in the audience as he gave an interview that was part chaos and part entertainment.

Golf had continued to produce great stories, with Sandy Lyle's seven iron from the bunker at the closing hole giving him the birdie he needed to become the first British winner at Augusta. A final round 65 gave Seve Ballesteros his third Open championship, at Royal Lytham and St Annes, and Curtis Strange needed a play-off at Brookline to beat Nick Faldo to the US Open title.

Sandy Lyle was acknowledged in the voting and took third place behind Adrian Moorhouse, but the strength of the snooker audience exerted the greatest influence. Steve Davis had figured in seven of the last eight snooker World Championship finals and in 1988 he had beaten Terry Griffiths to win his fifth title. Sir Arthur Gold made the announcement, but with Davis competing abroad Griffiths journeyed to Milan to make the presentation to snooker's first ever Sports Personality of the Year.

▶▶ Fortunately, 46 of the 49 winners winners have been in the studio to collect their awards. Apart from **Steve Davis**, **Jim Laker** was touring South Africa in 1956 and **Ian Botham** was in India in 1981.

▶▶ The unlikeliest competitors at the Winter Olympics were the **Jamaican bobsleigh team**. They survived a bad crash but later had their story told by Hollywood in the movie *Cool Runnings*.

Sporting roundup

Cricket Graeme Hick hit an undefeated 405 for Worcestershire against Somerset in the County Championship.

Football Celtic completed the double for the first time in 11 seasons.

Horse racing The Derby was won by Kahyasi and Rhyme 'N' Reason was first past the post at Aintree. This was also the year in which the Princess Royal unveiled a statue of Red Rum at the course, to commemorate the horse's three Grand National successes.

Motor sport Ayrton Senna won his first Formula One World Championship in a season when McLaren won 15 of the 16 races.

Rugby league Martin Offiah's 44 tries helped Widnes to the League and Premiership Double and Wigan beat Halifax to lift the Challenge Cup.

Tennis Mats Wilander won three of the Grand Slam titles. At Wimbledon, Stefan Edberg beat Boris Becker in the men's singles final.

1989

Date 17 December 1989 • Location Queen Elizabeth II Conference Centre, London • Presenters Desmond Lynam with Steve Rider • Editor John Rowlinson • Producer Martin Hopkins

1st **Nick Faldo** golfer
2nd **Frank Bruno** boxer
3rd **Steve Davis** snooker player

Overall winner

Nick Faldo was only the second golfer to win the award, following in the footsteps of Dai Rees in 1957. He has now won both the US Masters and the Open three times, as well as having a share in three Team of the Year awards with various Ryder Cup squads.

There were many reasons why the programme moved from its Television Centre base to the more contemporary surroundings of the Queen Elizabeth II Conference Centre in Westminster, and not all of them could be seen on the screen. *Sports Review of the Year* was now more than a big programme. It was also a major opportunity to greet, entertain and thank all the people in sport who had helped the BBC throughout the year. Not only did the conference centre provide a better environment for hospitality, it also offered producer Martin Hopkins and his designers the chance to give an imaginative new look to the programme.

It is the content that sets the tone of the programme and in 1989 it was potentially a sombre show, as the sporting year had been dominated by the tragedy of Hillsborough. The death of 95 Liverpool supporters at the FA Cup semi-final against Nottingham Forest was a disaster that changed English football.

A moving video tribute was played and the Liverpool manager, Kenny Dalglish, joined us in the studio, flanked by members of the Liverpool squad. He spoke of the family feeling that had built up in the city and that had culminated in Liverpool's emotional win in an all Merseyside FA Cup final. Having made the difficult decision to complete the season, the club then took part in an incredibly dramatic climax to the championship race, as Arsenal won the league with a Michael Thomas goal against Liverpool in the last minute of the last match.

There had been plenty of excitement in 1989, however, not least in golf. A wide-ranging report from Harry Carpenter covered Nick Faldo's success in the Masters at Augusta, Ian Woosnam's brave challenge in the US Open, and the first ever three-man, four-hole play-off in the Open Championship, which ended with victory for Mark Calcavecchia at Royal Troon.

Another dramatic Ryder Cup at the Belfry culminated in Christy O'Connor's famous two iron into the final green, the greatest shot of his career, and the putt from Jose Maria Canizares that meant Europe would retain the trophy. But at least the USA, after two successive defeats, managed to make it a tied match at 14 points apiece.

English cricket remained in turmoil after Allan Border had led Australia to a 4-0 win over England in the summer. It was the first time they had regained the Ashes here since 1934 and led to David Gower being sacked as captain for a second time. Graham Gooch took over.

Where once *Sports Review* would celebrate the rare British world title successes in boxing, the proliferation of governing bodies was now beginning to show and many fighters were featured. Dennis Andries, Duke McKenzie, Glenn McCrory and Dave McAuley all ended the year as world champions, although Lloyd Honeyghan had lost his welterwight title to Marlon Starling.

In tennis it became the year of the new generation when Michael Chang and Arantxa Sanchez both won the French Open, aged just 17. Monica Seles, at 15, was another rising star, which left the Wimbledon winners, Steffi Graf and Boris Becker, looking positively ancient at 20 and 21. Sadly, there was still no sign of a future British champion of any age and Henmania was still several years away.

The programme editor, John Rowlinson, decided to introduce some extra entertainment sections. One of these was a special film that saw some of the nation's best-loved commentators swap sports for the evening. We heard Dan Maskell commentate on boxing, Peter O'Sullevan on Formula One, Raymond Brookes-Ward on the 400m

Below Frank Bruno, always popular with the voting public and always a popular guest on the programme
Below right Peter O'Sullevan, the BBC's instantly recognizable voice of racing for several decades

Overseas winner

The big fight of the year had been the long awaited meeting of **Mike Tyson** and Frank Bruno in Las Vegas. Frank had his moments and for a brief few seconds he managed to wobble Tyson when he caught him with an explosive right hand, but the champion recovered and won in the fifth.

The two were reunited on a satellite link-up and Tyson offered Bruno the chance of a return any time in London. He also took the opportunity to tease Frank about his pantomime role in *Aladdin* by asking him to sing. Bruno declined, but when he wondered, 'Where's 'Arry?' he was out in Las Vegas, standing by to present the Overseas award to the undisputed heavyweight champion of the world.

Team winner

Although the influence of Steve Cram was waning, new javelin star Steve Backley had won the World Student Games, European Cup and World Cup, and all in all 1989 was a very good year for the **British men's athletic team**. This was proved with their first victory in the Europa Cup, appropriately in front of a home crowd at Gateshead. They also came third at the World Cup final in Barcelona.

Gordon Pirie, the 1955 Sports Personality of the Year, was called upon to present Linford Christie (above) and the squad with the Team award.

hurdles, Peter Alliss on three-day eventing, Bill McLaren on snooker and Murray Walker on the Grand National. Murray proved that his phrase 'and they're off' could indeed apply across the board.

Like so many editions of *Sports Review*, the 1989 show had its 'stunt'. This time it looked ahead to the World Cup as England, Scotland and the Republic of Ireland had all qualified for Italia 90. A special game of table football tried to put viewers in the mood, with Bob Wilson the commentator and adjudicator. Gary Lineker and Frank Bruno defeated David O'Leary and Christie O'Connor 2-0, before beating the Scottish pair of Stephen Hendry and Kenny Dalglish 1-0, thanks to a dubious handball by Bruno.

The Bishop of Liverpool, former test cricketer David Shepherd, was called upon to present the main award and, as expected, had supportive words for Liverpool FC and all those touched by the Hillsborough tragedy. He went on to announce that Steve Davis had come third, Frank Bruno was second, and Masters champion and Ryder Cup hero Nick Faldo was the 1989 Sports Personality of the Year.

▶▶ When **Steve Davis** collected his award it meant that he had been voted into the top three on a record five occasions. He was first in1988, second in 1981 and 1987, and third in 1984 and 1989.

▶▶ *Sports Review*'s first **telephone poll** was put together to identify the top British sporting moment of the decade. Votes were invited from a shortlist of ten (see right for options); proceeds from the 5p calls went to Children in Need; and Liverpool and Daley Thompson tied for first place, with 24 per cent of the vote each.

Opposite Kenny Dalglish (left) scores the winning goal against Chelsea to clinch the 1986 League Championship for Liverpool, a week before their FA Cup final victory over Everton wrapped up the double. This was viewers' favourite sporting moment of the 1980s

Sporting roundup

Football Rangers won the Premier League and the Skol Cup, but missed out on the treble when they lost to Celtic in the Scottish Cup final.

Horse racing Nashwan was the horse of the year. Ridden by Willie Carson, it won the Derby, the 2000 Guineas and the King George. Desert Orchid won the Gold Cup and Little Polvier was first in the Grand National.

Motor racing McLaren rivals Alain Prost and Ayrton Senna once again fought out the season before Prost clinched his third Formula One title.

Rugby league Wigan beat St Helens in the Challenge Cup final and Martin Offiah's tries helped Great Britain beat New Zealand 2-1.

Rugby union France won the Five Nations. The Lions had a successful tour of Australia and won the Test series 2-1.

Snooker Steve Davis beat John Parrott 18-3 to win his sixth world title.

Swimming Adrian Moorhouse set a new world record in the 100m breaststroke as he won gold at the European Championships.

Top British sporting moment of the 1980s: the options

- 1980 Coe v Ovett in the 1500m Olympic final
- 1981 Botham's Ashes win
- 1981 Aldaniti winning the Grand National
- 1983 Daley Thompson's World Championship gold
- 1984 Torvill and Dean's Olympic gold
- 1985 Europe regaining the Ryder Cup
- 1985 Dennis Taylor's snooker World Championship
- 1985 Barry McGuigan's world title fight
- 1986 Liverpool's Double
- 1988 British men's hockey team's Olympic gold

1990

Date 16 December 1990 • **Location** Queen Elizabeth II Conference Centre, London • **Presenters** Desmond Lynam with Steve Rider • **Editor** John Phillips • **Producer** Martin Hopkins

1st Paul Gascoigne footballer
2nd Stephen Hendry snooker player
3rd Graham Gooch cricketer

In 1990 the show had a new editor, John Phillips, who decided to experiment with the format. For the first time we looked back at the sporting year in monthly film packages, rather than on the traditional sport by sport basis. It was a bold and adventurous move, but it did sometimes make the narrative difficult to follow as many stories continued across several months.

Overall winner

Paul Gascoigne had recently reached number two in the charts with Lindisfarne and their special version of 'Fog on the Tyne'. Later, at the after-show party, he performed a stirring version of the track with the special Geordie Boys backing group of athletes Steve Cram and Brendan Foster.

Although the dominant story was that of Italia 90 and the incredible growth in the popularity of opera, thanks to the timely choice of Pavarotti singing *Nessum Dorma* on the BBC's World Cup programme titles, it had been a year when the individual had come to the fore. Nowhere was that better illustrated than in cricket, where England's captain, Graham Gooch, had the kind of summer that even Don Bradman would have admired.

Having led his team to their first Test win in the West Indies for 16 years, Gooch recovered from a broken finger to dominate the twin series against New Zealand and India and score over 1000 runs in the six Tests. His ascension into the ranks of cricketing immortals came at Lord's, when he hit the Indian attack for 333 and 123, breaking a host of records along the way.

It was another outstanding year for Nick Faldo. He retained the US Masters title after a play-off and then went to St Andrews, where he won his second Open Championship. At the age of 54, Lester Piggott returned to racing after a five-year break and promptly won the Breeders' Cup Mile. Meanwhile, at the other end of sports age scale, Stephen Hendry was only 21 when he lifted his first snooker World Championship trophy, having beaten Jimmy White 18-12. It was the first of five consecutive runner-up spots for the luckless Whirlwind, and the year was also a bad one for the Hurricane. Alex Higgins was banned for ten months for threatening to have fellow Irishman Dennis Taylor shot.

The biggest ever boxing upset saw Buster Douglas knock out Mike Tyson in the tenth round of their world heavyweight title fight. The undisputed 23-year-old champion didn't take his challenger seriously enough, although controversy surrounded claims that a long count allowed Douglas to recover when he should have been knocked out in the eighth. In October Douglas lost his first defence to Evander Holyfield, but reputedly collected around $24m for the experience.

It was an outstanding year for Britain's athletes, too, and it was incredibly unusual that none of them made it into the top three of the voting. Our best-ever performance at the European Championships saw nine gold medals won and Steve Backley, Colin Jackson, Kriss Akabusi and Linford Christie all doubled their success at the Commonwealth Games. Backley also became the first British athlete for 17 years to set a world record on home soil when he threw a borrowed javelin 90.98m at Crystal Palace.

In a year where men had dominated, I interviewed Tracy Edwards, the skipper of *Maiden*, about taking the first all-female crew on the Round the World yacht race. She hoped that their success would make it easier for other women, and it certainly helped pave the way for Ellen MacArthur a decade later.

Another woman still going strong was Martina Navratilova. She beat Zina Garrison to win her ninth and final Wimbledon singles title, and Stefan Edberg beat Boris Becker in their third consecutive Centre Court final in a year that saw eight different Grand Slam winners.

Top Lester Piggott got straight back in the saddle after his short sabbatical and won the Breeders' Cup on Royal Academy
Right Paul Gascoigne weeps – the picture that turned him into an icon. It was the result of a booking against Germany that meant he wouldn't have played in the World Cup final, had England got there

Team winner

In the Grand Slam decider at Murrayfield, Gavin Stanger's try against England secured a surprise 13-7 victory and gave the Five Nations Championship to the **Scotland rugby team**. They were the obvious choice for the Team award and turned up at the conference centre in their kilts to receive the trophy from Bill McLaren.

Overseas winner

The Australian rugby league captain, **Mal Meninga**, won the trophy after leading his team through a triumphant season in Britain, in which they had won the Test series 2-1. He went on to skipper Australia to victory against England in the 1992 World Cup final at Wembley. The award was presented to him in a dressing room by his raucous team-mates.

Domestic football had been dominated by Liverpool's Championship and Manchester United's FA Cup final replay victory over the unfancied Crystal Palace, but in 1990 all eyes were turned on Italy for a wonderfully successful World Cup.

England reached the semi-finals, only to lose on penalties to the eventual winners, West Germany. Stuart Pearce and Chris Waddle became infamous for their misses, but the abiding image of the competition was of Paul Gascoigne, the young midfield genius who had wept after learning that a booking in the match would have caused him to miss the final. England returned as heroes and Graham Taylor was appointed as the departing Bobby Robson's successor.

In a rare departure for this particular programme, Des interviewed Peter Shilton, who had retired from international football. He felt that his best moment was difficult to pick but that the two European Cups he had won with Brian Clough and the World Cup semi-final were amongst the highlights. Paul Gascoigne joined them and Des expressed a prophetic concern that his off-field interests might damage his football, but Gascoigne was confident that he would cope.

Come the end of the show, another English World Cup hero was on hand to dispense the awards. Neither Graham Gooch nor Stephen Hendry was in the studio, but Bobby Charlton was able to present the Sports Personality of the Year trophy to Paul Gascoigne.

▸▸ **Derek Warwick** had survived a very bad accident at the Italian Grand Prix; **Louise Aitken-Walker** had a lucky escape when her rally car rolled down a cliff and into a lake; and **Martin Donnelly** had a terrible crash in practice for the Spanish Grand Prix. All three were presented with special Good Sport of the Year awards.

▸▸ In December, Arsenal captain **Tony Adams** was jailed for nine months for drink-driving. His career could have been over, but he returned as a reformed character, led Arsenal to two doubles and a stack of trophies, and became an inspirational England captain.

Opposite Nigel Benn (left) fights Chris Eubank for the WBO world middleweight title in November 1990. On this occasion Eubank won, but the rivalry between the two boxers was famously intense

Sporting roundup

Boxing Nigel Benn, Dennis Andries and Dave McAuley all ended the year with world titles.

Darts An unknown 100-1 outsider called Phil Taylor won the World Championship.

Football Rangers won their second successive title and Aberdeen lifted both Scottish Cups.

Horse racing Mr Frisk won the Grand National, Pat Eddery rode Quest For Fame to victory in the Derby, and 47-year-old Willie Carson, on Salsabil, won the Oaks and 1000 Guineas.

Motor racing Ayrton Senna won his second World Championship after another fierce duel with Alain Prost, as McLaren dominated once again.

Rugby league Wigan beat Warrington and won their third consecutive Challenge Cup final.

Swimming Adrian Moorhouse equalled the 100m breaststroke world record.

1991

Date 16 December 1991 • **Location** Queen Elizabeth II Conference Centre, London • **Presenters** Desmond Lynam with Steve Rider • **Editor** Brian Barwick • **Producer** Martin Hopkins

1st Liz McColgan athlete
2nd Will Carling rugby union player
3rd Gary Lineker footballer

After the experiment of 1990 it was back to basics in 1991, with a new editor in the person of Brian Barwick, and we heard the opinions of past winners as they made their pick of the current heroes. Stirling Moss chose Nigel Mansell for the zest he had given modern Formula One. Barry McGuigan went for Graham Gooch's 154 not out at Headingly to give England their first home win against the West Indies for 22 years. Seb Coe selected the performance of Carl Lewis at the World Championships in Tokyo, where he took the title in the greatest 100m of all time and then played his part in the greatest ever long jump competition.

Among the others, Steve Davis picked out the goal-scoring feats of Gary Lineker and Henry Cooper went for the Ryder Cup in Kiawah Island, most notably the agonising putt that Bernhard Langer faced on the final green. Fatima Whitbread chose Liz McColgan, Britain's 10,000m gold medallist from Tokyo, and football's World Cup winner Bobby Moore selected the battling World Cup challenge of England's rugby union team.

In contrast to the 1990 programme, the whole shape and ingredients of the year had been laid before the audience in the space of five minutes, and a record 23 guests were to be interviewed. Then it was down

Overall winner

The highpoint of **Liz McColgan**'s career probably came in 1991 as her future performances were hampered by injury. She came fifth in the 10,000m at the 1992 Barcelona Olympics and was awarded the MBE in the same year. Previously, she had been Commonwealth champion in 1986 and Olympic silver medallist in 1988, and she went on to win the London marathon in 1996, before announcing her retirement five years later.

to the detail. Graham Gooch and Ian Botham welcomed England's recovery from a dismal winter in Australia to record two morale-boosting wins over the West Indies, their first at home since 1969, as they drew the series. Brian Johnston paid tribute to John Arlott, 'the voice of cricket', who had died the day before the programme.

Nigel Mansell had hounded Ayrton Senna all the way to the Brazilian's third world title. Senna's car was on display in the studio, but Mansell was live via a satellite link from Florida, promising that things would be different next year, as his first world title was now becoming overdue.

A fantastic year of golf had begun with Nick Faldo going for his third straight win at the Masters, but the four days at the Augusta National finished with him putting the Green Jacket on the shoulders of Ian Woosnam, as British domination of the season's first Major continued. Ian Baker-Finch won the Open, John Daly stormed onto the scene with his win in the USPGA, before Bernhard Langer saw his putt slide by at Kiawah Island and the Ryder Cup was back with the United States.

The thoughts of the world of boxing, and in particular Chris Eubank, were with Michael Watson, who remained on a life support machine after the critical injuries that he suffered in their world title fight in September. Eubank explained to Des that he had decided to carry on boxing as it was his living. Watson's recovery has amazed his doctors and in 2003 he stunned them further by completing the London marathon.

The heavyweight division saw the progress that Lennox Lewis was making as he took the British and European belts from a brave Gary Mason. Mike Tyson

Above right Liz McColgan strikes out in the 10,000m in Tokyo
Right Ian Baker-Finch's best seasons were undoubtedly 1990-91, when he amassed 15 top tens and won the Open at Royal Birkdale, defeating fellow Australian Mike Harwood by two strokes

was charged with rape, Evander Holyfield remained the man to beat and, and after two years of inactivity, Frank Bruno was back in action with a double-quick victory that lasted less than three minutes. In a startling maroon suit he had his annual verbal joust with Des to promote both his world title ambitions and tickets for his panto at the Bristol Hippodrome, where he was playing Robin Hood.

No single club dominated football in a season that saw Manchester United win the Cup Winners' Cup final against Barcelona, Arsenal regain the Championship and Spurs win the FA Cup for a record eighth time. Rangers topped the Scottish league yet again, while Motherwell collected the Scottish FA Cup for the first time since 1952.

The 1991 athletics World Championships took place in Tokyo and included what was undoubtedly the highest quality 100m in history. With the disgraced Ben Johnson relegated to watching from the stand, Carl Lewis set a new world record of 9.86 seconds, with six sprinters all inside 10 seconds. They included Linford Christie, whose time of 9.92 confirmed that he was the fastest ever European.

Left Will Carling took on the England captaincy at the tender age of 22 and led sides that beat all the major rugby-playing nations at least once

Below Gary Lineker missed a penalty against Brazil in 1992, which left him one short of Bobby Charlton's record of 49 goals for his country

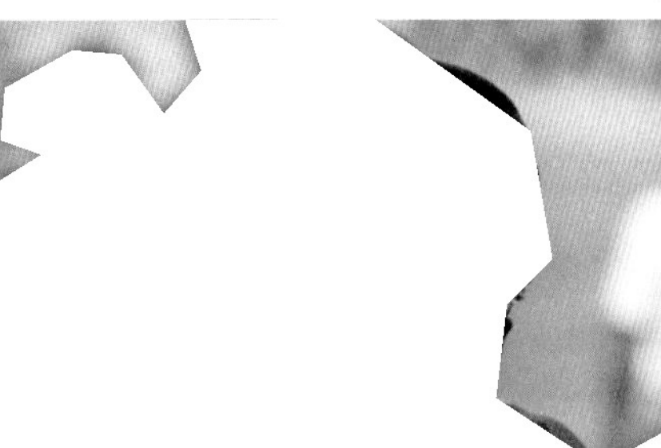

However, amid growing disappointment about the British team's performance it was Liz McColgan, recently returned to sport after the birth of her daughter, who gave Britain a much-needed gold medal with an inspiring run in the 10,000m. Brendan Foster described it as the best performance by any British distance runner he had ever seen or read about. Later in the year she won the New York marathon.

When Des interviewed Liz she admitted to being almost obsessed with running and had completed 15 miles at 7 a.m. that day, before flying to London. Sticking with a custom that went back to the earliest days of the show's history, Des concluded with a request that the audience acknowledge 'our golden girl'.

There were no 'stunts' this year, but a balance beam was wheeled out for a demonstration by the young star of the gymnastics World Championships, Kim Gwang Suk. She was just over four feet tall, weighed less than five stone and her journey from Korea to London had taken almost a week, but her performance stunned the studio and drew admiration from the great Nelli Kim, who was in the audience.

Above The final leg of the men's 4x400m relay final at the athletics World Championships in Tokyo (from left to right): John Regis passes the baton to Kriss Akabusi; Akabusi (left) crosses the line just ahead of the USA's Antonio Pettigrew to take the gold medal; Derek Redmond and Akabusi celebrate their win

Team winner 1

In the last event of the athletics World Championships there had been more British gold. Kriss Akabusi ran down Antonio Pettigrew on the final leg to bring euphoria for the **British 4x400m relay team** of Akabusi, Roger Black, Derek Redmond and John Regis.

In the studio Akabusi delivered his usual modest and entertaining analysis of his performance and Bob Beamon stepped forward to present the quartet with the Team trophy. There were chaotic scenes as they decided to shake hands with every rugby player in sight.

Team winner 2

It was an outstanding year for English rugby, with the Grand Slam success ahead of Britain's staging of the World Cup. Despite being criticized for their style and approach, England nevertheless battled through to the final, where they eventually lost to Australia. Their Australian arch enemy, David Campese, was in the studio to present the Team award to Will Carling's **England rugby union squad**, although several of the players did pointedly ignore him.

Overseas winner

Carl Lewis hadn't been beaten in the long jump for ten years and at the athletics World Championships he set the standard with the longest jump in history, past Bob Beamon's famous mark but wind assisted. Then down the runway came **Mike Powell**, the wind was legal and the jump was immense – 8.95m – and Beamon's astonishing jump at the Mexico Olympics had been surpassed.

A red carpet was rolled across the studio floor to show how the world long jump record had progressed and, sparing no expense on air fares, the programme brought former record-holders Ralph Boston, Igor Ter Ovanesian and Bob Beamon into the studio. Unfortunately the punch line was missing, because flight delays meant that Mike Powell was unable to make the leap across the Atlantic, but he joined the conversation via satellite.

He received the Overseas award from another great long jumper, Lynn Davies, who handed it to Bob Beamon for safe-keeping.

The 1991 award was announced by BBC director general, Michael Checkland. In third place was Gary Lineker, a cup winner that season with Spurs and now nearing the climax of his career; England rugby captain Will Carling was second when the votes were counted; and Scotland's star performer from the athletics World Championships, Liz McColgan, was the viewers' choice for Sports Personality of the Year.

▸▸ **Will Carling** is only the third rugby player to be voted into the top three. **Barry John** and **Willie John McBride** were each third in 1971 and 1974 respectively, but despite the large amount of airtime that the BBC gives to the game, individual personalities don't seen to make much of an impact.

▸▸ Rugby league club **Runcorn Highfield** ended one of sport's most unsuccessful runs when they beat Dewsbury 9-2 in March to register their first win in 76 attempts. Their previous taste of victory had been in October 1988.

Opposite Will Carling (second from right) in action, with Jeremy Guscott (left) in support, against Italy during the rugby World Cup

Sporting roundup

Athletics British athletics lost two of its great stalwarts when the BBC's much loved commentator, Ron Pickering, and the 1955 Sports Personality of the Year, Gordon Pirie, both died.

Boxing There was world title success for Dave MacAuley, Duke McKenzie and Paul Hodkinson.

Cricket Essex won the County Championship to take their haul of silverware to ten trophies in 13 glorious years.

Horse racing Generous was the horse of the year, winning the Derby, King George and Irish Derby. Garrison Savanah won the Gold Cup and came second in the Grand National, behind Seagram.

Rugby league Wigan had dominated the season as Ellery Hanley led them to a record fourth consecutive Challenge Cup victory. They also retained the League Championship. Hanley then shocked the club by signing for rivals, Widnes.

Snooker John Parrott beat Jimmy White to lift the World Championship trophy at the Crucible.

Tennis Boris Becker reached his sixth Wimbledon final, but lost in straight sets to his compatriot, Michael Stich, who had begun the fortnight as a 66-1 outsider. Steffi Graf beat Gabriela Sabatini to clinch her third title.

1992

Date 13 December 1992 • **Location** Queen Elizabeth II Conference Centre, London • **Presenters** Desmond Lynam with Steve Rider • **Editor** Brian Barwick • **Producer** Martin Hopkins

1st Nigel Mansell racing driver
2nd Linford Christie athlete
3rd Sally Gunnell athlete

I have no idea what Spain's equivalent programme was like in 1992, but the BBC's *Sports Review of the Year* could hardly have been more Spanish. The Barcelona Olympics had been a triumph on many fronts and, as Montserrat Caballe and Freddie Mercury's theme tune belted out, the Olympic heroes, both British and Spanish, entered the auditorium.

In fairness, the parade of champions was pretty impressive from the British point of view. There was the fastest man in the world, Linford Christie; the fastest man on a bike, Chris Boardman; our hurdling champion Sally Gunnell; two sets of rowing gold medallists; and Paralympians such as Tanni Grey and Chris Holmes.

Linford described the nervous agony he went through ahead of the 100m final and Sally Gunnell talked about the near-perfection of her 400m hurdles. Chris Boardman brought along his revolutionary new bike and explained the advantages that it had given him when he won gold in the 4000m individual pursuit.

In football, the main focus had been on the European Championships and the stunning and unexpected victory by a Danish side that was a late replacement for the war-torn Yugoslavia. Their success allowed John Motson to declare, 'It's dramatic, it's delightful, it's Denmark.' There was disappointment for England and, in particular, Gary Lineker. Graham Taylor's decision to substitute him during England's final match against Sweden had meant the end of his glorious international career.

In the domestic game, Liverpool beat Sunderland in the FA Cup final and Leeds won the last ever First Division title as football's revival began with the launch of the

Overall winner

Nigel Mansell became only the second person to win the Sports Personality of the Year award twice, following in the footsteps of Henry Cooper (1967 and 1970). Mansell retired from Formula One in 1995 with a record of 31 wins from 187 starts.

Premiership. Alan Shearer signed for Blackburn for a record fee of £3 million and Ally McCoist's 39 goals gave Rangers their first double for 14 years.

Rugby union saw England achieve the first back-to-back Grand Slam for 68 years and Bath continued to be dominant in the domestic game. Wigan won their fifth successive rugby league Challenge Cup, but in the studio their star player Martin Offiah talked of how the World Cup-winning Australians had set a standard that no one else could reach.

There had been great sadness at BBC Sport as we had lost two of our colleagues. On the show, tributes were paid to Raymond Brookes-Ward, who had been the voice of show-jumping for many years, and to the broadcasting legend, Dan Maskell, who finally retired in 1992 after covering 41 consecutive Wimbledon Championships.

At Muirfield, Nick Faldo won his third Open Championship and his fifth major. However, this was the toughest of the lot as he squandered a three-shot lead with eight holes to play and then, to win the title, had to make up three shots on the American John Cook in the last four holes. He joined the programme live from America to talk about the intense emotion he had felt at the final hole.

Des linked into the boxing by explaining that there were now 62 boxers claiming world titles. Britain had the likes of Chris Eubank, Nigel Benn, Colin McMillan, Duke McKenzie, Paul Hodkinson and Pat Clinton, all holding different versions, but the richest prize in sport was still the heavyweight crown and that division was in chaos. Lennox Lewis held the WBC title and, with Mike Tyson in prison, Riddick Bowe had taken the other heavyweight belts from Evander Holyfield.

In a vain attempt to clarify the situation, the programme had Riddick Bowe live in the studio, Lennox Lewis on a satellite link from Jamaica and Frank Bruno

Below Sally Gunnell strides home to take the top Olympic spot in the 400m hurdles. She is the only woman to have held European, World, Commonwealth and Olympic titles simultaneously
Below left Linford Christie, at the age of 32, ran a time of 9.96 – his only sub-10 seconds run that year – to win the 100m Olympic gold

ducking and diving on the fringes. No progress was made, but Bowe confessed that the Holyfield fight had been tougher than he had expected, although he said that the best thing about being world champion was getting to meet Des. For once Lynam looked slightly flustered, but he quickly went on to suggest that Bowe was ducking Lennox Lewis. Bowe refuted the charge. Inevitably, Bruno was then brought on. He said that he planned to beat Lewis and then Bowe, as he was convinced that 1993 was going to be his year. He didn't and it wasn't.

Above Riddick Bowe had a killer punch, but some say he never trained as hard as Lewis or Holyfield and so, despite his indisputable success, never quite fulfilled his potential
Opposite Chris Boardman was so fast he lapped his rival, Germany's Jens Lehmann, in the 4000m pursuit Olympic final. His specially designed bike was built by Lotus and weighed less than 20lbs

It was, however, a World Championship season that had gone right at last for Nigel Mansell. Driving for Williams he won the first five races, had an epic battle with Ayrton Senna at Monaco and then won at Silverstone, prompting a track invasion. Adding to his mass appeal was the fact that he had seemingly been discarded by Williams and was about to be replaced by their test driver, Damon Hill. But this was Nigel's finest hour and he hobbled up to the rostrum on crutches to accept the trophy from Riddick Bowe. Having beaten Sally Gunnell into third in the voting and Linford Christie into second, he had every reason to be pleased with himself.

▶▶ In a decade when the Sports Personality trophy was dominated by sportsmen, **Sally Gunnell** was consistently popular. She never won the main award, but was second in 1993, and third in 1992 and 1994.

▶▶ At 56, **Lester Piggott** rode his 30th British Classic winner to set a record that is unlikely ever to be beaten. It came at Newmarket when he won the 2000 Guineas on Rodrigo de Triano.

Overseas winner

The Overseas award went to another Centre Court star and in 1992 few had shone brighter than the charismatic **Andre Agassi**. In the year that Jimmy Connors bowed out of Wimbledon, Agassi's flowing blond hair and all-white outfits caught the eye and won in a pulsating five-set final over Goran Ivanisevic. John Barrett delivered the trophy to Agassi in Munich.

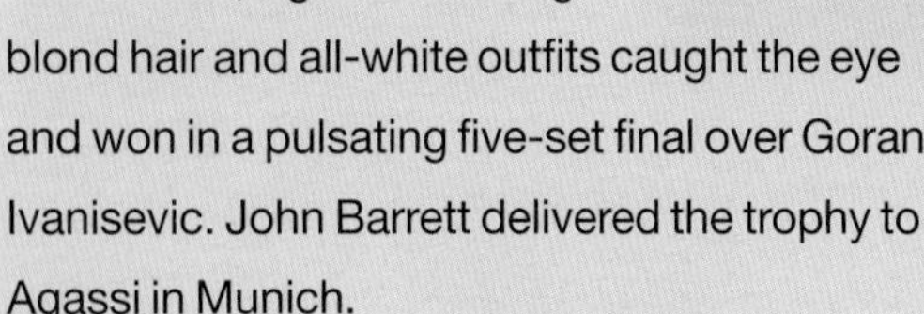

Team winner

Being an Olympic year there was, of course, the **British rowing team** – not just Steve Redgrave, now in partnership with Matthew Pinsent and winning gold medals number three and one respectively, but also the Searle brothers. Greg and Johnny, together with their tearful cox, Gary Herbert, had won gold in the coxed pairs. To the rowers fell the responsibility of performing the studio stunt, a four-way indoor rowing contest, which Steve Redgrave won. Their reward was the prestigious Team award, presented by the Spanish Olympians.

Sporting roundup

Cricket England's cricketers had won in New Zealand but lost 2-1 to Pakistan in the summer. In the World Cup in Australia, England lost in the final yet again, this time to Pakistan.

Horse racing Martin Pipe and Peter Scudamore dominated the National Hunt season, while the election year Grand National was won by Carl Llewelyn on Party Politics. Dr Devious was first home in the Derby.

Snooker Jimmy White was leading the final 14-8 and looked certain to claim the World Championship at last. He then lost ten frames in a row as Stephen Hendry picked up his second title.

Tennis Steffi Graf beat Monica Seles in a rain-affected match to win her fourth Wimbledon title.

1993

Date 12 December 1993 • **Location** Queen Elizabeth II Conference Centre, London • **Presenters** Desmond Lynam with Steve Rider • **Editor** Brian Barwick • **Producer** Martin Hopkins

1st Linford Christie athlete
2nd Sally Gunnell athlete
3rd Nigel Mansell racing driver

British athletics had another chance to impress in 1993 with the World Championships taking place in Stuttgart. That was the main set piece of the year, but *Sports Review* still had a lot of ground to cover and emphasized this with a prolonged opening that looked back at some of the great images of the past year. This ended with Neil Thomas, Britain's gymnastics world silver medallist, tumbling acrobatically into his seat in the auditorium.

From that point on it was headlong stuff, starting with a celebration of England's victory over the All Blacks at Twickenham just two weeks earlier. It was at the end of a rugby year that was memorable for a French Five Nations win and a 2-1 defeat for the Lions in New Zealand.

The boxing year was as complicated as ever, but Des attempted to clarify things by announcing that Britain, incredibly, could boast two claimants to the world heavyweight title, and they both made a live contribution to the programme. Michael Bentt, who had taken the WBO belt from Tommy Morrison, was in the studio and Lennox Lewis, who had successfully defended the WBC title against both Tony Tucker and Frank Bruno, was on a satellite link from Las Vegas. He announced that Evander Holyfield's WBA and IBF crowns were his next target. Holyfield had beaten Riddick Bowe on points in a bout that was interrupted by a crash-landing parachutist. Frank Bruno joined Des in the studio, resisted any thoughts of retirement and offered to fight just about everybody.

Overall winner

Linford Christie had been coming to the *Review of the Year* for many years and was a hugely popular winner among the sportsmen and women in the audience. He retained his European and Commonwealth 100m titles in 1994 and had the chance to repeat the feat in the 1996 Olympic Games, but was disqualified in the final for two false starts. Apart from one brief comeback, he retired from competition in 1997 after a glittering career and a vast collection of medals.

It was the 40th anniversary of the historic 6-3 victory by Hungary over England at Wembley, and to show the growing international ambitions of the programme, Ferenc Puskas was flown over to join Billy Wright in the studio. In the 1993 football season, Manchester United were the new Premiership champions, having won their first title since 1968, and Graham Taylor resigned as manager when England failed to make it through to the 1994 World Cup finals in the USA. However, under Jack Charlton the Republic of Ireland did get there.

The show also remembered one of its greatest heroes, Bobby Moore, who had died of cancer, aged just 51. Moore had collected the Team award in 1965 and 1966, as well the individual Sports Personality of the Year trophy in 1966, having led England to World Cup glory.

There were two extraordinary stories in 1993. One nearly fatal, the other plainly farcical. Tennis player Monica Seles, having won the Australian Open, was stabbed at a tournament in Hamburg by a deranged fan of Steffi Graf. It was a terrifying incident that seriously affected her career and took Seles many months to recover from.

The other story was less solemn and Des appeared in the Grand National starter's outfit of black bowler, brown raincoat and red flag. He mounted the Aintree rostrum, which had been reconstructed in the studio, and reminded the audience that at the Grand National there was the 'teeniest, weeniest bit of a cock-up'. Captain Keith Brown had to delay the start because of saboteurs and then there were two false starts when the tape got wrapped around the jockeys. Many failed to hear the second recall and ignored flag wavers, thinking that they were protesters. Esha Ness won 'the National that never was'.

It had been a troubled year once again for English cricket, with a bad series defeat on the winter tour to India. Shane Warne's devastating first ball in the Ashes series bowled Mike Gatting in outrageous fashion and gave an indication of how Australia were going to dominate the summer as they claimed a 4-1 victory.

Below Monica Seles, before the attack that halted her career
Bottom Alex Ferguson, Manchester United manager, with the first Premiership trophy – and it wouldn't be for the last time, either

Ian Botham, David Gower and Viv Richards had all announced their retirements during the year and were in the studio. Australia's captain, Allan Border, joined the show via a satellite link to add his helpful comments on where England were going wrong.

The flexibility of the conference centre location enabled the show to bring the late Graham Hill's 1962 BRM into the foyer, alongside his son Damon's Williams car. Damon offered a few reflections on how Grand Prix motor racing had developed and then went back into the auditorium to beat Sally Gunnell, David Gower and Nigel Mansell in a giant arcade racing game. It was a rare defeat for Nigel, who had proudly won that year's Indycar Championship, and the audience had earlier heard team boss Paul Newman paying tribute to Mansell's achievement. Tributes were also paid to James Hunt, the 1976 Formula One champion and BBC commentator, who had died aged 45.

It had been another great season for Sally Gunnell and British athletics, with the Stuttgart World Championships the highlight. Sally had won the 400m hurdles and told how she celebrated with a Coke and chocolate. Colin Jackson set a new world record in winning the 110m hurdles and Linford Christie was outstanding in beating Carl Lewis to the 100m gold in a time of 9.87.

At the end of the show, Bob Scott, who was trying to bring the Olympic Games to Manchester, made the awards to Nigel Mansell in third, Sally Gunnell in second and, perhaps a year overdue, the famous silver camera went to world and Olympic champion, Linford Christie.

Overseas winner

Greg Norman had seriously considered retirement 18 months earlier and said as much in his satellite link-up from Florida. But then came his momentous victory in the Open Championship at Royal St George's, a performance that gained him the Overseas award for the second time. He received the trophy from his Florida neighbour, Chris Evert Mills.

Team winner

Much discussion was prompted by the choice of the **England rugby team** for this award. There had been strong claims from Manchester United and also Arsenal, who had won the FA Cup and League Cup, and Wigan were still continuing their domination of rugby league. However, the memory of that victory over the All Blacks, and of Will Carling being chaired off by an ecstatic crowd, was still fresh and Bill Beaumont made the presentation.

▸▸ Although 16 athletes have been voted Sports Personality of the Year, **Linford Christie** is the only male sprinter to collect the trophy.

▸▸ **Steffi Graf** clinched Wimbledon for the fifth time in six years with an incredible come back against **Jana Novotna**. That led to a famous scene as the Duchess of Kent consoled Novotna as she sobbed on Centre Court. Five years later she finally won the trophy and got a hug from the Duchess.

Opposite The Grand National turns into a comedy of errors as, after the false start, Won't Be Gone Long, ridden by Richard Dunwoody, goes back with the tape still looped around him

Sporting roundup

Boxing Chris Eubank and Nigel Benn drew their world super-middleweight title fight at Old Trafford when the judges couldn't split them after 12 brutal rounds.

Football Walter Smith steered Rangers to the Scottish treble, with Aberdeen the runners-up in all three competitions.

Rugby league Wigan won their sixth successive Challenge Cup when they beat Widnes. Great Britain defeated New Zealand 3-0.

Tennis Pete Sampras beat Jim Courier to lift the men's trophy at Wimbledon for the first time. Former champion Arthur Ashe, who had also won the 1975 Overseas award, died aged 49.

1994

Date 11 December 1994 • **Location** Queen Elizabeth II Conference Centre, London • **Presenters** Desmond Lynam with Steve Rider and Sue Barker • **Editor** Brian Barwick • **Producer** Martin Hopkins

1st Damon Hill racing driver
2nd Sally Gunnell athlete
3rd Colin Jackson athlete

This was the 40th anniversary of *Sports Review of the Year* and that was reason enough for a celebration, which came with a parade of as many previous winners of the title as could be assembled. The gathering, which ranged from Christopher Chataway, Ian Black and Anita Lonsbrough to Linford Christie, Fatima Whitbread and Paul Gascoigne, was a vivid testament to the manner in which the programme had charted British sport since 1954.

Also in celebration, Sue Barker joined Desmond Lynam and I on the presentation team. She had already brought the Winter Olympics in Lillehammer to the largest single audience to watch a sporting event on British television. That audience had peaked at over 26 million as Jayne Torvill and Christopher Dean took to the ice to challenge for the Olympic ice dance title once again, having already regained their European crown. Jayne and Chris were in the studio to talk about the amazing public reaction to their performance in Lillehammer; a response that, unfortunately, wasn't shared by the judges, who only awarded them bronze. We also paid tribute to the 1976 Olympic gold medallist and Sports Personality of the Year, John Curry, who had died earlier in the year.

With three presenters flitting around the set, it was a busy programme and we had 25 interviewees to get through, either in the studio or via satellite. There was plenty to talk about, especially in Formula One. The season ended in an astonishing climax in Adelaide when Michael Schumacher seemingly barged his only championship challenger, Damon Hill, out of the way to claim the title. Damon was in the studio along with David Coulthard, and he also reflected on the tragic events of Imola, when first Roland Ratzenberger and then the great Ayrton Senna were killed on one of the worst weekends that Grand Prix motor racing had ever experienced.

The Jockeys' Championship was won by Frankie Dettori, who was regarded as one of the brightest stars in sport, but the older riders were still competitive and, at the age of 51, Willie Carson won his fourth Derby, on Erhaab. There were two great stories at the Grand

Overall Winner

Damon Hill went a stage better than his father, Graham, who had entertained the show for many years with his double act alongside Jackie Stewart. Graham had only once featured in the voting, coming second in 1968. When he received the award Damon paid a special tribute to the memory of his own late team-mate, Ayrton Senna.

National. Richard Dunwoody won on Miinnehoma, eight years after his last victory, and Des spoke to Rosemary Henderson, who had come in fifth, the best ever result by a woman jockey, on Fiddler's Pike.

Boxing, as usual, was complicated. Chris Eubank and Nigel Benn had retained their world super-middleweight titles but the heavyweights were in even greater chaos than the previous year. Evander Holyfield, Michael Moorer, Lennox Lewis, Oliver McCall, Michael Bentt and Herbie Hide had all been able to claim that they were world champion at some stage during the previous 12 months. And then George Foreman knocked out Michael Moorer to win the WBA and IBF titles and become the oldest ever champion at the age of 45.

Des interviewed Foreman live from Las Vegas, more than 20 years since he had last been champion. He said he planned to continue and wanted mandatory retirement for boxers at 65. Herbie Hide was in the audience and felt he could beat Foreman, but was first due to meet Riddick Bowe in March. He was sitting next to Frank Bruno but said he didn't want to fight him as he didn't want to hurt him. A loud snort was the reply. Bruno was confident that 1995 would deliver glory for him.

It had been the year of the Commonwealth Games in Canada and the World Cup in Los Angeles, with Brazil beating Italy on penalties to win the competition for the first time since 1970. Jack Charlton's gallant Irish were the closest that we had to a 'home nation' to follow and they provided great entertainment and excitement.

Elsewhere, Manchester United were happy to have claimed the double and manager Alex Ferguson was in the studio to promise more success ahead. They were only the fourth club to achieve the feat in the twentieth century and it had helped them to get over the loss that year of their talisman, Sir Matt Busby.

Sir Matt had been manager of Manchester United back in 1954, when *Sports Review* was first broadcast, and he would have recognised many of the outfits on show during the musical interlude that was staged in the centre of the studio. A long routine saw dancers split into pairs to represent each sport. One was in the garb of 1954, the

Left Colin Jackson had an exceptionally good year in 1994, winning titles, including both the 60m and 60m hurdles at the European Indoors Championships, and breaking records

Below Damon Hill, driving for Williams, locks his brakes as he chases Michael Schumacher's Benetton car in the Australian Grand Prix

Team winner

Wigan's long domination of rugby league was acknowledged by the presentation of the 1994 Team award. They had beaten Leeds in the Challenge Cup final as part of the Treble and then won the World Club Challenge in Australia. Wembley witnessed one of the greatest ties of all time when the mazy, tantalising run by Martin Offiah helped them secure the Challenge Cup.

Overseas winner

In cricket, the story of the year was **Brian Lara**, the West Indies star batsman. In the winter he had broken Sir Gary Sobers's Test match run-scoring record with his innings of 375 against England in Antigua, before completely rewriting the record books with his undefeated 501 for Warwickshire against Durham at Edgbaston. That broke the world record held by Hanif Mohammad and was one of six 100s that he made in his first seven championship innings for Warwickshire. One of his rewards was the Overseas trophy, which Sir Gary Sobers presented to Lara in India.

other in the kit of 1994, as they writhed in front of an appreciative but slightly startled audience of sporting stars.

Continuing the theme of the first show, Des interviewed three of the 'grand old men' of British athletics. Christopher Chataway, Chris Brasher and Sir Roger Bannister reminisced about the four-minute mile, with Brasher recalling how the race was arranged over tea in the Sloane Square Lyons Corner House. They were stuck on 61- second laps so Brasher and Bannister drove up to Glencoe in an Aston Martin, did some walking, came back and were running 59-second laps. It all sounded so simple.

British athletics had been more complicated in 1994 and we had to absorb the news of Diane Modahl's positive drugs test on the eve of the Commonwealth Games. It was the start of a long and costly legal battle for both Modahl and the sport, but her name was eventually cleared. The good news had come with the British performances in the European Championships in Helsinki, where there had been golds for Linford Christie, Sally Gunnell, Steve Backley, Colin Jackson, Duane Ladejo and the men's 4x400m relay squad.

This gave Gunnell second and Jackson third place in the voting for BBC Sports Personality of the Year, and the original winner of the award, Chris Chataway, was an appropriate person to make the presentations. However, the motor racing lobby had once again rallied around its hero – he wasn't world champion, but Damon Hill was very much the viewers' choice for first place.

▸▸ The arrival of previous winners was announced by **Len Martin**, who had been heard on many of the shows from 1954. Sadly, it was to be Len's final show as he died the following year after 36 years of announcing football scores and racing results on *Grandstand*.

▸▸ **Dermot Reeve**'s captaincy led Warwickshire to unprecedented cricketing success. They won the County Championship, Sunday League and the B&H Cup and were runners-up in the Nat West Trophy final. No domestic cricket team had ever been so dominant.

Opposite Stephen Hendry's 1994 World Championship win was all the more remarkable because he'd slipped at his hotel, fractured his elbow and had to wear his arm in a sling whenever he wasn't playing

Sporting roundup

Cycling Chris Boardman became the first British cyclist since Tommy Simpson to wear the Yellow Jersey in the Tour de France.

Football Arsenal won the European Cup Winners' Cup and Rangers continued their grip in Scotland with a sixth successive title.

Golf Nick Price, from Zimbabwe, won the Open at Turnberry.

Rugby union Wales won the Five Nations outright for the first time in 15 years.

Snooker For the third consecutive year Stephen Hendry defeated Jimmy White in the final of the World Championship. This was the closest of them all, 18-17.

Tennis Pete Sampras retained his Wimbledon title and Conchita Martinez won her first by beating Martina Navratilova.

Sue Barker, presenter,
remembers ...

My first memory of *Sports Review of the Year* is watching at home, debating with my sports-mad family who should win and why!

'Therefore it was such a huge honour to be invited as a 'guest' in the early to mid-1970s. I remember, as a junior, sitting alongside Ann Jones, Wimbledon champion in 1969, and Roger Taylor, then a British hero for playing at Wimbledon in the boycott year. It was great and guaranteed a picture or two of me on TV, which was so special back then, although the dress was a big mistake – a floral flop!

'Even though I lived in California, I always made the trip home to be at *Sports Review of the Year*. In 1978 we were presented with the Team award after our victory over the USA in the Wightman Cup at the Albert Hall. Virginia Wade couldn't be there, so I was the spokesperson, which was terrifying. It sounds crazy considering the number of interviews you give throughout your career, and maybe it was the number of household names surrounding you, but there was always something special or different about this evening.

'Everyone was watching the tennis video package while I had a microphone attached and Harry Carpenter moved next to me in the aisle. I had to wait a couple of minutes, but it seemed like two hours. The interview was short and sweet. Well, my answers were short and Harry was sweet – just as well the award had already been decided!

'Then I had to come forward to receive the trophy on behalf of the team from Prince Charles. The outfit was better that year because I kept to one colour, even though it was peach! At least afterward I could relax and enjoy the rest of the show.

'Then, on the 40th anniversary of the programme, I was asked to join Des and Steve on the show. That evening was the most nervous I've ever been as a presenter. Why? The opening music probably had a lot to do with it. When I heard that familiar tune and saw all those famous sportspeople arriving at the studio, I suddenly realized that the BBC had made me partly responsible for one of the biggest television nights of the year.

'When I heard that familiar tune ... I suddenly realized that the BBC had made me partly responsible for one of the biggest television nights of the year'

'It's still a nerve-wracking experience, but one I'm thrilled and proud to be a small part of, and what I love about *Sports Review of the Year* is mixing with my heroes and talking to the people whom I admire so much.

'My favourite moment was meeting the great man himself, Muhammad Ali – that's a photo I treasure – and another favourite was Olga Korbut, who inspired so many young girls to take up sport. Her story was so moving, and that's what makes *Sports Review of the Year* the event it is. When great heroes, role models and personalities from different decades get together under one roof, it's a formula for an evening to remember.'

1995

Date 10 December 1995 • **Location** Queen Elizabeth II Conference Centre, London • **Presenters** Desmond Lynam with Steve Rider and Sue Barker • **Editor** Brian Barwick • **Producer** Martin Hopkins

1st **Jonathan Edwards** athlete
2nd **Frank Bruno** boxer
3rd **Colin McRae** rally driver

Overall Winner

Jonathan Edwards described the award as the 'icing on the cake of an incredible year,' but his career continued to go from strength to strength and went on to win a host of medals, including the 1999 World Championship and gold at the 2000 Olympic Games in Sydney.

1995 was not a World Cup year and had neither an Olympics nor a Commonwealth Games, but BBC Sport threw absolutely everything at the *Sports Review* show and was rewarded with a programme that sometimes hit the target – and sometimes fell short. Take, for example, a rather gimmicky, studio-based attempt on the world standing long jump record. Unfortunately, despite the efforts of Steve Backley, Steve Ojomoh and Denise Lewis, one of sport's great barriers remained intact. Honourable mention must be made, though, of Steve Redgrave, who was just short of Jonathan Edwards's jump of 2.97m, and Martin Offiah, who went some way past it to win the event. This was *Sports Review* at its best – or as some critics would have it, its worst.

In a case of *Sports Review of the Year* meets *Blue Peter*, there was also an update on the standard Formula One wheel change studio stunt. At the start of the show, the Benetton team took delivery of their car in 750 pieces and were given the duration of the programme to put it all together. Regular checks were made on their progress.

But there were also serious stories to tell. Rugby union was dominated by the image of Nelson Mandela in a Springbok shirt and Francois Pienaar who had lifted the World Cup for the hosts South Africa. Jonathan Davies had headed back from rugby league to rugby union, with Cardiff, and was one of those set to benefit as union moved into the professional era. Rob Andrew was in the studio and talked with great optimism about what

Above Frank Bruno (right) lays into Oliver McCall. Bruno had built up a large score card lead and survived a late revival by his opponent
Right Colin McRae (right) with co-driver Derek Ringer. McRae was the youngest driver to win the rally World Championship. His father, Jim, was British champion five times

lay ahead, especially at his new club Newcastle, and he said he would be on a recruiting mission for them at the after-show party.

There was certainly plenty of talent around. Martin Offiah was representing Wigan rugby league club, who had won the championship for the sixth straight year, but he talked with frustration about the failure to overcome Australia in the World Cup finals that Britain had hosted.

The heavyweight boxing scene was as complicated as ever, but after more than a decade of speculative interviews on the programme, it was a great to be able to introduce, 'Frank Bruno, world heavyweight champion'. Frank had at last gained a world crown at his fourth attempt, having beaten Oliver McCall at Wembley to claim the WBC title. But elsewhere Tyson was out of prison, Hide lost his WBO title to Riddick Bowe, Selden was WBA Champion and Botha held the IBF belt. Lewis was left frustrated and Foreman was still fighting, while Holyfield was on the prowl. It needed Frank Bruno in a striking blue suit to try to make sense of it all. While he was looking forward to another meeting with Tyson, Chris Eubank had hung up his gloves – but not his breeches, monocle and silver-topped cane. He struck a pose in the studio and told the unsurprized audience, 'I'm an exhibitionist ... I can't help it.'

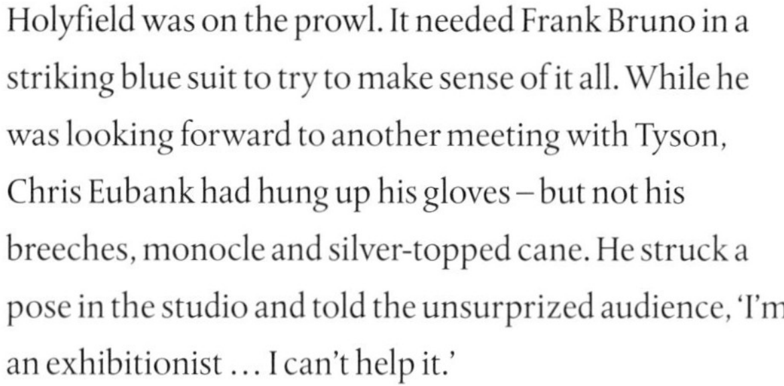

In the year that the great Fred Perry died, we all noticed the name of a young British player at Wimbledon. Unfortunately, Tim Henman made it into the headlines for the wrong reasons, when he hit a ball girl with an angry shot. Steffi Graf won her sixth title after a classic final with Sanchez-Vicario, and Pete Sampras continued his march into the record books by beating Boris Becker to become the first American to win three in a row.

English cricket rallied in the summer, following the by-now-traditional loss of the Ashes. Mike Atherton's team drew with the West Indies in an entertaining series that was notable for Brian Lara's batting and Dominic Cork's bowling. On his debut at Lord's, Cork picked up 7 for 43 in the second innings and in only his third match, at Old Trafford, he took England's first Test hat-trick since 1957. He was immediately cast as the latest in a long line of 'new Bothams'.

Horse racing had a prominent role in the show and Jenny Pitman flirted with Des as she relived her Grand National success with

Above Left Jenny Pitman was the first woman to train a Grand National winner, her success in the race earning her the soubriquet First Lady of Aintree
Left Dominic Cork (right) had been desperate to break into the England team, but since 1995 his career with the national side has been somewhat erratic
Opposite Jonah Lomu (right) fends off Tony Underwood as the All Blacks play England in the rugby union World Cup. The final score was 45-29 to New Zealand

Royal Athlete, one of her six runners. Jenny told him that she looked at horses the way men look at women, saying, 'Phwoar, I could fancy that.' She then admitted, 'I must say that I have had more luck with my horses than my men!' For once Des struggled to reply and hastily moved on.

The most famous National winner of all, Red Rum, had died and his trainer, Ginger McCain, was back in the studio nearly 20 years after his last famous appearance, to reveal that he had turned down an offer of $1 million to sell the horse to America after he retired. Frankie Dettori spoke with Sue, live from Hong Kong, to review a year in which he had won the St Leger, the Oaks, the King George and the Arc to establish himself as the leading flat jockey of his generation.

The Premiership title went to the final day and once again Kenny Dalglish emerged a winner as Blackburn pipped Manchester United. It was a frustrating year for Alex Ferguson as his team were also runners-up in the FA Cup to Everton and lost Eric Cantona to a lengthy ban following his attack on a Crystal Palace fan. The television rights money was filtering through to the clubs, though. Andy Cole had moved to Old Trafford for £7 million and Stan Collymore to Liverpool for £8.5 million as wages and fees began to spiral.

Special award

Lester Piggott finally retired, aged 60, having ridden more than 5000 winners in a 47-year career. In recognition of his unique talents, Peter O'Sullevan presented him with a Special Award. It was the second such award that he had collected, as he had been given a similar special trophy in 1984. He told Sue that the best horse he had ridden was Sir Ivor, his 1968 Derby winner.

The Athletics World Championships in Gothenburg yielded comparatively little from the British point of view, but did underline the triple jump dominance of Jonathan Edwards, who had taken the title and broken the world record as well. Indeed, it was his exploits that prompted that studio attempt on the world standing long jump record.

Overseas winner

The astonishing All Black **Jonah Lomu** had been the dominant figure of the rugby union World Cup tournament and his four tries had bulldozed England to defeat in the semi-finals. Just 20 years old, Lomu stood 6 foot 5 and weighed over 19 stone, but was also incredibly fast with a best 100m time of 10.8 seconds. He was duly presented with the Overseas award by one of the enduring stars of the British game, Jonathan Davies.

Team winner

Once again Wigan were strong candidates for the Team award but were beaten to it by the **European Ryder Cup team**, who had produced one of the great performances in the history of the competition to win the cup on American soil. The victory at Oak Hill had been a personal triumph for captain Bernard Gallagher, who was in the studio with Howard Clark, Ian Woosnam, David Gilford and Sam Torrance, with Seve Ballesteros joining the celebration via satellite from Spain as Henry Cooper presented the award.

While all that was going on the Benetton engineers had completed the assembly of their Formula One car and team boss Flavio Briatore duly praised their efforts. Michael Schumacher had taken the car to his second successive world title in 1995. From the British point of view the big motor sport achievements had been Carl Fogarty successfully defending his world superbike title and Colin McRae becoming Britain's first ever rally world champion.

The motor sport lobby duly mobilized themselves to give McRae third place in the voting for Sports Personality of the Year, and Frank Bruno took second from a shortlist that also included Rob Andrew, Mike Atherton and Stephen Hendry. It was, however, the clean cut Jonathan Edwards, world champion and world record holder, who was posing with the famous trophy at the end of the show.

And when the programme had concluded and the press photographers had all the shots of Edwards they wanted, they drifted off one by one to surround Chris Eubank. He had remained motionless in his seat, his hands clasped around his cane, staring through his monocle into the middle distance. It was a strange sight and a strange evening.

▶▶ **Jonah Lomu** is the only rugby union player to win the Overseas award. He is also the only New Zealander to collect it.

▶▶ **Will Carling** had led England to their third Grand Slam in five years, but their World Cup preparations had been disrupted when he was sacked and reinstated after calling the sport's administrative body, the Rugby Football Union (RFU), '57 old farts'.

Opposite Miguel Indurain dominated the Tour de France during the 1990s. He was known for his competitiveness and his bravery, and his physique was unusual in that he had a resting heartbeat of just 29 beats per minute and lungs which could hold 8l of air

Sporting roundup

Boxing Naseem Hamed stopped Steve Robinson in the eighth round to win the WBO featherweight title.

Cycling Miguel Indurain won his fifth successive Tour de France.

Football Rangers won their seventh title in a row and Celtic won the Scottish FA Cup, their first trophy for six years.

Golf The Open was won by John Daly at St Andrew's.

Horse racing Walter Swinburn on Lammtarra won the Derby. It was his third victory.

Snooker Stephen Hendry made two televised maximums, one in the World Championship semi-final against Jimmy White, before beating Nigel Bond to clinch his fifth title.

1996

Date 15 December 1996 • Location Queen Elizabeth II Conference Centre, London • Presenters Desmond Lynam with Steve Rider and Sue Barker • Editor Dave Gordon • Producer Martin Hopkins

1st **Damon Hill** racing driver
2nd **Steve Redgrave** rower
3rd **Frankie Dettori** jockey

This was the year of the Atlanta Olympics and Euro 96 and the *Sports Review* team produced big names from both. There was Olympic sprint champion Donovan Bailey plus the legendary one-lap king Michael Johnson. Evander Holyfield was brought on and there were some British stars too, who included gold medallist rowers Steve Redgrave and Matthew Pinsent, Formula One champion Damon Hill and jockey Frankie Dettori.

Overall winner

Damon Hill looked overwhelmed as he stepped forward for the second time in three years and said, 'I'm enormously proud to receive this award. To stand here among the cream of this country's sportsmen is a very humbling experience.' Only Henry Cooper and Nigel Mansell have also been double winners of Sports Personality of the Year.

Damon Hill remembers ...

'In my opinion my father should have won the Sports Personality of the Year award when he was racing, but then I came along and won it twice. The main reason is because Grand Prix motor racing had become far more of a television event in the 1980s and 1990s compared to the 1960s and 1970s. People enjoyed seeing my father on the programme, but they got few opportunities to see him race on live television.

'All I can remember was being slightly embarrassed on both occasions I won and to look back now and recall that I got the vote ahead of Sally Gunnell still makes me a bit embarrassed. After all, I hadn't even won the World Championship.

'The second time I won it, at least I was world champion, but to beat a multiple Olympic champion like Steve Redgrave made me feel a bit uncomfortable. However, I was getting the benefit of having won the world title in a fairly exciting battle just a month or so before the end of the programme. So there I was with the trophy again, feeling a bit strange alongside the biggest man in the audience, Steve Redgrave, and the smallest Frankie Dettori.'

Frank Skinner, David Baddiel and the Lightning Seeds sang 'Three Lions' in the studio to recreate the party spirit of Euro 96. It was a little more successful than the penalty shoot-out that came later. Alan Shearer and Terry Venables were the studio spokesmen for an England team that, despite a glorious victory against Holland, had been unable to prevent the relentless progress of the eventual winners, Germany. Gareth Southgate's miss in the penalty shoot-out had meant that England were unable to make that last step into the final.

Away from the international game it had been a thrilling domestic season. Manchester United won their third title in four years, then beat Liverpool in the FA Cup final to be the first team to win the double twice, while north of the border Rangers completed their eighth successive title as part of their double.

There were many great stories in 1996, all reflected in the two-hour show. Nick Faldo was live by satellite from Florida, still hardly able to believe how he had won his third Green Jacket at Augusta by overhauling Greg Norman's six-shot final round lead.

Frankie Dettori received a chocolate horse's head cake, complete with magic candles, from Willie Carson and Walter Swinburn in honour of his 26th birthday, but the main celebration was for Dettori's astonishing perfect seven rides at the Ascot Festival that consolidated his reputation as both a performer and a personality.

British tennis suddenly had new heroes in Tim Henman and Greg Rusedski. Henman climbed into the world's top 30 and became the first British man to reach the last eight at Wimbledon for 23 years. Sue spoke with him about his new-found fame and the burden of expectation that now existed. In the real world, Richard Krajicek beat Mal Washington in the Wimbledon men's final and Steffi Graf won her seventh title.

The Summer Olympics in Atlanta had been a pretty disheartening experience both for followers of British sport and supporters of the Olympic movement. Linford Christie had been disqualified in the final of the 100m, Sally Gunnell pulled up injured in the 400m hurdles and, although we did pick up a handful of medals in athletics, tennis, swimming, cycling, sailing and rowing, it was one of our poorest ever games.

However, Britain did have a very successful Paralympics and Sue interviewed Simon Jackson, Sarah Baily and Steve Peyton in the studio. The irrepressible Jackson was now unbeaten in his last 86 judo bouts.

The other great story was in Formula One when, for a season at least, the dominance of Michael Schumacher was halted and Damon Hill claimed the title many felt should have been his two years earlier.

Lifetime Achievement award

Frank Bruno was the recipient of the Lifetime Achievement award, Mike Tyson having signalled the end of Bruno's long career with a brutal defeat in Las Vegas in March. The presence in the studio of Tyson's conqueror, Evander Holyfield, only served to remind Bruno of what might have been, as Harry Carpenter presented his old friend with a special trophy. In his final interview with Des, Frank revealed that he was glad it was all over as he had achieved his own aim. He wouldn't fight again for £100 million and was now doing panto in Bradford.

Overseas winner 1

Evander Holyfield has had one of the most enduring and unpredictable boxing careers of all time and he has held versions of the world heavyweight title on four separate occasions.

He knocked out Buster Douglas to become champion in 1990; beat Riddick Bowe to reclaim the title in 1993; and defeated Mike Tyson in 1996 to win the WBA belt and become a three-time champion to rank alongside Muhammad Ali. Having lost his titles to Lennox Lewis, he won his fourth crown, the vacant WBA belt, against John Ruiz in 2000. Frank Bruno presented the award to him.

Team winner

When spirits were at their lowest in Atlanta, amid all the transport chaos and the aftermath of the city centre bomb, it was once again **Steve Redgrave and Matthew Pinsent** who delivered the kind of perfomance that only the Olympics can provide.

Steve won his fourth gold medal and Matthew his second with another immaculate performance in the coxless pairs. The strong expectation was that Steve would walk away with the Sports Personality of the Year award. Whether that would happen or not was beyond the programme's control, but the decision was taken that a coxless pair constituted a team and Steve's wife, Ann, the rowing team doctor in Atlanta, gave them the Team award. However, Steve still refused to be drawn on whether he would now retire or continue on to Sydney.

At the end of the programme, Jonathan Edwards announced the top three names. Frankie Dettori was third and Steve Redgrave's fourth Olympic gold medal made him second, although there was less than 5 per cent of the votes between him and the man taking the trophy for the second time. Damon Hill had emulated his father's world title and maybe made up for the Sports Personality of the Year award that his father never won.

▸▸ After 20 years at the helm, in a reign that dated back to Virginia Wade's win in 1977, 1997 was the final show for **producer** Martin Hopkins.

▸▸ **Scotland** beat Estonia in the World Cup when they were the only team to turn up after a dispute over the match's start time. Billy Dodds kicked off and passed the ball to captain John Collins, the referee blew his whistle and the game was abandoned.

Opposite Steve Redgrave and Matthew Pinsent glide towards gold as they win their heat and head for the final of the Olympic coxless pairs in Atlanta

Overseas winner 2

In 1996 **Michael Johnson** was the star of the Atlana Olympic Games, setting a new 200m world record of 19.32 as he became the first man to complete the Olympic 200m/400m double at the same games. The sight of those golden shoes scorching round the Olympic Stadium was the enduring image of Atlanta and Johnson received his award from Frank Bruno.

Sporting roundup

Boxing Henry Akinwande won the WBO version of the heavyweight title, Steve Collins beat Nigel Benn, Naseem Hamed defended his featherweight title four times and Robbie Reid won the WBC super-middleweight crown.

Cricket England lost the winter series in South Africa 1-0 and were knocked out of the World Cup in the quarter-finals by the eventual winners, Sri Lanka. In the summer, England beat India 1-0 and lost to Pakistan.

Football Newcastle paid Blackburn a world record £15 million for Alan Shearer.

Golf Tom Lehman won the Open at Royal Lytham.

Horse racing The Grand National was won by the favourite, Rough Quest, and Shaamit was first home in the Derby.

Rugby league The sport moved to summer and launched Super League. Bradford beat St Helens 40-32 in the Challenge Cup final.

Rugby union Will Carling retired, having led England to the Five Nations trophy for a fourth time.

Hunting Holyfield ...

On the trail of a special guest

Viewers take for granted the studio presence of some of the great names in sport, but nowadays, when the superstars have round-the-year commitments, it is increasingly difficult to persuade the big international stars to attend.

Usually, after the initial agreement, a producer is sent off to help the big star get to the studio on time. In 1996, senior producer Chris Lewis (below, right) was charged with making sure that Evander Holyfield arrived at the Queen Elizabeth II Conference Centre by 8 p.m. on the Sunday at the absolute latest. Lewis takes up the tale.

'Evander had an engagement in Atlantic City on the Saturday night which he couldn't break. The only way to get him across was on the Sunday morning Concorde at 9.30 a.m. from New York. I booked him a limo to take us from Atlantic City at midnight, and on the Saturday evening went to meet Holyfield and his entourage at their hotel.

'At 12 a.m. I was told that Evander wouldn't be available until 1.30 a.m., and come that time I was summoned to the casino reception and taken across to one of the tables and introduced to no less than the billionaire businessman, Donald Trump, who guaranteed that he would make his private jet available at 8.15 a.m. to get Holyfield to JFK in time for Concorde.

'I waited in Holyfield's suite and at about 3.30 a.m. he finally arrived, complaining that he had lost $24,000. He disappeared into his room and slammed the door. At 5.30 a.m., he re-emerged in a tracksuit and bobble hat and

went straight back into the casino to win his money back. Sure enough, he returned with a bulging tracksuit and emptied $24,000 onto his bed.

'After a short nap he was ready to go and we finally found ourselves climbing aboard Donald Trump's ludicrously luxurious jet. The time was 8.45 a.m. and I then realized that we weren't going to make Concorde. I rang ahead to the Concorde lounge and explained that I had the world champion with me and could they hold the flight? This is never possible I was told, but on this one occasion the plane happened to be full of boxing fans and they agreed to a short delay, as long as Holyfield gave each one of them an autograph, which he duly did.

'He finally arrived, complaining that he had lost $24,000. He disappeared into his room'

'The rest should have been plain sailing, except that Holyfield didn't appear for our 7.15 p.m. rendezvous at his London hotel. On ringing his room I was told he had just sent his suit to be pressed and was waiting for it to come back – 45 minutes to on-air and he sent his suit to be pressed!

'I virtually ripped the suit from the hotel laundry but it was still 7.50 p.m. before we left. Ten minutes to on-air and the team were re-writing the top of the show to cope with Holyfield's absence. We screamed up to the front door of the conference centre as the titles were running.

'Security was tight, but I just yelled, "He's Evander Holyfield – let him through," and as he disappeared I could hear Desmond Lynam announcing, "I am delighted that the world champion can be with us here tonight."

'Not half as delighted as I was ...'

David Vine, presenter, remembers ...

'It was occasionally my job to sit in a sound booth when the show was on air and act as a backup presenter, in case there was a catastrophical technical problem.

'Mercifully this never happened, but we had a few problems in 1974 when we kept losing a satellite link to Muhammad Ali in America. When the link was finally up again I had to keep the great man talking to make sure the line didn't disappear before we handed over live to Harry Carpenter.

'Unfortunately, though, Ali was under the impression that I was the interviewer and started using all his best material in our conversation. Eventually I was able to interrupt him and explain that we weren't actually on air yet because we were waiting for the cricket sequence of the programme to finish; a sequence that I must admit was going on a bit.

'Ali then demanded to have the rules of cricket explained to him, which I was happy to do, but he got more and more confused and bored, which was why, when he actually got to go live he was pretending to be fast asleep.

'In those days you didn't get the opportunity to out-talk Muhammad Ali very often, but at least we were able to reassure ourselves that the satellite link was up and running.'

1997

Date 14 December 1997 • Location Queen Elizabeth II Conference Centre, London • Presenters Desmond Lynam with Steve Rider and Sue Barker • Editor Dave Gordon • Producer Malcolm Kemp

1st Greg Rusedski tennis player
2nd Tim Henman tennis player
3rd Steve Redgrave rower

After the highs of 1996 it had been a quieter year for British sport and the lack of outstanding individuals was reflected in the fact that there were some gaps in the audience just before the programme went on air. Every year it is inevitable that some sports stars who have accepted invitations fail to turn up, so there is a small army of BBC Sport producers hovering at the side of the set waiting to dive into the spare seats a couple of minutes before transmission. That's why you might have spotted some faces who are prominent in every show but seem to change sports, sitting in the middle of the rugby players one year, becoming a boxer the next and then a member of the racing community the following season.

Overall winner

This year was probably the peak of **Greg Rusedski's** career to date. Born in Montreal but with an English mother, the former Canadian junior champion had switched nationalities to play for Great Britain in 1995. In 1998 Rusedski beat Pete Sampras in the final of the Paris Open, but he has since been troubled regularly by injury.

Famous faces who did attend included Greg Rusedski and Tim Henman, who held out the tantalising prospect of British success at Wimbledon. Hyperactive Ryder Cup captain Seve Ballesteros was also there and swept into the studio on his Valderrama buggy. Seve had inspired Europe towards the retention of the cup in Spain and he joined me to look back at that triumph with fellow team members Darren Clarke, Lee Westwood and Colin Montgomerie.

The Open at Royal Troon had been won by the previously unknown American, Justin Leonard, and a candidate for Overseas personality would have been Tiger Woods, who had won his first major title at 21. He broke ten Masters scoring records in taking victory at Augusta.

Mike Tyson, by contrast, had lost his chance to win when he bit a chunk out of Evander Holyfield's ear. His career, and to an extent boxing as well, was in crisis. Although Norwich's Herbie Hide had knocked out Tony Tucker to claim the vacant WBO heavyweight crown, it had been Lennox Lewis's year and he won all three of his world title fights. Lennox joined us live from Miami and we also linked up with Naseem Hamed, who was in New York, about to defeat Kevin Kelly for his fifth straight win of the year.

In 1997 the programme also maintained its long association with the fringes of sporting endeavour and Andy Green's land speed record-breaking *Thrust SS6*, capable of 763mph, drew the crowds when it was parked outside the conference centre.

At Wimbledon, Tim Henman, Greg Rusedski and, for once, the weather helped make it a memorable Championships, when rain delays forced play to take place on the normally vacant middle Sunday. This became People's Sunday with the show courts packed and noisy and watched by 13 million TV viewers. Both Tim and Greg would eventually go out in the quarter-finals, allowing Pete Sampras to win the title for the fourth time in five years.

Both had already had their most successful seasons to date, though. Henman had collected his first title, in Sydney, and Rusedski had won in Nottingham and clinched the Swiss Open. He then built on his efforts by becoming the first British player to reach the US Open final in New York for 61 years. He was beaten by Pat Rafter, but did climb to number six in the world rankings.

Lifetime Achievement award

The European Ryder Cup team, who had successfully defended the trophy in Spain, were strong contenders again for the Team award. Instead, **Seve Ballesteros**, who covered every square yard of the course and dispensed constant advice, both wanted and unwanted, was presented with a Lifetime Achievement award by Colin Montgomerie. The man who had energized European golf for the past two decades was a hugely popular recipient. It was his fifth trophy, having been given the Overseas award in 1984 and been part of three winning teams.

Right Tim Henman and Greg Rusedski happen to share a birthday – 6 September – although Tim was born in 1974, a year after Greg
Below Andy Green, a fighter pilot by day, set the land speed record of 714.144mph in the Black Rock Desert, north of Reno, Nevada. He achieved speeds of 700.661mph and 728.008 in two runs, less than an hour apart, on a 13-mile course, and these were averaged

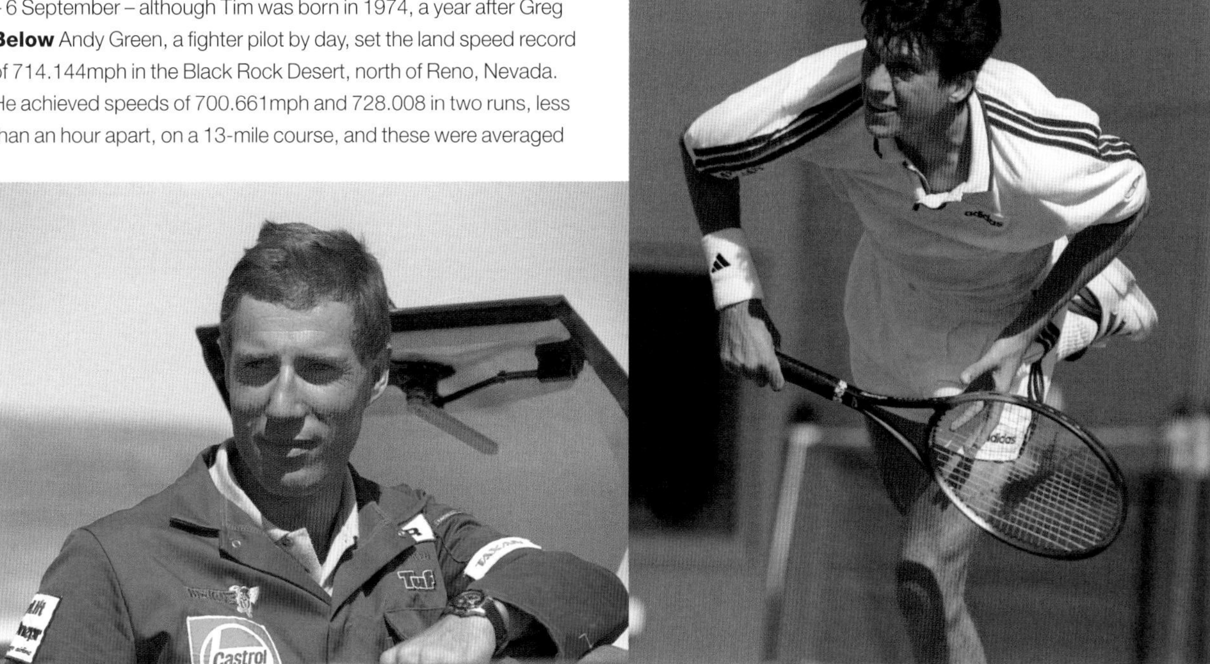

Sue interviewed both Henman and Rusedski who said that their rivalry helped them and was healthy for British tennis. I'm not sure how healthy it was to then see them humiliated in an impromptu table tennis match against 13-year-old phenomenon Casey Parker, as the curse of the *Sports Review* stunt struck for the first time in the show.

Overseas winner

The Wimbledon women's title was won by an eye-catching new star – 16-year-old Swiss prodigy, **Martina Hingis**. She had already won the Australian Open in 1997 and would go on to add the US title as well. When she beat Jana Novotna in the final on Centre Court, she became the youngest winner of the century. Martina was in New York where she received the Overseas award from Pam Shriver.

Team winner

The **British Lions'** 2-1 victory in South Africa was a performance of character and flair. Their character was shown by the defensive commitment of the team in the face of huge Springbok pressure in Durban, but the flair came with a late drop goal from Jerry Guscott that gave the Lions victory and an unbeatable series lead. A great Lion of the past, Willie John McBride, presented the Team award.

It was soon followed by a second when the production team decided it would be great to recreate Jeremy Guscott's famous drop goal for the Lions – in a TV studio, with non-rugby players. It was a brave decision. Roger Black, Nasser Hussain, Denise Lewis, Matthew Pinsent and Lee Westwood all soon proved that they had chosen wisely in not pursuing a career in that particular sport.

The Grand National made the headlines for all the wrong reasons once again, this time when it was delayed by two days because of a bomb warning. The race was eventually won by Lord Gyllene, but in the studio we celebrated a different kind of hero, including Phil Sharpe, the stable lad of Sonny Boy, who stayed behind on his own to look after all the horses.

Steve Redgrave was also taking on a significant personal challenge. He had decided to continue to the Sydney Olympics, now in a four with Matthew Pinsent, Tim Foster and James Cracknell, but at the end of 1997 his diabetes was also first diagnosed. He was very much in the public's mind when votes were cast and Steve once again found himself in the top three. But he was behind second-placed Tim Henman and Greg Rusedski, who was presented with the silver trophy by the BBC's recently retired racing commentator, Peter O'Sullevan.

▶▶ **Julian Wilson** recorded his final horse racing feature for the programme, having been one of its longest serving contributors. His first racing roundup had appeared back in 1967.

▶▶ **Ronnie O'Sullivan** made a maximum break of 147 in just five minutes and 20 seconds during the snooker World Championship.

Opposite Jacques Villeneuve drives past the chequered flag to win the Luxembourg Grand Prix. In 1997, Villeneuve was determined to better his 1996 runner-up Championship position, which he did, despite a hard-fought contest with Michael Schumacher

Sporting roundup

Athletics The World Championships proved disappointing with no British golds but silvers for Denise Lewis, Jonathan Edwards, Steve Backley and Colin Jackson.

Cricket England started the year well by beating New Zealand 2-0, but the inevitable reverse occurred when Australia toured and retained the Ashes 3-2.

Football Manchester United won their fourth title in five years, Chelsea beat Middlesbrough in the FA Cup final, Paul Gascoigne helped Rangers to their ninth title in a row and Kilmarnock won the Scottish FA Cup.

Motor racing Jacques Villeneuve became the first Canadian Formula One champion.

Rugby league St Helens beat Bradford Bulls in the Challenge Cup final for the second year running.

Rugby union England claimed the Triple Crown but lost to France, the Grand Slam winners.

Snooker Steve Davis won the Masters title in his 98th final in front of ten million television viewers. Ken Doherty defeated Stephen Hendry in the World Championship final.

1998

Date 13 December 1998 • **Location** Queen Elizabeth II Conference Centre, London • **Presenters** Desmond Lynam with Steve Rider and Sue Barker • **Editor** Dave Gordon • **Producer** Paul Davies

1st Michael Owen footballer
2nd Denise Lewis athlete
3rd Iwan Thomas athlete

The most significant innovation in 1998 came from editor Dave Gordon, who instigated the first ever telephone poll. The aim of this was to streamline the voting system and give more people the opportunity to influence the choice of Sports Personality of the Year. Calls cost 10p and the choice was between Tony Adams, Tim Henman, Denise Lewis, Michael Owen, Greg Rusedski and Iwan Thomas.

This reflected a year that had seen both the World Cup in France and the Commonwealth Games in Kuala Lumpur. The Winter Olympics had also taken place in Nagano, Japan, and Britain's only medal, a bronze, came on the last day, from the four-man bob team. Paul Attwood, Courtney Rumbolt, Dean Ward and Sean Olsson, plus their machine, were in the studio to talk about the Formula One technology that they hoped would take the sport to further success.

England had gone out of the World Cup in the second round, but only after a match against Argentina that saw David Beckham desolate after his sending off and David Batty in despair following his penalty miss. But a great new star had emerged and Michael Owen had announced his arrival with a spectacular goal against the Argentinians. Des interviewed him and asked what it was like 'to have everything you ever wanted at the age of 19?' France went on to win the World Cup in style, beating Brazil in the final.

Both Tim Henman and Greg Rusedski had made good progress in 1998, with Rusedski reaching number four in the world rankings having won a competition in Paris in which he beat Pete Sampras in the final. Tim still hadn't worked out a way past Pistol Pete, but he did become the first Britain to reach the semi-final at Wimbledon since Roger Taylor in 1973. Unfortunately, he then lost to Sampras, who went on to win the title for the fifth time.

Overall winner

Michael Owen was the second youngest winner of the trophy and only the third footballer, following Bobby Moore in 1966 and Paul Gascoigne in 1990. He was also third in 2001.

Henman had, however, won a couple of competitions and entered the world's top ten, and the nation's tennis fans discovered new hope when he and Rusedski inspired Britain's Davis Cup team to victory over India for a return to the World Group. They were both in the studio to look back on their year with Sue.

Despite losing in the West Indies and struggling in Australia, it had been a memorable summer for England as Alec Stewart led them to victory against South Africa. It was their first major series win in 12 years, but Sri Lanka won the one-off Test when Muttiah Muralitharan took 16 wickets at the Oval, the fifth best bowling figures of all time.

Comedian Kevin Connelly made several very entertaining appearances during the show, beginning with his cricket impressions. As someone who thankfully escaped ridicule, it was fascinating to watch his victims at such close quarters, as they squirmed under fixed smiles.

The 16th Commonwealth Games had been held in Kuala Lumpur amidst chaotic facilities, riots and civil disorder, but 70 nations took part and, for the first time, team sports were allowed. The All Blacks had won the rugby sevens and South Africa collected the cricket gold. Our sportsmen and women had won almost 170 medals and many took a bow in the studio.

British athletes also had an excellent European Championships and brought back nine gold medals. Iwan Thomas and Denise Lewis reflected on their successes and those of their team-mates, including Colin Jackson and Steve Backley, who had each won their third titles.

In motor sport it had been a good year for the Finnish competitors. Mika Hakkinen won the Formula One title and Tommi Makinen the world rallying championship, but Britain had some outstanding success stories as well. Carl Fogarty followed in the footsteps of many other biking legends when he clinched his third superbikes championship. Webster and James retained the sidecar crown, Alan McNish won Le Mans and Nigel Mansell went for a comeback in touring cars.

With so many governing bodies, a whole host of British boxers could claim to be world champions in 1998. The one

Below Denise Lewis, heptathlete, in action in the 100m hurdles
Bottom Alec Stewart (centre) takes a boundary on the way to his 150 in the third Test against South Africa, at Old Trafford

man who rose above the confusion was Lennox Lewis, who had won both his fights and was now preparing to face Evander Holyfield in March. On the inevitable satellite link, Lewis thought he had a chance to become the best heavyweight on the planet and planned to, 'Go into the ring with one belt and come out with three.'

Des's final show also saw him placed in his most uncomfortable situation, as he was required to interview the winning connections of Earth Summit, in a Grand National race simulator out in the car park. Sue had it easier when she spoke to the irrepressible jockeys Frankie Dettori and Olivier Peslier, who were in Hong Kong.

In line with every edition of *Sports Review*, there was a film that rounded up many of the other British sporting achievements of the year. When Des announced that this had been voiced by Helen Rollason, there was instant applause. Helen was fighting her own battle against illness and sadly this proved to be her last appearance on the show.

When the telephone lines closed, Iwan Thomas and Denise Lewis took the third and second spots respectively, but David Hemery, the 15th winner, stepped up to present the trophy to Michael Owen, the 45th Sports Personality of the Year.

Opposite Simon Haughton (centre) of Wigan Warriors is tackled by Sheffield Eagles' Dale Laughton, Keith Senior and Nick Pinkney in the Challenge Cup final. Sheffield Eagles won 17-8

▶▶ This was the 16th and final show presented by **Des Lynam**. He made his debut in 1982, but in 1999 moved to ITV to present its football coverage.

▶▶ At Royal Birkdale, **Justin Rose**, a 17-year-old amateur golfer from Hampshire, emerged as the new British hope. He came fourth in the Open and his final shot at the 18th hole, when he chipped in from 45 yards, was possibly the shot of the year.

Overseas winner

On film, Ernie Els gave the trophy to **Mark O'Meara**, following an astonishing year in which, at the age of 41, O'Meara had won both the US Masters and the Open Championship at Royal Birkdale. He is the oldest player ever to win two Majors in the same year and he rounded off the season by beating Tiger Woods to clinch the World Matchplay Championship. When I interviewed him, O'Meara was still celebrating his dream year. 'The ball sitting on the grass doesn't know how old you are,' he remarked.

Team winner

Football had two strong contenders this year. Gianluca Vialli had led Chelsea to the League Cup, the European Cup Winners' Cup and the Super Cup, but the award went to double winners **Arsenal**.

Arsène Wenger's team had beaten Newcastle 2-0 in the FA Cup final and Des interviewed several of the Arsenal players, who had brought the trophies with them. Tony Adams (above right) felt that their success was due to the strength of the squad and the all-round team effort. Glenn Hoddle presented Adams with the Team award.

Sporting roundup

Football After nine years, Celtic broke Rangers' grip on the Scottish Championship. Rangers won the League Cup and Hearts the Scottish FA Cup.

Rugby league The Challenge Cup saw one of its biggest ever upsets when Sheffield Eagles beat Wigan.

Rugby union On the way to their second Grand Slam in a row, France beat Wales 51-0. It was the biggest ever Five Nations win.

Snooker John Higgins was the new world champion, beating Ken Doherty in the final.

Tennis To great acclaim from the Centre Court crowd, Jana Novotna finally won Wimbledon when she defeated Natalie Tauziat in straight sets.

1999

Date 12 December 1999 • **Location** Television Centre, London • **Presenters** Steve Rider with Sue Barker, Gary Lineker, John Inverdale and Clare Balding • **Editor** Philip Bernie • **Producer** Paul Davies

1st **Lennox Lewis** boxer
2nd **David Beckham** footballer
3rd **Colin Jackson** athlete

Trying to fit 12 months of sporting highlights into a single programme is always challenging, but in 1999 the new editor, Philip Bernie, had an almost impossible task. As the world began to celebrate the start of the year 2000 and the dawn of a new millennium, the programme also set out to review an entire century of sporting achievement.

Bernie also had to cope with Des Lynam's surprise move from BBC to ITV Sport five months earlier. This robbed the programme of a man who had set its style and tone through two decades. However, the production team's response was to beef up the presentation line-up with Clare Balding and John Inverdale joining myself, Gary and Sue. And reinforcements were certainly essential with the range of action we were required to cover as we returned to studio one at Television Centre for the first time since 1988. The name of the show also changed to *Sports Personality of the Year*, rather than *Sports Review of the Year*, to reflect a greater emphasis on the awards themselves.

For a start, the number of awards had been doubled with new trophies for Young Sports Person of the Year and Coach of the Year, plus the special award that would

Overall winner

Although he had been either world champion or a contender for most of the previous six years and undoubtedly commanded great respect, it had taken a long time for **Lennox Lewis** to gain the affection of the British public. However, 1999 changed that and his award demonstrated that he had finally been accepted.

be made at the end of the evening to the viewers' choice of the Sports Personality of the Century. And with the death of Helen Rollason five months earlier, an annual award in her memory would be made for courage and fortitude in sport. To select the winners of these we had a special judging panel that consisted of Trevor Brooking, Shar ron Davies, Denise Lewis, Richard Littlejohn, Hugh McIlvanney and Cliff Morgan.

In what was easily the biggest gathering of sportsmen and women in the history of the show, we attempted to capture the flavour and excitement of the previous hundred years of sport. Memories and montages formed the heart of the programme and many great sporting names and previous winners joined us in the studio. The poet laureate, Andrew Motion, had composed a new work about the Olympics, and Olga Korbut looked back to the 1972 games, while Steve Redgrave spoke about the tantalising prospect of a fifth gold in Sydney.

Peter Alliss selected his key golfing personalities and moments in a year that had seen an extraordinary Open, when Paul Lawrie won after Jean Van de Velde had waded into the water at the 18th in a desperate attempt to salvage his lead. Two former award winners, Seve Ballesteros and Nick Faldo, were present to pick their own high points.

The 1988 Sports Personality of the Year, Steve Davis, was back to look at the great names of snooker, while from the world of horse racing, Richard Dunwoody and Frankie Dettori selected Lester Piggott and John Francome

Below Colin Jackson lunges for the line to win gold in the 110m hurdles at the World Championships in Seville

Coach of the Year

Sir Alex Ferguson was perhaps the inevitable choice in the year that he had been knighted. Seve Ballesteros handed him the trophy.

Helen Rollason award

Our much loved colleague, Helen Rollason, had lost her courageous fight against cancer in 1999 and as a tribute to her memory there was to be a new award for outstanding courage and achievement in the face of adversity. **Jenny Pitman** had herself overcome cancer and, in the year of her retirement from training racehorses, she was presented with the award by Helen's daughter, Nicky.

as the best jockeys of the century. Motor racing legends Jackie Stewart and Stirling Moss remembered Juan Fangio and Ayrton Senna as the greatest drivers from their sport, and after John McEnroe had talked us through the tennis greats, Illie Nastase and Virginia Wade told Sue about their own Wimbledon memories.

Andre Agassi was unlucky not to receive the Overseas award. He had made a comeback from 2-0 and 2-1 down to win the French and US Opens and end the year as world number one, though he was unable to defeat Pete Sampras in the Wimbledon final. However, Lindsay Davenport did manage to overcome Steffi Graf to lift the women's trophy.

Two generations of English footballing heroes came together to talk about the international game when Gary spoke to Jack Charlton about 1966 and Michael Owen looked forward to Euro 2000. In rugby, it was two great tries that were the main focus: Gareth Edwards's classic try for the Barbarians against the All Blacks in 1973 and Martin Offiah's unforgettable sprint down the full length of the Wembley pitch in the 1994 Challenge Cup final.

Below Jesse Owens, the legendary American athlete, was one of the names in contention for Sports Personality of the Century. This picture shows him winning the long jump, one of four gold medals he won at the 1936 Olympics in Berlin

Athletics has usually featured strongly in the end-of-year voting and Sue chatted with Seb Coe and Sally Gunnell about the sport's impact on the public. Seb thought the attraction is that at a very fundamental level it pits man against man and woman against woman. Colin Jackson had once again beaten all comers at the athletics World Championship to win gold in the 110m hurdles.

Boxing had always played a central role in the show and the legendary Sugar Ray Leonard looked back at the great fighters he had admired. But, as had happened so many times down the years, the programme was dominated by the heavyweights. Evander Holyfield and Lennox Lewis walked down the ramp to join John Inverdale and review their two contests from that year. The first ended in a contentious draw, but Lewis had won the second to become the undisputed champion. In a very honest interview, Holyfield confided that he was happy that he had done his best but felt that Lewis was genuinely the best in the world.

Rumours of a very special guest had been rife and John then made the introduction that the entire audience had been waiting for, announcing, 'Would you welcome the undisputed, undisputed heavyweight champion of all time – Muhammad Ali.' Ali walked down the ramp to a massive ovation. There were extraordinary looks and smiles on the faces of the audience. For once it was all genuine and a mixture of awe, love and admiration.

Newcomer of the Year

Canvey Island's 21-year-old decathlete, **Dean Macey**, was presented with this award by Denise Lewis, after he had won a surprise silver medal at the World Championships.

For the first time in the long history of the show, the presentation of the Sports Personality of the Year trophy was not to be the climax of the evening. That was reserved for a unique award – a special gold trophy destined to go to the person who had made the greatest impact on the global audience in the twentieth century.

The poll had been conducted early so that arrangements could be made to bring the winner to the studio. The leading contenders had emerged as **Muhammad Ali**, George Best, Don Bradman, Jack Nicklaus, Jesse Owens and Pele. Ali, it has to be said, was the winner by a considerable margin, and was keen to come, but there was concern over his health, as everyone remembered how frail he had appeared at the Atlanta Olympics opening ceremony – and this was three years on.

Backstage, the presenters and production team were awestruck to be in the presence of the greatest icon in twentieth century sport. Parkinson's disease had taken its toll and it was hard to believe that we would shortly be inviting this apparently vague, shambling figure to accept the title of Sports Personality of the Century.

Our apprehension was heightened by the fact that the set designers had constructed a 20m aerial walkway to bring guests on and off, and one of Ali's minders confided in me that the short walk would physically exhaust the great man. In fact, he said Ali had spent the previous four hours preserving all his strength for the exertion to come.

The doubts were unfounded, though, and when he first came on to be interviewed by John Inverdale, Muhammad Ali made the kind of spine-chilling entrance that was the equal of anything he had manufactured in his days in the ring. It was ponderous but proud and brought the star-studded audience to its feet for the most sustained ovation the programme had ever heard.

When it came to the final award, it was only appropriate that Harry Carpenter, who had interviewed him many times on this very show, should make the announcement and pay tribute to Muhammad Ali, as Evander Holyfield stepped forward to hand him the trophy.

After a seemingly endless standing ovation by an audience who felt truly privileged to have been in the studio that evening, Ali managed a short speech: 'I want to thank the British people for giving me such a big welcome. I want to thank all concerned for the award. I had a good time boxing, I enjoyed it ... and I may come back.'

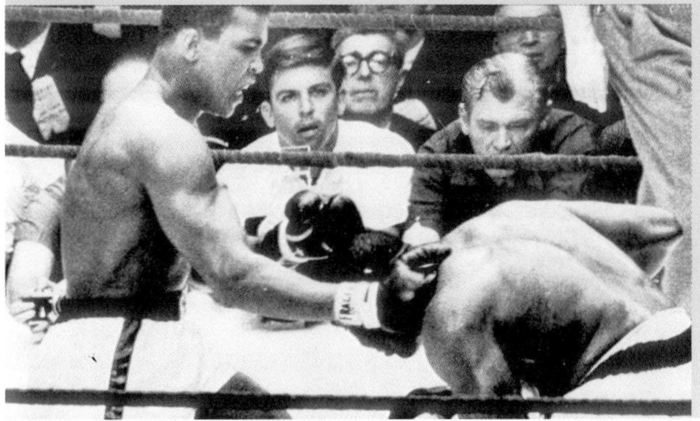

Left Muhammad Ali, or Cassius Clay as he was then known, bangs a right to Sonny Liston's left shoulder during their world heavyweight bout in 1964. It was a controversial fight, but Ali emerged the champion after a technical knockout in the seventh round

Overseas winner

The Kansas Cannonball, **Maurice Greene**, was presented with the award in the studio by the legendary hurdler Ed Moses, after Greene had broken Donovan Bailey's 100m world record to set a new best of 9.79.
In an outstanding season, Greene had also won the world indoor 60m title and taken all three sprint golds at the World Championships.

Team winner

There was only ever one real candidate for this award and, to the sound of David Bowie's 'Heroes', Sir Alex Ferguson proudly led **Manchester United** into the studio. They had won the Champions League, the Premiership and the FA Cup. They all regarded the win in Barcelona, a victory secured by two dramatic injury-time goals against Bayern Munich, as their greatest achievement, and the 1999 squad followed in the footsteps of Sir Matt Busby's 1968 players when they were presented with the Team award by Seve Ballesteros.

Opposite Carl Fogarty, known as Foggy to his legions of fans, won his 50th race in 1999, but retired in 2000 after a serious crash

Ali didn't speak at this stage in the show but sat smiling as Lewis and Holyfield paid tribute to him. Holyfield described him as, 'Someone who took a sport and changed people's lives to motivate them to be the very best they can be. That outweighs the boxing. Ali's been able to do that and it's a great accomplishment.' Completing a unique collection of boxing heroes, they were joined on the sofa by Naseem Hamed, Frank Bruno, Barry McGuigan and Chris Eubank.

It was hard to top that moment but the telephone lines had been open and the contenders for Personality of the Year were David Beckham, Stephen Hendry, Colin Jackson, Lennox Lewis and Colin Montgomerie. In the year that Ali was in the studio, the voters helped to provide this memorable programme with what was literally the perfect punch-line – and Lennox Lewis was presented with the famous trophy by Michael Owen.

As the credits rolled the Manchester United players formed a queue for Muhammad Ali's autograph. Despite their fame and fortune, he was a hero to them, and I'm sure this was exactly the kind of magical moment that Peter Dimmock and Sir Paul Fox had in mind some 45 years earlier when they first conceived the show.

▶▶ The move away from a straightforward review of the year was seen when the 1999 show broke two of its own records. There were **more stars** interviewed and **more awards** presented than ever before. Between us we spoke to no fewer than 41 guests and handed out seven trophies.

▶▶ **Martina Hingis** won her third successive Australian open but threw an extraordinary and unprecedented strop in the French final. With Steffi Graf on match point, Hingis decided to serve underarm, before storming off the court after Graf had completed her sixth victory.

Sporting roundup

Football Rangers won the double in Scotland.

Motor cycling Carl Fogarty became world superbikes champion for the fourth time in six years.

Motor racing Mika Hakkinen retained the Formula One World Championship.

Rugby union Scotland lifted the last ever Five Nations trophy and a drab World Cup final saw Australia beat France.

Snooker Stephen Hendry beat Mark Williams in the final of the World Championship at the Crucible to become champion for a record seventh time.

Gary Lineker, presenter, remembers ...

'I have probably been to the Sports Personality of the Year presentation as many times as a studio guest as I've been as a presenter – and in either role it's a very nerve-wracking experience indeed.

'I'd been fancied to win it a few times and finished in the top six on a couple of occasions, including in 1986 when I was the top scorer in the World Cup and lost out to Nigel Mansell, who hadn't even won the World Championship! But good luck to him – he was the one who had to make the speech and I was very relieved to let him do it.

'There was another time on which I got close, too, but that was in 1991, after my son, George, had been diagnosed with leukaemia, and I felt that if I had won that year it would have been for the wrong, non-sporting kind of reasons.

'Then, when I joined Steve, Sue and the rest of the team as a presenter, I was far more nervous than I had ever been as a contender. Walking out to perform in front of an audience of your sporting peers and heroes really concentrates the mind – until you realise that, because of the nature of the occasion, the audience are as nervous as you are.

'A highlight for me was interviewing the likes of David Beckham and Michael Owen in the *Sports Personality of the Year* studio after the 2002 World Cup. Getting players like that together is a special thing.

'Walking out to perform in front of an audience of your sporting peers and heroes really concentrates the mind'

'I try to be as light-hearted as possible, because you're never going to get anything of great significance from an interview in these circumstances. Sven Goran Eriksson was with us as well, and ahead of the World Cup he, of course, was as much in the gossip columns as the sports pages. I was wondering how to touch on this, so I said, "Well, Sven, you had a busy summer – and then there was the World Cup as well ..." but instead of a laugh there was a sharp intake of breath from the audience and I thought, blimey, what have I said!

'I like to think that response was a result of the audience being tense and uptight, so if there was one thing I would change about Sports Personality of the Year, it would be to try to get a few more members of the public and sports fans into the audience. It would give them an insight into what an amazing occasion it is – and it might help me get a few laughs as well!'

2000

Date 10 December 2000 • Location Television Centre, London • Presenters Steve Rider with Sue Barker, Gary Lineker, John Inverdale and Clare Balding• Editor Philip Bernie • Producer Paul Davies

1st Steve Redgrave rower
2nd Denise Lewis athlete
3rd Tanni Grey-Thompson wheelchair athlete

Overall winner

Steve Redgrave claimed another record that evening – for the longest acceptance speech in the show's history. For six minutes he spoke with great passion about his sport and those who had supported him. He remembered, 'When I was ten I dreamed of being an Olympic champion when I saw Mark Spitz winning seven golds. In 1984, that dream came true and I came to the *Sports Review of the Year* and something else caught my eye. I've been to these awards 16 times and been short-listed six times, but I had to hint at retiring to win!'

Steve Redgrave remembers ...

'I wouldn't say winning the award came as a surprise, but you take nothing for granted when you have been prominent in the voting so often and not come out on top. I remember in 1996 after the gold medal in Atlanta, I finished behind Damon Hill in the top three and even Damon's mother, Bette, came up to me after the programme and said, "I'm delighted for Damon, but you should have won it." But then she is a rowing fan.

'In 1996 and in 2000 the press, and especially the rowing press, were full of campaigns urging people to vote for me, which was appreciated, but it did emphasize how important it was to the sport of rowing that I should do well in the voting.

'A lot of people wondered whether I had my winner's speech prepared well in advance, because it did seem to flow quite naturally, but I had hardly given it a thought until during the programme, when John McEnroe made a comment like, "If that man hasn't got your votes this year then something's wrong." That was when I first thought that maybe I'd won it and it was only then that the idea of a speech got my attention.

'I suppose in a way the speech was a product of having sat through so many editions of the programme in the past, and seeing how so many previous winners handled things, but the main thing I was conscious of was the significance of the moment.'

If Muhammad Ali had claimed the glory in the twentieth century, the twenty-first century was only a couple of hundred days old when another sporting hero, this time British, entered sporting legend. Steve Redgrave had been coming to the show for 16 years, but at the end of this particular edition he would step from the audience for an honour and celebration long overdue.

Before that, though, the programme was one big celebration of everything that had been achieved at the spectacular Sydney Olympics. The British team had brought home its biggest haul for 80 years – 28 medals in all – and every one of the British medallists was introduced at the start of the show. The final tally was seven bronze, ten silver and 11 gold, and they were all there, as were many of our Paralympians, who had won 131 medals.

The space behind the set was very cramped and the choreography to bring each medallist on was complicated. The main problem, though, was that behind the scenes it was a massive Sydney reunion. Audley Harrison, in particular, nearly scuppered the whole sequence by going walkabout to greet all the athletes . However, we made it and it set a rousing tone for what was to follow.

The programme took on a very different style for the new millennium and moved away from a literal recall of the year's sporting achievements to one that was more personality-led. Michael Schumacher reviewed Formula One after a season when he had guided Ferrari to their first title in 21 years and David Coulthard had survived a plane crash in France.

Frankie Dettori and Ray Cochrane also had a lucky escape from a plane crash, one that claimed the life of

Below Jason Queally's first sport was water polo. Then he switched to the triathlon, before settling on cycling in his mid-twenties
Right Great Britain's Matthew Pinsent, Tim Foster, Steve Redgrave and James Cracknell (left to right) go for gold in the men's coxless four final
Below right Audley Harrison (right) squares up to Kazakhstan's Mukhtarkhan Dildabekov for gold in the Olympic 91+kg category

Tanni Grey-Thompson remembers ...

'Firstly, to get third place was a huge thing for me and for disability sport, but then when my name was called the problem was obvious. There were a few big guys around me who I think were offering to lift me up, and Sally Gunnell offered to help but she was pregnant, and when Alan Shearer was called forward to present the award the BBC knew they were in trouble.

'I was amazed at the reaction that followed. In the next few days it was just endless phone calls from newspapers and radio stations, and even the BBC themselves wanted me to come on *Points of View*. When I said I might not be able to make it they said that Terry Wogan would make himself available for an interview at any time.

'I made the incident the opening chapter in my book and even now, when I go to speaking engagements, it's the one topic that people want to talk about. It was embarrassing for the BBC but in reality it turned into a huge night for disabled sport in terms of the award and all the publicity that followed.'

their pilot. Sinndar was the horse of the year, winning the Derby, Irish Derby and the Arc, and the Grand National was won by the Irish horse, Papillon. Clare interviewed the trainer and jockey, Ted and Ruby Walsh.

In boxing, they don't come much bigger than Evander Holyfield and he considered the fortunes of Lennox Lewis, Mike Tyson, Naseem Hamed and the new Olympic super heavyweight champion, Audley Harrison.

The football section was unrecognizable from any that had gone before, as it was in the style of a comic strip, which enabled it to reflect a wide range of stories. These included Kevin Keegan's resignation as England manager and Rio Ferdinand's transfer to Leeds for £18m, as well as Rangers' 11th title in 12 years and Martin O'Neill's move to Celtic having won the League Cup with Leicester City.

An impressive lineup of managers joined Gary to look back at those issues, as well as Manchester United's Championship success and Chelsea's victory in the last Cup final at the old Wembley. Peter Taylor, David O'Leary, Craig Brown and Mick McCarthy all gave their views.

The other main sporting event of the year had been Euro 2000 and Alan Shearer, Dennis Bergkamp and Thierry Henri reviewed the tournament. England failed to make it past the group stage, having lost 3-2 to both

Helen Rollason award

Tanni Grey-Thompson had won four gold medals at the Paralympics and competed in the wheelchair 800m in the main games. Sydney had taken a very different approach to the event and she felt that 'for the first time we were treated as athletes'. The award was presented to Tanni by Jenny Pitman.

Portugal and Romania. Their only satisfaction had come with victory over Germany at Charleroi. France beat Italy 2-1 in the final.

At the conclusion of the first Six Nations Championship, there was similar frustration for the England rugby team as they were beaten for the second year running at the final hurdle of a Grand Slam. This time defeat came at the hands of Scotland at Murrayfield and in the studio the respective captains, Andy Nicol and Matt Dawson, gave their own version of events.

The BBC's long-serving commentator, David Vine, had retired and looked back at his 25 years of presenting memories from the snooker World Championships, where Mark Williams had won the 2000 title.

Yorkshire's Darren Gough chipped in with his thoughts on the cricket season in which Nasser Hussain had led England to a series victory over the West Indies for the first time in 31 years. They'd also beaten both New Zealand and Pakistan.

Venus Williams dominated the tennis year, winning the singles and doubles at both Wimbledon and Sydney, in addition to the US Open. She spoke on film about wanting to entertain the crowds and put on a good show. Pete Sampras beat Pat Rafter in one of the latest ever finishes – at 8.57 p.m. – to clinch his seventh Wimbledon crown.

Coach of the Year

Following the Olympic success of the coxless fours, this award went to their coach, **Jurgen Grobler**, and was one of the few trophies in 2000 that Steve Redgrave handed over rather than received.

Newcomer of the Year

Jackie Stewart presented the trophy to Britain's newest and, at just 20, youngest Formula One driver, **Jenson Button**, following his successful first season driving for Williams.

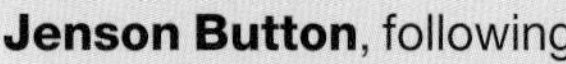

All these were sideshows to the main event, though, and the joyful images of Sydney dominated. Britain had enjoyed so much success that the stories of the winners were broken up into several segments, as the audience heard from all the gold medallists. Denise Lewis and Jonathan Edwards summarised the track and field events; Jason Queally, who had won our first gold, in cycling, talked about how the games had changed his sport's profile; and I spoke with the gold medal rowing eight who were reunited for the first time since the final. Shirley Robertson, Ben Ainslie and Ian Percy all won sailing golds, and Richard Foulds and Stephanie Cooke completed the lineup, having been champions in shooting and modern pentathlon.

Left Eric Moussambani found the second 50m tough and thought he wasn't going to finish. He did, though, in a time of 1.52 – about a minute slower than the other heat winners

However, the whole programme was built towards the gold medal that had been won by the coxless four and it was seen through the eyes of various celebrities who had joined the millions of viewers at home, watching at midnight. Ricky Tomlinson, Louise Redknapp, Michael Parkinson, Paul Gascoigne and Tim Henman shared their thoughts – and then it was time for the famous quartet to step forward.

Steve Redgrave confirmed that he had definitely retired this time; James Cracknell had felt good during the race but thought the other lads were tired; Tim Foster believed that technically they were the best crew and had a lot of spirit; and Matthew Pinsent, who possessed three gold medals himself, talked about the emotion and the pressure that had built up before the final and how they had used it to their advantage.

And so it came to the presentations to the top three in the voting, and here there was at least a surprise, although it was an uncomfortable one for the production team and myself. When I announced that Tanni Grey-Thompson had come third, it was quite clear that there was no ramp and no way of getting her wheelchair onto the stage to receive the award. I ushered Alan Shearer forward to present it in the auditorium, but the damage was done. We paid the price in the national press in the days to come and Tanni, quite correctly, used the incident to make some very forthright points about disabled access and rights.

Denise Lewis's gold in the heptathlon secured her second place, but no one was surprised when, finally, and by an overwhelming margin, Steve Redgrave, the five times Olympic champion, was named as the 2000 Sports Personality of the Year.

Opposite Denise Lewis moved into the lead in the Olympic heptathlon when she threw 50.19m with her final javelin. This was despite an injured foot sustained in the long jump

Overseas winner

Tiger Woods collected the award after winning the Open Championship for the first time with an astonishing 19 under par at St Andrews. Having already won the 1997 Masters and 1999 US PGA, Woods dominated world golf in 2000. As well as the Open, he also won the US Open and the US PGA. Ken Brown was seen presenting Woods with the trophy.

Team winner

Normally there are a dozen or so people at the most who can claim to be part of the winning team, and the largest had been rugby squads. All that changed in 2000 as I handed the award to Matthew Pinsent on behalf of the several hundred members of the **British Olympic and Paralympic teams**.

▸▸ **Steve Redgrave** took his award tally to six when he lifted the main trophy and claimed a share in the Team award. He had already received those in 1992 and 1996, as well as being voted second in 1996 and third in 1997.

▸▸ **Eric Moussambani**, otherwise known as Eric the Eel, unintentionally became a star of the Olympic Games when the other competitors were disqualified from his heat and he had to swim the 100m freestyle alone. What made his tale even more extraordinary was that he had only learnt to swim that year and his landlocked country, Equatorial Guinea, had only one small swimming pool.

Sporting roundup

Cricket Gloucestershire won all three one-day trophies under the captaincy of Mark Alleyne.

Golf Europe's women won the Solheim Cup.

Rugby league Bradford won the Challenge Cup for the first time in 51 years and Australia became world champions when the World Cup was held in the UK and France.

2001

Date 9 December 2001 • Location Television Centre, London • Presenters Steve Rider with Sue Barker, Gary Lineker and Clare Balding • Editor Philip Bernie • Producer Paul Davies

1st David Beckham footballer
2nd Ellen MacArthur sailor
3rd Michael Owen footballer

After the broad canvas of the millennium show, the 48th edition of *Sports Review of the Year* saw the programme committed to the solid ingredients of high profile studio guests, imaginative video packages and strong presentation.

David Beckham, Sven Goran Eriksson and Sir Alex Ferguson were all there, as it was clear that football would play a big part in the show. This was the year that Sven had resurrected England's hopes of qualifying for the World Cup, Michael Owen had struck a hat-trick in an outrageous 5-1 win over Germany, and Beckham had secured qualification with a dramatic last-gasp free kick against Greece.

In a break with tradition, many sports were reviewed by enthusiasts rather than the BBC's own commentary teams. This meant that Clare Balding's interview with racing fan, Sir Alex Ferguson, formed the basis of the review of the racing year, with special emphasis on the progress of his horse, Rock of Gibraltar.

The golfing year, in which Tiger Woods held all four Majors after his win at the Masters, was reviewed by Alan Hansen; Jamie Theakston and Shane Warne looked back at a cricket season in which Australia had comfortably retained the Ashes; and Keith Wood tried to give a Christmas goodwill theme to the rugby story, even though Ireland had denied England the Grand Slam.

The purists, though, were none too sure about the way in which the show treated boxing and rugby league. The boxing story was told with animated models of Lennox Lewis, Audley Harrison and Naseem Hamed, while comedian Johnny Vegas joined his idols at St Helens for a training session. This was very funny, but conveyed little detail and no doubt the sport was hoping for a little more coverage, particularly after St Helens had beaten Bradford 13-6 to win the 100th Challenge Cup final.

Overall winner

Despite the claims of George Best and Bobby Charlton, **David Beckham** was the first Manchester United player to win the main award. Like Michael Owen in 1998, Paul Gascoigne in 1990 and Bobby Moore in 1966, Beckham's success was down to the fact that his appeal stretched way beyond the partisanship of club football and he had emerged as a national sporting icon.

Lennox Lewis had lost to Hasim Rahman, but quickly regained his world title to equal Ali as a three-time champion, and as Gary spoke to Lennox live in Los Angeles he admitted that he hadn't taken the first fight seriously, but now planned to meet and beat Mike Tyson.

Matthew Pinsent and James Cracknell were candidates for team of the year, having won the coxed and coxless pairs world titles within two hours on the same day. They explained about their need to put themselves under pressure. The athletics World Championships in Edmonton had been disappointing for Britain, as only Jonathan Edwards won gold and Dean Macey, bronze.

At the end of the evening, however, there was one supreme example of how inspiration in the video editing suite can add perspective to even the most familiar piece of action. I was standing next to David Beckham in the wings as the big screens started to replay the famous moments from the win in Germany. He gave it a glance but he'd seen it a hundred times before. Then came his astonishing free kick against Greece, with the camera seemingly exploring his psyche as the most important strike of his life was lined up. All the good and bad things that had happened over the last few years were replayed, in particular the sending off against Argentina. Watching this, Beckham, like everyone else in the studio, was transfixed. When the kick went in he turned to me and punched the air again.

Helen Rollason award

Ellen MacArthur had spent three months racing around the world single-handedly, and her video diaries from on board *Kingfisher* captured all the physical demands and stark fear that she had to confront. She received the Helen Rollason Award for courage and achievement from Tanni Grey-Thompson.

Below Goran Ivanisevic gets acrobatic in the final against Pat Rafter. He had had to request a wildcard to enter the tournament

Team winner

Liverpool had won a staggering five trophies in 2001 and the UEFA Cup, FA Cup, League Cup, Charity Shield and Super Cup were all on display at Anfield, from where Gérard Houllier and Phil Thompson spoke live with Gary. Everyone was relieved to see that Houllier was recovering from his heart surgery. He explained that he had ignored the symptoms because, as a manager, he hadn't wanted to show signs of tiredness or weakness. However, he could draw strength from the passion of his team and, after such a successful year, Ian Rush presented him with a sixth trophy to add to his collection – the Team of the Year award.

Minutes later, from a shortlist which also included Jonathan Edwards, Tim Henman and Lennox Lewis, the results were announced and it was Michael Owen in third, Ellen MacArthur in second and David Beckham in first. He stepped forward to collect the trophy from Sven Goran Eriksson.

Opposite Michael Owen (centre) gets Liverpool's winning goal in the last minute of the FA Cup final. Arsenal's Tony Adams (right) and David Seaman can only watch as the trophy slips out of their grasp

▶▶ Ellen MacArthur's second place meant that **sailing** became the twentieth different sport to be represented in the top three of the voting.

▶▶ **Foot and mouth** hit the sports season heavily, especially racing, and the Cheltenham festival had to be cancelled. It also meant that the Six Nations tournament, which England won, was extended into the autumn.

Coach of the Year

Having taken England to the 2002 World Cup finals and inspired the astonishing wins against Germany and Greece that had lifted the entire nation, manager **Sven Goran Eriksson** was presented with the Coach of the Year award by Sir Bobby Charlton. The feelings of all football fans were, as ever, summed up by John Motson: 'Oh, this is getting better and better and better – one, two, three for Michael Owen.'

Lifetime Achievement award

This had been awarded twice before, to Lester Piggott in 1995 and Frank Bruno in 1996, but from this year onwards it was established as a permanent category. Peter Schmeichel presented it to his old boss, **Sir Alex Ferguson**, as he had announced that he would be retiring having led Manchester United to their seventh title in nine seasons.

Young Sports Personality of the Year

This new award replaced the Newcomer of the Year that had been presented for the previous two years. The first winner was 16-year-old sprinter, **Amy Spencer**, and Michael Owen gave her the trophy. The runners-up were wheelchair athlete, Lee Lower, and hockey player, Alex Danson.

Overseas winner

When **Goran Ivanisevic** lifted the 2001 Wimbledon trophy at the age of 29, he became one of the most extraordinary champions in the long history of the men's singles. He had lost all three of his previous finals and, ahead of the Championship, had dropped to number 128 in the world and was unseeded.

The Croatian beat Tim Henman over three days in a rain-affected semi-final and then triumphed against Pat Rafter in an epic battle that, also because of rain, was played on the Monday, in front of a raucous crowd. He received the Overseas award from Boris Becker.

Sporting roundup

Boxing Naseem Hamed had been beaten for the first time in his career – by Marco Berrera.

Football Martin O'Neill won the treble in his first season at Celtic.

Golf The Open had been won by David Duval. Ian Woosnam had been in great form but was penalized when his caddy put an extra club in his bag.

Horse racing The Grand National was won by Richard Guest on Red Marauder, the 33-1 shot. Only three other horses finished. Galileo won the Derby with Mick Kinane in the saddle.

Snooker Ronnie O'Sullivan beat John Higgins 18-14 to win the world title.

Swimming The women's 4x200m freestyle gold was the first for Britain at a World Championships since David Wilkie 26 years before.

Tennis Jennifer Capriatti's incredible comeback continued as she won the Australian and French Opens. Venus Williams won her second Wimbledon title and then beat Serena in the US Open final.

And the winner is ...

How the nation voted

Every year the voting becomes a national obsession and for the producer, trying to organize all the elements of *Sports Personality of the Year*, this can come as a great shock.

Suddenly, around the last week of November or the first week in December, the producer of *Sports Personality of the Year* is reminded that the programme has a national responsibility, not only for revealing the public's choice, but also for making sure the public gets it right. Whoever the nation chooses, though, the choice is always perceived to be that of the BBC.

Giles Smith of the *Daily Telegraph*, a diligent observer of the programme, wrote in 2001: 'What happens to the votes cast for this prestigious and gratefully received award? We simply do not know. It is one of the great political scandals of our time. For the duration of the award's 48-year history, the BBC have espoused an electoral process which would seem shady, even by the standards of destabilized countries in South America. Every year, we, the public, have been encouraged to vote. Every year the BBC have announced a winner. Yet not once have the results of our voting been published.'

In the same year, *The Times* commented: 'The trouble is that the BBC Sports Personality of the Year award almost always goes to the wrong person, or the right person in the wrong year. Nigel Mansell got it the year Linford Christie won the Olympic 100m; Damon Hill got it the year Steve Redgrave won his fourth Olympic gold.'

The production team would have drawn no comfort either from Peter Corrigan in the *Independent on Sunday*, who wrote: 'The terms of reference for deciding the winner have always been vague. The word "personality" widens the field beyond pure accomplishment, and comparing achievements across various sports is a difficulty they overcome by a viewers' voting system conducted in absurd secrecy, which is bound to excite suspicion unless you get a momentous hero like Sir Steve Redgrave.'

You can bet that when Paul Fox persuaded his family to help him count the votes on the living room carpet one evening back in 1954, he knew that there were problems ahead. Indeed, within months he was firing off memos insisting on secretarial help to handle this onerous task in years to come. And as for the integrity of the vote, after just one year of the programme, Peter Dimmock became aware of approaches from agents and managers, who realized the potential of the award to advance their clients' commercial profiles. Almost from day one the award was the subject of debate and suspicion.

'... When Paul Fox persuaded his family to help him count the votes on the living room carpet one evening back in 1954, he knew there were problems ahead'

For the first 30 years of the programme, voting was by coupons cut out from the *Radio Times*, but once that publication lost its right to exclusive BBC listings, the voting system was broadened to postcards and the peculiar compromise of 'a stuck down envelope'. It was Dave Gordon who, more than any other producer, worked to drag the voting system into the modem era of transparency; and that was possibly because Dave had suffered more than most at the hands of what might be called 'rogue voting'.

Through the 1970s there had been huge, organized votes on photocopied voting slips for the likes of speedway rider Barry Briggs. These had been clumsy and clearly against the spirit of the award. On one occasion footballer Justin Fashanu figured high in the voting, posthumously, after a campaign by students, and Carlisle goalkeeper Jimmy Glass emerged a strong challenger for Personality of the Century after another orchestrated vote.

'Through the 1970s there had been huge, organized votes on photocopied voting slips ... These had been clumsy and clearly against the spirit of the award'

Dave became the target of abuse after a campaign to advance the claims of fishing champion Bob Nudd. 'I got abuse for not supporting anglers and fishermen in the voting anyway, and when Bob Nudd was ruled out a columnist in the *News of the World* wrote of my role, "I've got a 4m pole in my bag and I know precisely where to stick it." I had experience in previous years of getting boxes of votes for one person and instinctively you knew this couldn't be allowed. My great concern through it all was that one day the programme would get a winner that was clearly wrong and how damaging this would be for British sport. It's one thing being able to reflect the unpredictable preferences of the voters, but it's quite another to get a completely irrelevant winner.'

So Dave, and others, set about sharpening up the voting system. In the mid-1990s, faxes and emails were included in the voting, the prelude to dropping the postal vote altogether. In 1998, a phone vote was introduced. This upset a lot of purist fans, but Dave was careful to only open the lines in the last 15 minutes of the programme, to ensure that every candidate had received exposure. Even then, over half a million phone votes were cast in that short period.

In 1999, as Phil Bernie took over as the new editor, the phone lines were opened at the beginning of the show, but the voting was concentrated on the shortlist of six that had been defined by an earlier poll. The system was now protected from abuse and there was no BBC involvement in the vote, but even so the criticism continued, driven partly by the strong betting market around the event.

As Dave Gordon recalls, 'I felt quite bitter about the betting involvement, partly because at times my integrity was questioned, especially when a bookmaker would say in the press, "We're not taking bets because the whole thing is rigged." There was no way it was rigged and no reason for it being rigged.'

The question of revealing the number of votes polled was finally confronted in 2002. Until then, I was a firm believer that it did nothing for the dignity of the second- and third-placed personalities if it was revealed that they bad been beaten by a landslide margin. I also had no desire to read out the figures like a returning officer.

However, by 2002 it seemed appropriate and, when I opened the gold envelope in the finale and, without my glasses, struggled to decipher the huge numbers generated by the phone vote, I was reassured. Although the programme had become a little more complicated, the electorate could rest easy in the knowledge that Paula Radcliffe had been voted Sports Personality of the Year with the huge majority that she deserved.

2002

Date 8 December 2002 • Location Television Centre, London • Presenters Steve Rider with Sue Barker and Gary Lineker • Editor Philip Bernie • Producer Paul Davies

1st Paula Radcliffe athlete
2nd David Beckham footballer
3rd Tony McCoy jockey

Sporting endeavour has remained essentially the same across the decades and the performances that earned Paula Radcliffe the *Sports Personality of the Year* award in 2002 are equivalent to those of Chataway and Bannister back in 1954. However, compared to 50 years ago, there are so many opportunities to view sporting highlights on a day-to-day basis, so the production team feels it must provide a fresh angle and perspective, rather than just replaying a goal or tennis rally in its standard form.

Overall Winner

When Michael Johnson gave the famous trophy to **Paula Radcliffe** it capped a truly extraordinary year. She was born in Cheshire in 1973, five days after Jackie Stewart had been handed the award by Mary Peters, and had been running ever since joining Bedford Athletics Club when she was nine years old. With her husband, Gary Lough, never far from her side, Paula has rewritten the record books and continued her form into 2003 by smashing her own world record in the London marathon.

As soon as the rough content of a particular sport's year is known, a producer is briefed to come up with a treatment for the video, and he or she is encouraged to be as imaginative as possible. Typical of this was the kung fu fighter treatment of Peter Ebdon's snooker World

Championship final win against Stephen Hendry. This used a helicopter in a cliff-top location, and it worked brilliantly and, most importantly, Peter Ebdon had great fun in getting involved with the shoot. Once again the programme was strongly fulfilling its near 50-year-old brief to bring the audience a bit closer to the personalities and characters of sport.

In 2002 it was reasonable to expect that the World Cup would provide plenty for the programme to feature, although in the end it didn't quite produce the stories that English and Irish football wanted. Bringing in comedian Ricky Gervais for an *Office*-style parody of the art of football management was another inspired idea.

In the same vein were features on the family behind Tony McCoy, who had passed Richard Dunwoody's record of National Hunt winners; actor Ewan McGregor joined Suzi Perry to talk motor sport; and, for some reason, Sue Barker took Tim Henman into the ladies' locker room at Wimbledon.

It didn't need too much gimmickry, however, to do justice to the spectacle and success of the Commonwealth Games in Manchester. Likewise, the unexpected drama of the curling gold for Rhona Martin and her team in Salt Lake City did not require too much embellishment, as it was clear once again why six million late-night viewers had become so hooked on the sport. It was Britain's first gold at the Winter Olympics since Torvill and Dean, 18 years earlier.

For the first time the voting figures for the Sports Personality of the Year award were announced, although everyone knew it wasn't a close-run thing. In the voting, as in her sport, no one could keep up with Paula Radcliffe. In addition to her Commonwealth gold, European gold and a world marathon record, Paula became the 16th athlete to win the

Below Tony McCoy (left), on Mighty Montefalco, at Uttoxeter, heads for the winning post of his 1700th race. This also won him the record for the jump jockey with the highest number of first places – ever

Opposite Paula Radcliffe on her way to winning the London marathon and setting a new European record

Young Sports Personality of the Year

Everton's 17-year-old striker, **Wayne Rooney**, broke through into their first team in August and has already been capped by the man who handed him the trophy, Sven Goran Eriksson.

trophy and, even considering Chataway, Coe, Ovett and Thompson, perhaps the greatest. But that's another debate.

▶▶ **Paula Radcliffe** and **Michael Owen** are the only two winners to be born in December, but there is no great correlation between date of birth and winning the trophy, although July, August and September have each produced six winners.

▶▶ BBC Sport and Comic Relief combined to launch **Sport Relief**, which raises money for youngsters at home and abroad. With Sir Steve Redgrave at the helm, a special show on BBC1 in July raised more than £14.4 million. Sport Relief 2 takes place in July 2004.

Helen Rollason award

Paula Radcliffe presented this to **Jane Tomlinson**, a 38-year-old mother of three who was terminally ill with cancer but raised funds by running the London marathon, a triathlon and the Great North Run. She had only taken up running in 2001. Her family were in the audience as she thanked them.

Coach of the Year

Arsenal had won their second double in five years. They defeated Chelsea in the FA Cup final and clinched the Premiership with a 1-0 win at Old Trafford in the last game of the season. Patrick Vieira presented the trophy to his manager, **Arsène Wenger**.

Overseas winner

Ronaldo's extraordinary performance in the 2002 World Cup helped him to become only the third footballer to win the Overseas award, following Eusebio and Pele.

It was in the Far East that the Brazilian star was finally able to put the ghosts of France 98 behind him. Having suffered from a string of injuries and a lack of first-team football at Inter Milan, the Brazilian striker made a triumphant return in Japan and Korea and won the Golden Boot award with eight goals, as Brazil won their fifth World Cup. He has subsequently moved to Real Madrid. Gary Lineker presented him with the award.

Lifetime Achievement award

The Lifetime Achievement award acknowledges the prowess of someone who, for one reason or another, has been overlooked by the voters down the years, and **George Best**, frail and recovering from his liver transplant, received a huge ovation as testament to his legendary talent.

Opposite Rhona Martin (centre) watches intently as team-mates Janice Rankin (left) and Fiona MacDonald sweep furiously in front of her stone. In fact, this turned out to be the throw that won both the game and the gold medal for curling in Salt Lake City

Sporting roundup

Boxing Lennox Lewis knocked out Mike Tyson in the eighth round of their fight in June.

Cricket England drew with India and beat Sri Lanka during the summer.

Football The Scottish honours all went to Glasgow. Celtic retained the championship and Rangers lifted both cups.

Golf Ernie Els beat Thomas Levet in a play-off to win the Open at Muirfield.

Horse racing Bindaree was first home in the Grand National, while High Chaparral won the Derby.

Motor racing Michael Schumacher clinched his fifth world title as Ferrari dominated, winning 15 of the 17 races.

Rugby league Great Britain drew their series with New Zealand and Wigan beat St Helens in the Challenge Cup final.

Rugby union France won the Grand Slam, but England managed a clean sweep in the autumn by defeating Australia, New Zealand and South Africa.

Tennis Lleyton Hewitt and Serena Williams were Wimbledon champions.

2002 Sports Personality of the Year: the voting

Paula Radcliffe	619,577
David Beckham	113,539
Tony McCoy	87,972

2003

Date 14 December 2003 • Location Television Centre, London • Presenters Steve Rider with Sue Barker and Gary Lineker • Editor Philip Bernie • Producer Paul Davies

And so to the 50th presentation of the coveted award – a year still in progress and, as far as the programme is concerned, a work still in progress.

For editor Philip Bernie there has been no time to switch off. As soon as the 2002 set was taken down and the debris cleared from the after-show reception, his thoughts will have turned to 14 December 2003. From the second the 2002 programme faded from the screen, every British sporting achievement that followed has had to be considered for inclusion in 2003, and with the broader international perspective of the show, every world-wide star and champion must be reviewed as a potential guest.

There was an immediate contender for the Overseas award when Andre Agassi, the 1992 winner, won his fourth Australian Open, but Martina Navratilova staked her claim when she partnered Leander Paes to doubles success in both Australia and at Wimbledon. Martina is the oldest Grand Slam winner in history and, like Agassi, could follow Greg Norman and Muhammad Ali as a repeat winner of the Overseas award.

Philip Bernie will have made an effort to get agents to pencil 14 December into the contenders' diaries, and will certainly have done that with the inspirational American cyclist Lance Armstrong, who had won the Tour de France for the fifth consecutive year.

Along with the high-tech aspects outlined by producer Paul Davies overleaf, the problem of getting high-profile guests into the studio is the starkest contrast with the way the show was put together 50 years ago. Back in 1954, sportsmen and women seemed to have close seasons, which fortuitously coincided with early December. Nowadays their careers and commercial obligations run 12 months a year.

And as the year draws to a close, the top global stars will have received dozens of invitations to similar awards evenings, some genuinely prestigious, others more self-serving, and they can be forgiven for putting all the invitations, including ours, into the pending tray.

I remember going to Sun City in South Africa in 1998 to help orchestrate the

Right Paula Radcliffe, the current golden girl of British athletics, won the Sports Personality of the Year trophy in 2002 and, after her second London marathon victory, some tip her to do it again in 2003
Opposite top Jonny Wilkinson (left), famous for training hard and practising every day, fends off Scotland's Nathan Hines as the English take on the Scots in the Six Nations Championship
Opposite bottom Roger Federer during his final against Mark Philippoussis in the 2003 Wimbledon men's singles

presentation of the Overseas award to Mark O'Meara. Most of the world's top players agreed to get involved, except Tiger Woods who didn't do awards ceremonies unless a dozen agents and lawyers had been consulted. However, it was gratifying to hear Ernie Els take him to one side and explain that this one was different. Tiger immediately joined in the presentation and, once it was all over, spent longer than most examining the trophy. Two years later he won it himself.

It has to be said that 2003 hasn't been a great year for the golfing superstars, but it's been a splendid year for the dreamers and supposed underdogs, and Philip Bernie will be aware that the astonishing Open Championship victory by Ben Curtis, then ranked 396th in the world, is just the kind of story that *Sports Personality of the Year* revels in.

South African cricket captain Graeme Smith also had a dream summer, underlining his reputation as an international player of class with his double centuries in the first two Tests against England. But England, under the new captaincy of Michael Vaughan, made a fight of it, in contrast to the 4-1 winter series defeat by Australia, who added World Cup success a few weeks later.

England's cricketers were perhaps not the strongest contenders for the Team award, but England's rugby team certainly were, even before the start of the rugby World Cup in Australia in the autumn. Their Six Nations campaign, completed with an emphatic 42-6 win in Dublin, gave them their first Grand Slam in eight seasons. They then went on, in the first few weeks of the summer, to land their epic victories in New Zealand and Australia, and Jonny Wilkinson and a few others were already identifying themselves as strong challengers for the 50th Sports Personality of the Year award.

How appropriate it would be, in this landmark year, if the sport of rugby could land its first ever Sports Personality award, but what the programme and the viewers want most of all is competition for the title. One year, for example, we sat in a production meeting in October and the lineup of contenders looked so bleak that someone suggested making it a roll-over year and presenting two awards at once 12 months later.

This is surely not a problem we will have in 2003. Former winners such as David Beckham and Lennox Lewis will have their supporters, as will Mark Williams, after winning his second World snooker title. The 2003 winner, Paula Radcliffe, promised much with her London marathon win, only for injury to force her out of the World Championships, but she remains the undoubted star of women's sport in Britain.

Then there are other British world champions. Could swimmers James Gibson and Katy Sexton persuade the voters to go for their sports, as they did with Ian Black and Anita Lonsbrough all those years ago? Or will the winner come from one of the high-profile television sports?

Below Lance Armstrong, seldom seen in anything but the yellow jersey, in the closing stages of the 2003 Tour de France
Right Ben Curtis takes a swing at the Open in Sandwich
Opposite Michael Vaughan, who in the summer of 2003 took on the often thankless job of England cricket captain

The debate will be in full flow by November and if past press attention is anything to go by it will be a full-scale argument by December.

However, one thing is certain – on the night itself, and in the programming that surrounds it, due tribute will be paid to those who helped Sports Personality of the Year into the public consciousness, notably Peter Dimmock and Frank Bough, Harry Carpenter and David Coleman, and Des Lynam, along with all the great stars of British sport who have found inspiration and satisfaction in that shiny silver TV camera trophy.

Paul Davies, producer, remembers …

'In 1954 a one-page memo requested a desk, a chair, a black telephone, an in-tray and an out-tray as props. By contrast, the planning for the 2003 programme began as far back as March.

'Around then the technical team was brought together, including the studio supervisors, sound, lighting and camera technicians. These people have to be booked early because *Sports Personality of the Year* is broadcast around the time of all the Christmas specials and the best are in demand.

'I prefer to have a mix of the very best studio cameramen and the best sports outside broadcast cameramen, because even in the studio it's important to have cameramen who can react and provide shots of individuals at very short notice.

'The other aspect I have tried to concentrate on is the provision of screens, so that viewing the programme in the studio is a sophisticated experience. For the 2000 programme we took a risk and brought in a huge, very high-tech, four-way split screen, like those used in big pop concerts.

'For 2002 it was an equally complex series of strip screens that created a subtle lighting effect for each item – green for Wimbledon, red for Manchester United and so on. The experience and staging was more dynamic for the studio audience and hopefully that carried through to the television audience. Of course, we have some exciting effects planned for 2003 as well.

'The technical requirements and the design are the first components in the planning of the programme, and a specialist studio design consultant is brought in at least six months before the programme goes live. The other ingredients, though, are totally dependent on who does what that year.'

Facts and figures

Sports Personality of the Year winners

1954	Chris Chataway, athlete
1955	Gordon Pirie, athlete
1956	Jim Laker, cricketer
1957	Dai Rees, golfer
1958	Ian Black, swimmer
1959	John Surtees, motor cyclist
1960	David Broome, show-jumper
1961	Stirling Moss, racing driver
1962	Anita Lonsbrough, swimmer
1963	Dorothy Hyman, athlete
1964	Mary Rand, athlete
1965	Tommy Simpson, cyclist
1966	Bobby Moore, footballer
1967	Henry Cooper, boxer
1968	David Hemery, athlete
1969	Ann Jones, tennis player
1970	Henry Cooper, boxer
1971	Princess Anne, three-day eventer
1972	Mary Peters, athlete
1973	Jackie Stewart, racing driver
1974	Brendan Foster, athlete
1975	David Steele, cricketer
1976	John Curry, ice skater
1977	Virginia Wade, tennis player
1978	Steve Ovett, athlete
1979	Sebastian Coe, athlete
1980	Robin Cousins, ice skater
1981	Ian Botham, cricketer
1982	Daley Thompson, athlete
1983	Steve Cram, athlete
1984	Jayne Torvill and Christopher Dean, ice skaters
1985	Barry McGuigan, boxer
1986	Nigel Mansell, racing driver
1987	Fatima Whitbread, athlete
1988	Steve Davis, snooker player
1989	Nick Faldo, golfer
1990	Paul Gascoigne, footballer
1991	Liz McColgan, athlete
1992	Nigel Mansell, racing driver
1993	Linford Christie, athlete
1994	Damon Hill, racing driver
1995	Jonathan Edwards, athlete
1996	Damon Hill, racing driver
1997	Greg Rusedski, tennis player
1998	Michael Owen, footballer
1999	Lennox Lewis, boxer
2000	Steve Redgrave, rower
2001	David Beckham, footballer
2002	Paula Radcliffe, athlete

- Since 1954, **38** men and **ten** women have won the trophy. Torvill and Dean (1984) are the only couple to have won it.

- Men have filled the first **three** positions on **21** occasions. Women have filled them only **once**, in 1962, when Anita Lonsbrough, Dorothy Hyman and Linda Ludgrove topped the voting.

- The only people to have won **twice** are Henry Cooper (1967 and 1970), Nigel Mansell (1986 and 1992) and Damon Hill (1994 and 1996).

- The average age of the winners is **28**. Racing drivers have been the oldest winners, with an average age of **34.66**.

- At **44**, Dai Rees (1957) is the oldest male winner and Ian Black (1958), at **17**, is the youngest. The oldest female winner is Mary Peters (1972), who was **33**, and Princess Anne (1971) is the youngest, at **21**.

- The winners have represented **14** different sports.
All the winners have been in the studio to collect the trophy in person except Jim Laker (1956), Ian Botham (1981) and Steve Davis (1988). All three were competing overseas and had the trophy flown out and presented to them on film.

- The winners' nationalities break down like this: English (**42**); Scottish (**3**); Northern Irish (**2**); and Welsh (**2**)

Breakdown of winners' sports

Athletics (16 winners)

1954	Christopher Chataway
1955	Gordon Pirie
1963	Dorothy Hyman
1964	Mary Rand
1968	David Hemery
1972	Mary Peters
1974	Brendan Foster
1978	Steve Ovett
1979	Sebastian Coe
1982	Daley Thompson
1983	Steve Cram
1987	Fatima Whitbread
1991	Liz McColgan
1993	Linford Christie
1995	Jonathan Edwards
2002	Paula Radcliffe

Motor racing (6 winners)

1961	Stirling Moss
1973	Jackie Stewart
1986	Nigel Mansell
1992	Nigel Mansell
1994	Damon Hill
1996	Damon Hill

Football (4 winners)

1966	Bobby Moore
1990	Paul Gascoigne
1998	Michael Owen
2001	David Beckham

Boxing (4 winners)

1967	Henry Cooper
1970	Henry Cooper
1985	Barry McGuigan
1999	Lennox Lewis

Cricket (3 winners)

1956	Jim Laker
1975	David Steele
1981	Ian Botham

Ice skating (3 winners)

1976	John Curry
1980	Robin Cousins
1984	Jayne Torvill and Christopher Dean

Tennis (3 winners)

1969	Ann Jones
1977	Virginia Wade
1997	Greg Rusedski

Show-jumping/three-day eventing (2 winners)

1960	David Broome
1971	Princess Anne

Golf (2 winners)

1957	Dai Rees
1989	Nick Faldo

Presenters

Principal presenters

1961–85 Harry Carpenter (25 shows)

1964–82 Frank Bough (19 shows)

1959–71, 1979–84 David Coleman (19 shows)

1986–2002 Steve Rider (17 shows)

1983–98 Desmond Lynam (16 shows)

1954–63 Peter Dimmock (10 shows)

1994–2002 Sue Barker (nine shows)

1999–2002 Gary Lineker (four shows)

Other presenters

1976–77, 1979–84 Jimmy Hill (eight shows)

1961–64, 1967 Peter West (five shows)

1999–2001 Clare Balding (three shows)

1999–2000 John Inverdale (two shows)

1959, 1965 Brian Johnston (two shows)

1967, 1971 Cliff Morgan (two shows)

1955 Max Robertson (one show)

1963 Alun William (one show)

1965 Kenneth Wolstenholme (one show)

Team winners

1960	Cooper motor racing team
1961	Tottenham Hotspur
1962	BRM motor racing team
1963	West Indies cricket team
1964	England Youth football team
1965	West Ham
1966	England football team
1967	Celtic
1968	Manchester United
1969	Great Britain's women's athletics squad
	Great Britain's Ryder Cup team
1970	Nijinsky horse racing team
1971	British Lions rugby union squad
1972	Great Britain's Olympic three-day event team
1973	Sunderland
1974	British Lions rugby union squad
1975	Great Britain's men's swimming team
1976	Great Britain's modern pentathlon team
1977	Liverpool
1978	Davis and Whiteman Cup tennis teams
1979	British show-jumping team
1980	England rugby union squad
1981	Bob Champion and Aldaniti horse racing team
1982	Jayne Torvill and Christopher Dean
1983	Jayne Torvill and Christopher Dean
1984	Great Britain's hockey team
1985	European Ryder Cup team
1986	Liverpool
1987	European Ryder Cup team
1988	Great Britain's hockey team
1989	Great Britain's men's athletics squad
1990	Scottish rubgy union squad
1991	England rugby union squad
	Great Britain's men's 4x400m relay team
1992	Great Britain's Olympic rowing pairs
1993	England rugby union squad
1994	Wigan rugby league team
1995	European Ryder Cup team
1996	Great Britain's Olympic rowing pairs
1997	British Lions rugby union squad
1998	Arsenal
1999	Manchester United
2000	Team Great Britain – Olympic and Paralympic teams
2001	Liverpool
2002	European Ryder Cup team

Overseas winners

1960	Herb Elliott, athlete, Australia
1961	Valeriy Brumel, athlete, USSR
1962	Donald Jackson, ice skater, Canada
1963	Jacques Anquetil, cyclist, France
1964	Abebe Bikila, athlete, Ethiopia
1965	Ron Clarke, athlete, Australia
	Gary Player, golfer, South Africa
1966	Eusebio, footballer, Portugal
	Gary Sobers, cricketer, Barbados
1967	George Moore, jockey, Australia
1968	Oleg Protopopova and
	Ljudmilla Belousova, ice skaters, USSR
1969	Rod Laver, tennis player, Australia
1970	Pele, footballer, Brazil
1971	Lee Trevino, golfer, USA
1972	Olga Korbut, gymnast, USSR
1973	Muhammad Ali, boxer, USA
1974	Muhammad Ali, boxer, USA
1975	Arthur Ashe, tennis player, USA
1976	Nadia Comaneci, gymnast, Romania
1977	Niki Lauda, racing driver, Austria
1978	Muhammad Ali, boxer, USA
1979	Bjorn Borg, tennis player, Sweden
1980	Jack Nicklaus, golfer, USA
1981	Chris Evert, tennis player, USA
1982	Jimmy Connors, tennis player, USA
1983	Carl Lewis, athlete, USA
1984	Seve Ballesteros, golfer, Spain
1985	Boris Becker, tennis player, West Germany
1986	Greg Norman, golfer, Australia
1987	Martina Navratilova, tennis player, USA
1988	Steffi Graf, tennis player, West Germany
1989	Mike Tyson, boxer, USA
1990	Mal Meninga, rugby league player, Australia
1991	Mike Powell, athlete, USA
1992	Andre Agassi, tennis player, USA
1993	Greg Norman, golfer, Australia
1994	Brian Lara, cricketer, Trinidad
1995	Jonah Lomu, rugby union player, New Zealand
1996	Evander Holyfield, boxer, USA
	Michael Johnson, athlete, USA
1997	Martina Hingis, tennis player, Switzerland
1998	Mark O'Meara, golfer, USA
1999	Maurice Greene, athlete, USA
2000	Tiger Woods, golfer, USA
2001	Goran Ivanisevic, tennis player, Croatia
2002	Ronaldo, footballer, Brazil

In addition to the Sports Personality, Team and Overseas awards, a number of different trophies have been handed out down the years

Manager of the Year

1969	Don Revie, Leeds United

Special Achievement

1981	Dennis Moore, athlete
1984	Lester Piggott, jockey
1994	Lester Piggott, jockey

International Team

1983	Alan Bond and the crew of *Australia II*, sailing

Special Team

1986	Great Britain men's 4x400m team, athletes

Good Sport

1990	Derek Warwick, Martin Donnelly and Louise Aitken-Walker, motor sports

Lifetime Achievement

1996	Frank Bruno, boxer
1997	Seve Ballesteros, golfer
2001	Sir Alex Ferguson, football manager
2002	George Best, footballer

Coach of the Year

1999	Sir Alex Ferguson, football
2000	Jurgen Grobler, rowing
2001	Sven-Goran Eriksson, football
2002	Arsène Wenger, football

Helen Rollason award

1999	Jenny Pitman, horse racing
2000	Tanni Grey-Thompson, wheelchair athletics
2001	Ellen MacArthur, sailor
2002	Jane Tomlinson, athlete

Sports Personality of the Century

1999	Muhammad Ali, boxer

Newcomer of the Year

1999	Dean Macey, athlete
2000	Jenson Button, racing driver

Young Sports Personality of the Year

2001	Amy Spencer, athlete
2002	Wayne Rooney, footballer

- The Overseas award was first presented in 1960. Since then, 39 men and six women have won the trophy. Oleg Protopopov and Ludmila Belousova (1968) are the only couple to have won it.

- Only two people have won the Overseas award more than once: Muhammad Ali (1973, 1974 and 1978) and Greg Norman (1986 and 1993).

- There have been three sets of Overseas joint-winners: Ron Clarke and Gary Player (1965); Eusebio and Gary Sobers (1966); and Evander Holyfield and Michael Johnson (1996).

- The average age of Overseas winners is 27.87.

- At 44, George Moore (1967) was the oldest Overseas male winner and Boris Becker (1985), at 18, was the youngest male winner. The oldest Overseas female winner was Ludmila Belousova (1968), who was 33, and Nadia Comaneci (1976) was the youngest, at 15.

- The Overseas winners have represented 13 different sports and 19 different countries: USA (18); Australia (7); USSR (3); Brazil and Germany (2); and Austria, Barbados, Canada, Croatia, Ethiopia, France, New Zealand, Portugal, Romania, South Africa, Spain, Sweden, Switzerland and Trinidad (1).

- The Overseas winners' sports break down like this: tennis (11); athletics and golf (8); boxing (5); football (3); gymnastics, ice skating and cricket (2); and cycling, horse racing, motor racing, rugby league and rugby union (1).

Breakdown of top threes' sports

Athletics (39 top threes)

1954	Christopher Chataway, 1st
1954	Roger Bannister, 2nd
1955	Gordon Pirie, 1st
1960	Don Thompson, 2nd
1962	Dorothy Hyman, 2nd
1963	Dorothy Hyman, 2nd
1964	Mary Rand, 1st
1964	Ann Packer, 3rd
1968	David Hemery, 1st
1972	Mary Peters, 1st
1974	Brendan Foster, 1st
1975	Alan Pascoe, 2nd
1978	Steve Ovett, 1st
1978	Daley Thompson, 2nd
1979	Sebastian Coe, 1st
1980	Sebastian Coe, 2nd
1980	Daley Thompson, 3rd
1981	Sebastian Coe, 3rd
1982	Daley Thompson, 1st
1982	Steve Cram, 3rd
1983	Steve Cram, 1st
1983	Daley Thompson, 3rd
1984	Sebastian Coe, 2nd
1985	Steve Cram, 3rd
1986	Fatima Whitbread, 2nd
1987	Fatima Whitbread, 1st
1991	Liz McColgan, 1st
1992	Linford Christie, 2nd
1992	Sally Gunnell, 3rd
1993	Sally Gunnell, 2nd
1993	Linford Christie, 1st
1994	Sally Gunnell, 2nd
1994	Colin Jackson, 3rd
1995	Jonathan Edwards, 1st
1998	Denise Lewis, 2nd
1998	Iwan Thomas, 3rd
1999	Colin Jackson, 3rd
2000	Denise Lewis, 2nd
2002	Paula Radcliffe, 1st

Football (18 top threes)

1958	Bobby Charlton, 2nd
1958	Nat Lofthouse, 3rd
1959	Bobby Charlton, 2nd
1966	Bobby Moore, 1st
1966	Geoff Hurst, 3rd
1969	George Best, 3rd
1970	Bobby Moore, 3rd
1971	George Best, 2nd
1972	Gordon Banks, 2nd
1979	Kevin Keegan, 3rd
1986	Kenny Dalglish, 3rd
1990	Paul Gascoigne, 1st
1991	Gary Lineker, 3rd
1998	Michael Owen, 1st
1999	David Beckham, 2nd
2001	David Beckham, 1st
2001	Michael Owen, 3rd
2002	David Beckham, 2nd

Motor racing (11 top threes)

1961	Stirling Moss, 1st
1963	Jim Clark, 3rd
1965	Jim Clark, 2nd
1968	Graham Hill, 2nd
1973	Jackie Stewart, 1st
1976	James Hunt, 2nd
1986	Nigel Mansell, 1st
1992	Nigel Mansell, 1st
1993	Nigel Mansell, 3rd
1994	Damon Hill, 1st
1996	Damon Hill, 1st

Swimming (9 top threes)

1958	Ian Black, 1st
1959	Ian Black, 3rd
1960	Anita Lonsbrough, 3rd
1962	Linda Ludgrove, 3rd
1962	Anita Lonsbrough, 1st
1963	Bobby McGregor, 2nd
1975	David Wilkie, 3rd
1976	David Wilkie, 3rd
1988	Adrian Moorhouse, 2nd

Boxing (8 top threes)

1961	Billy Walker, 2nd
1967	Henry Cooper, 1st
1970	Henry Cooper, 1st
1974	John Conteh, 2nd
1985	Barry McGuigan, 1st
1989	Frank Bruno, 2nd
1995	Frank Bruno, 2nd
1999	Lennox Lewis, 1st

Cricket (8 top threes)

1956	Jim Laker,1st
1975	David Steele,1st
1977	Geoff Boycott, 2nd
1978	Ian Botham, 3rd
1979	Ian Botham, 2nd
1981	Ian Botham, 1st
1985	Ian Botham, 2nd
1990	Graham Gooch, 3rd

Show-jumping/three-day eventing (8 top threes)

1954	Pat Smythe, 3rd
1960	David Broome, 1st
1965	Marion Coakes, 3rd
1967	Harvey Smith, 3rd
1968	Marion Coakes, 3rd
1971	Princess Anne, 1st
1972	Richard Meade, 3rd
1973	Paddy McMahon, 3rd

Snooker (7 top threes)

1981	Steve Davis, 2nd
1982	Alex Higgins, 2nd
1984	Steve Davis, 3rd
1987	Steve Davis, 2nd
1988	Steve Davis, 1st
1989	Steve Davis, 3rd
1990	Stephen Hendry, 2nd

Golf (6 top threes)

1957	Dai Rees, 1st
1969	Tony Jacklin, 2nd
1970	Tony Jacklin, 2nd
1987	Ian Woosnam, 3rd
1988	Sandy Lyle, 3rd
1989	Nick Faldo, 1st

Tennis (6 top threes)

1961	Angela Mortimer, 3rd
1969	Ann Jones, 1st
1973	Roger Taylor, 2nd
1977	Virginia Wade, 1st

1997	Tim Henman, 2nd
1997	Greg Rusedski, 1st

Ice skating (4 top threes)

1976	John Curry, 1st
1980	Robin Cousins, 1st
1983	Jayne Torvill and Christopher Dean, 2nd
1984	Jayne Torvill and Christopher Dean, 1st

Rowing (3 top threes)

1996	Steve Redgrave, 2nd
1997	Steve Redgrave, 3rd
2000	Steve Redgrave, 1st

Rugby union (3 top threes)

1971	Barry John, 3rd
1974	Willie John McBride, 3rd
1991	Will Carling, 2nd

Cycling (2 top threes)

1965	Tommy Simpson, 1st
1967	Beryl Burton, 2nd

Horse racing (2 top threes)

1996	Frankie Detorri, 3rd
2002	Tony McCoy, 3rd

Motor cycling (2 top threes)

1959	John Surtees, 1st
1977	Barry Sheene, 3rd

Speedway (2 top threes)

1964	Barry Briggs, 2nd
1966	Barry Briggs, 2nd

Rallying (1 top three)

1995	Colin McRae, 3rd

Sailing (1 top three)

2001	Ellen MacArthur, 2nd

Wheelchair athletics (1 top three)

2000	Tanni Grey-Thompson, 3rd

▸▸ Since 1954, 112 of the top three places have gone to men and 29 have gone to women. (No record of the second and third place winners survives for 1955–57 and Torvill and Dean are counted as separate individuals.)

▸▸ Graham and Damon Hill are the only example of members of the same family coming in the top three.

▸▸ The sportspeople voted into the top three places have represented 20 different sports.

▸▸ Highest number of top three places:
Steve Davis (5)
Ian Botham, Sebastian Coe and Daley Thompson (4)
David Beckham, Steve Cram, Sally Gunnell, Nigel Mansell and Steve Redgrave (3)

▸▸ Breakdown of top threes' nationalities:
English (110); Scottish (14); Welsh (7); Northern Irish (7); and other (3)

Production teams

Editors

1954-60 Paul Fox
1961-62 Ronnie Noble and Leslie Kettley
1963 Phil Pilley and Cliff Morgan
1964 Cliff Morgan
1965-76 Alan Hart
1977-80 Jonathan Martin
1981-84 Harold Anderson
1985-89 John Rowlinson
1990 John Phillips
1991-95 Brian Barwick
1996-98 Dave Gordon
1999- Philip Bernie

Producers

1954, 1956 Dennis Monger
1955 Alan Rees
1957-62 Brian Cowgill
1963-64 Alec Weeks
1965-66 Richard Tilling
1967-68 Fred Viner
1969-76 Brian Venner
1977-96 Martin Hopkins
1997 Malcolm Kemp
1998- Paul Davies

Locations

1954-56 Savoy Hotel, London
1957-58 Grosvenor House Hotel, London
1959 Television Theatre, London
1960-64 Television Centre, London
1965-76 Television Theatre, London
1977 New London Theatre, London
1978-88 Television Centre, London
1989-98 Queen Elizabeth II Conference Centre, London
1999- Television Centre, London

Index